TREASURES
FROM THE
BAPTIST HERITAGE

TREASURES
FROM THE
BAPTIST HERITAGE

James P. Boyce

COMPILED WITH FOREWORD BY TIMOTHY GEORGE
TIMOTHY AND DENISE GEORGE, EDITORS

B&H
BROADMAN
& HOLMAN
PUBLISHERS
Nashville, Tennessee

4212-61
0-8054-1261-1

Dewey Decimal Classification: 286
Subject Heading: xxxxxxx / xxxxxxx
Library of Congress Card Catalog Number: 96-xxxxx

Scripture is from the King James Version.

Acquisitions and Development Editor: John Landers
Interior design by Leslie Joslin
Cover Design by Steve Diggs & Friends

Library of Congress Cataloging-in-Publication Data

Treasures from the Baptist heritage / Timothy & Denise George, general
editors.
    p. cm. — (Library of Baptist classics ; vol. 10)
    Includes bibliographical references and index.
    ISBN 0-8054-1252-1
    1. xxxxxxxxxxx. 2. xxxxxxxxxxxx. 3. xxxxxxxxxxx. 4. xxxxxxxxxx.
I. George, Timothy. II. George, Denise. III. Series.

BX6335.B29 1996
238'.6—dc20   96-xxxxx

CIP

01 02 03 04 05 00 99 98 97 96

Contents

Introduction

by
Timothy George

The Library of Baptist Classics offers a panorama of writings that have influenced the life, thought, and devotion of the people of God called Baptists during the past two centuries. The Southern Baptist Convention is the largest Protestant denomination in America, and other volumes in this series have focused on formative writings in this stream of the Baptist heritage. In this anthology we have brought together a discrete collection of classic works, most of them now long forgotten, that demonstrate the passion and depth of the Baptist spirit in diverse ways. With two exceptions, all of these writings come from the pretwentieth-century period. Some of these texts have had an incalculable influence on subsequent developments in Baptist life. Others illustrate the life and piety, the struggles and achievements, of Baptist Christians in an earlier era. Together they demonstrate the crucial importance of an unstinted commitment to Jesus Christ, a compelling burden for missions and evangelism, and the necessity for faithfulness amidst adversity—all distinctive marks of the Baptist tradition at its best.

William Carey was a poor journeyman shoemaker whose primary credential for missionary service was an inextinguishable conviction that God had called him to devote his life to "the conversion of the heathens." On June 13, 1793, Carey, his wife Dorothy, and their four children, including a nursing infant, sailed from England on a Danish ship headed for India. Carey remained in India for forty-one years translating the Scriptures into numerous languages and dialects, preaching the gospel, planting churches, establishing schools, working to reform horrible abuses in society, and influencing thousands of others to follow in his trail. Today he is rightly remembered by evangelical Christians everywhere as "the Father of Modern Missions."

Before leaving England, Carey had preached a stirring missionary sermon based on Isaiah 54. His summary of this text, "Expect great things from God; attempt great things for God," became the wake-up call for the missionary movement among Christians of various denominations. While still in England, Carey also published a treatise outlining his vision for carrying the gospel to those who had never heard the name of Christ. *An Enquiry into the Obligations of Christians to Use Means for the Conversion of the Heathens, in Which the Religious State of the Different Nations of the World, the Success of Former Undertakings, and the Practicability of Further Undertakings Are Considered* was first published at Leicester in 1792. This work, which reflects Carey's careful study of the world and his passionate commitment to fulfill the Great Commission, became the manifesto of the modern missionary movement.

Carey also had a strong personal influence on Luther Rice and Adoniram Judson, pioneers of the missionary awakening among Baptists on the American side of the Atlantic. Carey's *Enquiry*, along with his letters from India, were read eagerly by Baptists in America. Inspired by his example, they met in Philadelphia in May 1814 to organize "The General Missionary Convention of the Baptist Denomination of the United States for Foreign

Missions." Known as the Triennial Convention from its habit of meeting every three years, this cooperative venture was a major step in the process that led to the formation of the Southern Baptist Convention in 1845.

Carey's *Enquiry* also anticipated more recent and more sophisticated missionary manuals, such as the *World Christian Encyclopedia* and *Operation World*. What Carey wrote about the fulfillment of the Great Commission two hundred years ago is still valid, and even more compelling, today: "Some attempts are being made, but they are inconsiderable in comparison with what might be done if the whole body of Christians entered heartily into the spirit of the divine command on this subject." Today Southern Baptists are in the forefront of those who take seriously the great challenge of world evangelization, which Carey described so powerfully in this classic document.

John Leland had a long and productive career as a Baptist pastor, evangelist, champion of religious liberty, and a prolific writer. Included in this volume is an excerpt from one of his works, *The Virginia Chronicle*, first published in 1790. Leland was a native of Massachusetts and spent most of his life in New England, except for fifteen eventful years in Virginia from 1776 to 1791. *The Virginia Chronicle* is his firsthand account of religious life as he encountered it in the Old Dominion during the last decades of the eighteenth century.

While some Baptist leaders in the antebellum South defended the institution of slavery, others realized the terrible sin and evil consequences of this inhumane practice. Leland tried to improve the condition of slaves and openly advocated their emancipation. Leland died in 1841, two decades before the Civil War, but his words were prophetic of that wrenching struggle: "Something must be done! May Heaven point out that something, and may the people be obedient. If they are not brought out of bondage, in mercy, with the consent of their masters, I think that they will be, by judgment, against their consent." Leland also observed that the Christian faith had taken deep root among many of the slaves; he celebrated the genuine work of grace and distinctive patterns of worship he witnessed among these oppressed people of God.

Leland's *Chronicle* is also important for its placement of the Baptists among other denominational groups of the time. Leland provides valuable information about the Episcopalians, Presbyterians, Methodists, Quakers, Dunkers, and Mennonites, as well as the Baptists. Leland himself was a staunch advocate of religious liberty and worked closely with James Madison and other political leaders to make sure that the First Amendment was included at the head of the Bill of Rights. At the same time, Leland realized that the human conscience, clouded as it is by sin, was a fallible guide in matters of faith. "Though conscience should be free from human control," he wrote, "yet it should be strict subordination to the Law of God."

John Leadley Dagg was born in Middleburg, Virginia, in 1794, three years after Leland had left the state. Dagg was ordained to the ministry in 1817, and in 1825 he accepted a call to serve as pastor of the prestigious Fifth Baptist Church in Philadelphia. He later served as president of the Alabama Female Athenaeum in Tuscaloosa and Mercer University in Penfield, Georgia. Despite his failing health, including a broken voice and impaired vision, Dagg became the most prolific writing theologian among Baptists in the South. In this collection we have included two brief selections from his celebrated *Manual of Theology*, first published in 1857. These two selections demonstrate well Dagg's general approach to the study of theology, which he elsewhere described in this way:

> The study of religious truth ought to be undertaken and prosecuted from a sense of duty, and with a view of the improvement of the heart. When learned, it ought not to be laid on the shelf, as an object of speculation; but it should be deposited deep in the heart, where its sanctifying power ought to be felt. To study theology, for the purpose of gratifying curiosity, or preparing for a profession, is an abuse and profanation of what ought to be regarded as most holy. To learn things pertaining to God, merely for the sake of amusement, or secular advantage, or to gratify the mere love of knowledge, is to treat the Most High with contempt.

In keeping with this approach, Dagg introduced each of the eight sections of his *Manual of Theology* with a brief description of the duty that particular doctrine required.

In all of his writings, Dagg magnified the sovereignty of God and the good news of salvation through faith in Jesus Christ. Like the great Puritan divine William Ames, Dagg believed that theology was the "science of living in the presence of God." Thus there could be no divorce between intellect and piety, no separation between the devotion of the heart and the careful study of divine truth. Significantly, Dagg's *Manual of Theology* was adopted as the first textbook in systematic theology when Southern Baptists founded their first theological seminary at Greenville, South Carolina, in 1859.

"Three Changes in Theological Institutions" was first presented by James Petigru Boyce as an inaugural address before the board of trustees of Furman University on July 31, 1856. At the time Boyce was only twenty-nine years of age, but he was already recognized as one of the leading shapers of Baptist life in the South. A native of Charleston, South Carolina, he had been well educated at Brown University and Princeton Theological Seminary. His address to the Furman trustees would later be described by John A. Broadus as "epic-making in the history of theological education among Southern Baptists." A. M. Poindexter, secretary of the Foreign Mission Board, who was present on this occasion, claimed that this address was "the ablest thing of the kind he had ever heard."

Boyce's triad of "Changes" were revolutionary in the context of nineteenth-century ideals for theological education. He called for *openness*—a seminary for everybody called by God regardless of prior academic training; *excellence*—a course of instruction second to none in high scholarly standards; and *confessional integrity*—a statement of doctrinal principles that every professor would heartily embrace and in accordance with which he would teach. This address proved to be the catalyst in the formation and organization of The Southern Baptist Theological Seminary, which held its first session in the fall of 1859. Like Dagg, Boyce was a strong advocate of Reformed theology, which he taught at Southern Seminary for many years. The fruit of his classroom labors was eventually published in textbook form under the title *Abstract of Systematic Theology*.

In addition to his theological and pastoral work, Boyce was also a great parliamentarian and denominational statesman. He served nine terms as president of the Southern Baptist Convention! Although it was neglected for many years, Boyce's "Three Changes" has reemerged as a formative programmatic statement for theological educators today.

In one section of his "Three Changes" Boyce defended at length the use of confessions of faith among Baptists. The reluctance of some Baptists to adopt a specific doctrinal standard was related to the influence of Alexander Campbell, whose slogan "No Creed but the Bible" had lured many Baptists away from their traditional confessional moorings. Campbell had decried the use of confessions as an infringement upon the rights of conscience. Campbell was a powerful speaker, and his movement found fertile ground among many Baptists, especially in the "frontier" states of Kentucky and Tennessee.

S. M. Noel was moderator of the Franklin Baptist Association in Kentucky when the Campbellite movement became a matter of debate within that fellowship. To stem the tide of this divisive movement, Noel wrote a circular letter in 1826 that was sent to all the churches within his association. While opposing the imposition of any creedal statements by civil authorities, Noel strongly defended the historic Baptist acceptance of confessions of faith as a valid means for preserving "the unity, purity and peace of the church." Baptists frequently discussed important doctrinal and practical matters in their annual association meetings and often commissioned a respected pastor to draft a circular letter for dissemination among the congregations. In this way the faith of Baptist believers, who were sometimes scattered over many miles and able to come together only infrequently, could be strengthened and confirmed.

During his thirty-seven-year ministry at the Metropolitan Tabernacle in London, Charles Haddon Spurgeon became the most popular Protestant preacher in the world. While he was not a trained theologian, Spurgeon was very well read in the theology of earlier reformers, a fact that prompted William Gladstone to call him "The Last of the Puritans."

Spurgeon was indeed a strong advocate of the sovereignty of God and the doctrine of grace. However, early in his ministry, Spurgeon had encountered a strain of hyper-Calvinism, which he felt was antithetical to a strong evangelistic and missionary outreach. In no way did Spurgeon's commitment to the biblical doctrine of predestination inhibit his forthright proclamation of salvation by grace through faith in Jesus Christ, a message he strongly believed should by openly declared to all persons everywhere. One of the most eloquent and passionate statements of Spurgeon's "evangelical Calvinism" is his sermon of 1884, "High Doctrine and Broad Doctrine," based on one of his favorite biblical texts, John 6:37: "All that the Father giveth me shall come to me; and him that cometh to me I will in no wise cast out." Spurgeon's sermons were reprinted and widely read by Baptists on both sides of the Atlantic. We have included this sermon both as an example of Spurgeon's powerful preaching and also because of its intrinsic theological merit.

The next two selections are both sermons preached at annual Baptist associational meetings. In 1857 the Bracken Baptist Association, meeting at Millersburg, Kentucky, heard a message by John W. Brown on "The Duties of Pastors to Their Churches." This was a follow-up sermon to an earlier message on "The Duties of Churches to Their Pastors." Brown lists ten specific responsibilities that each pastor owes to his congregation. These ten "marks" of a faithful pastor still ring true more than one hundred years after they were first presented.

"Dangers of Denominational Prosperity" was delivered in 1843 by Jacob R. Scott before the Portsmouth Baptist Association in Virginia. Presented just two years before the definitive split between Northern and Southern Baptists, this prophetic message also has a timeless quality. Scott's final point about the prevalence of ingratitude is surely an important warning for any group of Christians so wondrously blessed by God as the Baptists.

S. G. Hillyer published *Reminiscences of the Old-time Baptists* in 1902. In some ways Hillyer's anecdotal survey of Georgia Baptist life in an earlier epoch resonates with Leland's even sketchier account of Baptist developments in Virginia. Neither account should be taken as an infallible guide to Baptist practice, but they both present snapshots and glimpses of Baptist worship, beliefs, social mores, and self-understandings. While Baptist life in the "good old days" was certainly not all "good" by contemporary standards, we may justly lament the loss of theological integrity, community spirit, and strong sense of purpose, which still shines through these descriptions.

Our concluding selection is a famous speech delivered by George Washington Truett before an audience of some fifteen thousand on the steps of the national Capitol in Washington, D.C., on May 16, 1920. With great eloquence and power, Truett rang the changes on the theme of religious liberty, showing how deeply rooted this theme was in Baptist history and calling on his fellow Baptists to be vigilant in holding forth the torch of freedom for a new generation. In a day when many take for granted the liberties won by others at so dear a price, we need to hear again both the promise and the warning of Truett's words. Now, as then, Baptists believe in a free church in a free state, knowing all the while that true freedom cannot be defined in political terms alone but must flow from a personal relationship with Jesus Christ, the source and goal of all freedom, whom to know and know aright is life eternal.

Chapter One

An Enquiry into the Obligations of Christians to Use Means for the Conversion of the Heathens, in Which the Religious State of the Different Nations of the World, the Success of Former Undertakings, and the Practicability of Further Undertakings Are Considered (1792)

WILLIAM CAREY

For there is no difference between the Jew and the Greek;
for the same Lord over all,
is rich unto all that call upon Him.
For whosoever shall call on the name of the Lord
shall be saved.
How then shall they call on Him,
in whom they have not believed?
And how shall they believe in Him
of whom they have not heard?
And how shall they hear without a preacher?
And how shall they preach except they be sent?

ROM. 10:12–15

Introduction

As our blessed Lord has required us to pray that His kingdom may come, and His will be done on earth as it is in heaven, it becomes us not only to express our desires of that event by words, but to use every lawful method to spread the knowledge of His name. In order to do this, it is necessary that we should become in some measure acquainted with the religious state of the world; and as this is an object we should be prompted to pursue, not only by the gospel of our Redeemer, but even by the feelings of humanity, so an inclination to conscientious activity therein would form one of the strongest proofs that we are the subjects of grace, and partakers of that spirit of universal benevolence and genuine philanthropy which appear so evident in the character of God Himself.

Sin was introduced amongst the children of men by the fall of Adam, and has ever since been spreading its baneful influence. By changing its appearances to suit the circumstances of the times, it has grown up in ten thousand forms, and constantly counteracted the will and designs of God. One would have supposed that the remembrance of the deluge would have been transmitted from father to son, and have perpetually deterred mankind from transgressing the will of their Maker; but so blinded were they, that in the time of Abraham, gross wickedness prevailed wherever colonies were planted, and the inquiry of the Amorites was great, though not yet full. After this, idolatry spread more and more, till the seven devoted nations were cut off with the most signal marks of divine displeasure. Still, however, the progress of evil was not stopped, but the Israelites themselves too often joined with the rest of mankind against the God of Israel. In one period the grossest ignorance and barbarism prevailed in the world; and afterwards, in a more enlightened age, the most daring infidelity, and contempt of God; so that the world which was once overrun with ignorance, now "by wisdom knew not God, but chanted the glory of the incorruptible God" as much as in the most barbarous ages, "into an image made like to corruptible man, and to birds, and four-footed beasts, and creeping things" (1 Cor. 1:21; Rom. 1:23). Nay, as they increased in science and politeness, they ran into more abundant and extravagant idolatries.

Yet God repeatedly made known His intention to prevail finally over all the power of the devil, and to destroy all His works, and set up His own kingdom and interest among men, and extend it as universally as Satan had extended his. It was for this purpose that the Messiah came and died, that God might be just, and the justifier of all that should believe in him. When He had laid down His life, and taken it up again, He sent forth His disciples to preach the good tidings to every creature, and to endeavor by all possible methods to bring over a lost world to God. They went forth according to their divine commission, and wonderful success attended their labors; the civilized Greeks, and uncivilized barbarians, each yielded to the cross of Christ, and embraced it as the only way of salvation. Since the apostolic age many other attempts to spread the gospel have been made, which have been considerably successful, notwithstanding which a very considerable part of mankind is still involved in all the darkness of heathenism. Some attempts are still being made, but they are inconsiderable in comparison with what might be done if the whole body of Christians entered heartily into the spirit of the divine command on this subject. Some think little about it, others are unacquainted with the state of the world, and others love their wealth better than the souls of their fellow-creatures.

In order that the subject may be taken into more serious consideration, I shall (1) enquire, whether the commission given by our Lord to His disciples be not still binding on us, (2) take a short view of former undertakings, (3) give some account of the present state of the world, (4) consider the practicability of doing something more than is done, and (5) the duty of Christians in general in this matter.

An Enquiry Whether the Commission Given by Our Lord to His Disciples Be Not Still Binding on Us

Our Lord Jesus Christ, a little before His departure, commissioned His apostles to "Go," and "teach all nations" (Matt. 28:19); or, as another evangelist expresses it, "Go into all the world, and preach the gospel to every creature" (Mark 16:15). This commission was as extensive as possible, and laid them under obligation to disperse themselves into every country to the habitable globe, and preach to all the inhabitants, without exception, or limitation. They accordingly went forth in obedience to the command, and the power of God evidently wrought with them. Many attempts of the same kind have been made since their day, and which have been attended with various success; but the work has not been taken up, or prosecuted of late years (except by a few individuals) with that zeal and perseverance with which the primitive Christians went about it. It seems as if many thought the commission was sufficiently put in execution by what the apostles and others have done; that we have enough to do to attend to the salvation of our own countrymen; and that, if God intends the salvation of the heathen, He will some way or other bring them to the gospel, or the gospel to them. It is thus that multitudes sit at ease, and give themselves no concern about the far greater part of their fellow sinners, who to this day, are lost in ignorance and idolatry. There seems also to be an opinion existing in the minds of some, that because the apostles were extraordinary officers and have no proper successors, and because many things which were right for them to do would be unwarrantable for us, therefore it may not be immediately binding on us to execute the commission, though it was so upon them. To the consideration of such persons I would offer the following observations.

First, if the command of Christ to teach all nations be restricted to the apostles, or those under the immediate inspiration of the Holy Ghost, then that of baptizing should be so too;

and every denomination of Christians, except the Quakers, do wrong in baptizing with water at all.

Secondly, if the command of Christ to teach all nations be confined to the apostles, then all such ordinary ministers who have endeavored to carry the gospel to the heathens, have acted without a warrant, and run before they were sent. Yea, and though God has promised the most glorious things to the heathen world by sending His gospel to them, yet whoever goes first, or indeed at all, with that message, unless he have a new and special commission from heaven, must go without any authority for so doing.

Thirdly, if the command of Christ to teach all nations extend only to the apostles, then, doubtless, the promise of the divine presence in this world must be so limited; but this is worded in such a manner as expressly precludes such an idea. "Lo, I am with you always, to the end of the world" (Matt. 28:20).

That there are cases in which even a divine command may cease to be binding is admitted. As for instance, if it be repealed, as the ceremonial commandments of the Jewish law; or if there be no subjects in the world for the commanded act to be exercised upon, as in the law of septennial release, which might be dispensed with when there should be no poor in the land to have their debts forgiven (Deut. 15:4); or if, in any particular instance, we can produce a counter-revelation, of equal authority with the original command, as when Paul and Silas were forbidden of the Holy Ghost to preach the word in Bythinia (Acts 16:6–7); or if, in any case, there would be a natural impossibility of putting it in execution. It was not the duty of Paul to preach Christ to the inhabitants of Otaheite, because no such place was then discovered, nor had he any means of coming at them. But none of these things can be alleged by us in behalf of the neglect of the commission given by Christ. We cannot say that it is repealed, like the commands of the ceremonial law; nor can we plead that there are no objects for the command to be exercised upon. Alas! The far greater part of the world, as we shall see presently, is still covered with heathen darkness! Nor can we produce a counter-revelation, concerning any particular nation, like that to Paul and Silas, concerning Bythinia; and, if we could, it would not warrant our sitting still and neglecting all the other parts of the world; for Paul and Silas, when forbidden to preach to those heathens, went elsewhere, and preached to others. Neither can we allege a natural impossibility in the case.

It has been said that we ought not to force our way, but to wait for the openings and leadings of Providence; but it might with equal propriety be answered in this case, neither ought we to neglect embracing those openings in providence which daily present themselves to us. What openings of providence do we wait for? We can neither expect to be transported into the heathen world without ordinary means, nor to be endowed with the gift of tongues, etc., when we arrive there. These would not be providential interpositions, but miraculous ones. Where a command exists nothing can be necessary to render it binding but a removal of those obstacles which render obedience impossible, and these are removed already. Natural impossibility can never be pleaded so long as facts exist to prove the contrary. Have the popish missionaries surmounted all those difficulties which we have generally thought to be insuperable? Have not the missionaries of the Unitas Fratrum, or Moravian Brethren, encountered the scorching heat of Abyssinia, and the frozen climes of Greenland, and Labrador, their difficult languages, and savage manners? Or have not English traders, for the sake of gain, surmounted all those things which have generally been counted insurmountable obstacles in the way of preaching the gospel? Witness the trade to Persia, the East Indies, China, and Greenland, yea even the accursed Slave Trade on the coasts of Africa. Men can insinuate themselves into the favor of the most barbarous clans, and uncultivated tribes, for the sake of gain; and however different the circumstances of trading and preaching are, yet this will prove the possibility of ministers being introduced there; and if this is but thought a sufficient reason to make the experiment, my point is gained.

It has been said that some learned divines have proved from Scripture that the time is not yet come that the heathen should be converted; and that first the "witnesses" must be slain (Rev.

11:1–13), and many other prophecies fulfilled. But admitting this to be the case (which I much doubt) yet if any objection if made from this against preaching to them immediately, it must be founded on one of these things: either that the secret purpose of God is the rule of our duty, and then it must be as bad to pray for them, as to preach to them; or else that none shall be converted in the heathen world till the universal down-pouring of the Spirit in the last days. But this objection comes too late; for the success of the gospel has been very considerable in many places already.

It has been objected that there are multitudes in our own nation, and within our immediate spheres of action, who are as ignorant as South-Sea savages, and that therefore we have work enough at home, without going into other countries. That there are thousands in our own land as far from God as possible, I readily grant, and that this ought to excite us to ten-fold diligence in our work, and in attempts to spread divine knowledge among them is a certain fact; but that it ought to supersede all attempts to spread the gospel in foreign parts seems to want proof. Our own countrymen have the means of grace, and may attend on the word preached if they choose it. They have the means of knowing the truth, and faithful ministers are placed in almost every part of the land, whose spheres of action might be extended if their congregations were but more hearty and active in the cause: but with them the case is widely different, who have no Bible, no written language (which many of them have not), no ministers, no good civil government, nor any of those advantages which we have. Pity therefore, humanity, and much more Christianity, call loudly for every possible exertion to introduce the gospel amongst them.

Containing a Short Review of Former Undertakings for the Conversion of the Heathen

Before the coming of our Lord Jesus Christ the whole world were either heathens, or Jews; and both, as to the body of them, were enemies to the gospel. After the resurrection the disciples continued in Jerusalem till Pentecost. Being daily engaged in prayer and supplication, and having chosen Matthias to supply the place of Judas in the apostolic office, on that solemn day, when they were assembled together, a most remarkable effusion of the Holy Spirit took place, and a capacity of speaking in all foreign languages was bestowed upon them. This opportunity was embraced by Peter for preaching the gospel to a great congregation of Jews and proselytes, who were from Parthia, Media, Elam, Mesopotamia, Judea, Cappadocia, the proconsular Asia, Phrygia, Pamphilia, Egypt, Lybia, Crete, Arabia, Rome, etc., and at the first effort God wrought so powerfully that three thousand were converted, who immediately after were baptized, and added to the church. Before this great addition they consisted of but about "an hundred and twenty persons" (Acts 1:15), but from that time they constantly increased (Acts 2). It was but a little after this that Peter and John, going up to the temple, healed the lame man; this miracle drew a great multitude together, and Peter took occasion while they stood wondering at the event to preach Jesus Christ to them (Acts 3). The consequence was that five thousand more believed (Acts 4:4).

This was not done without opposition; the priests and Sadducees tried all the methods they could invent to prevent them from preaching the gospel. The apostles, however, asserted their divine warrant, and as soon as they were set at liberty addressed God, and prayed that a divine power might attend their labors, which petition was heard, and their future ministry was very successful. On account of the needs of those who were engaged in this good work, those amongst them who had possessions, or goods, sold them, and devoted the money to pious uses (Acts 4).

About this time a man and his wife, out of great pretense of piety, sold an estate, and brought part of the money to the apostles, pretending it to be the whole; for which dissimulation both he and his wife were struck dead by the hand of God. This awful catastrophe however was the occasion of many more men and women being added to the church. The miracles wrought by the apostles, and the success attending their ministry, stirred up greater envy in the priests and Sadducees, who imprisoned them;

from which confinement they were soon liberated by an angel; upon which they went immediately as they were commanded and preached in the temple: here they were seized, and brought before the council, where Gamaliel spake in their favor, and they were dismissed. After this they continued to prosecute their work, rejoicing that they were counted worthy to suffer shame for the name of Christ (Acts 5).

By this time the church at Jerusalem was so increased that the multiplicity of its temporal concerns was the occasion of some neglects, which produced a dissatisfaction. The apostles, therefore, recommended to the church to choose seven pious men, whose office it should be to attend upon its temporal affairs; that "they might give themselves to prayer, and the ministry of the word" (Acts 6:4). Seven were accordingly chosen, over whom the apostles prayed, and ordained them to the office of deacons by imposition of hands: and, these things being settled, the church increased more and more (Acts 6). One of these deacons, whose name was Stephen, being a person of eminent knowledge and holiness, wrought many miracles, and disputed with great evidence and energy for the truth of Christianity, which raised him up a number of opponents. These soon procured his death, and carried their resentment so far as to stir up such a persecution that the church, which till now had been confined to Jerusalem, was dispersed, and all the preachers except the apostles were driven thence, and went everywhere preaching the word (Acts 8:1, 4).

A young man whose name was Saul was very active in this persecution; he had been educated under Gamaliel, a member of the Sanhedrin, was a person of promising genius, by profession a Pharisee, and much attached to the Jewish ceremonies. When Stephen was stoned he appeared much pleased with it, and had the custody of the clothes of His executioners; and from that time was fired with such a spirit of persecution himself, that he went about dragging some to prison, and compelling others to blaspheme the name of the Lord Jesus. Neither was he contented with exercising his rage at Jerusalem, but went to the chief priests and obtained testimonials of authority to carry on the same work at Damascus. But on His way, as he was almost ready to enter into the city, the Lord changed His heart in a very wonderful manner; so that instead of entering the town to persecute, he began to preach the gospel as soon as he was able. This presently brought upon him the same persecution which he had designed to exercise upon others, and even endangered His life, so that the brethren found it necessary to let him down the city wall in a basket by night, and so he escaped the hands of His enemies. From thence he went to Jerusalem where he preached the word, but being persecuted there he went to Caesarea, and from thence to Tarsus (Acts 9:1–30).

In the time of this trouble in the church, Philip went and preached at Samaria with great success, nay so great was the work that an impostor, who had deceived the people with legerdemain tricks for a long time, was so amazed, and even convinced, as to profess himself a Christian, and was baptized; but was afterwards detected, and appeared to be an hypocrite. Besides him a great number believed in reality, and being baptized a church was formed there. Soon after this the Lord commanded Philip to go the way which led from Jerusalem to Gaza, which he did, and there found a eunuch of great authority in the court of Ethiopia, to whom he preached Christ, who believed, and was baptized; after which Philip preached at Ashdod, or Azotus (Acts 8).

About the same time Peter went to Lydda, or Diospolis, and cured Eneas of a palsy, which was the means of conversion not only of the inhabitants of that town, but also of the neighboring country, called Saron, the capital of which was Lasharon; and while he was there, a circumstance turned up which tended much to the spread of the truth. A woman of Joppa, a sea-port town in the neighborhood, died and they sent to Lydda for Peter, who went over, and when he had prayed she was raised to life again; which was an occasion of the conversion of many of that town. Peter continued preaching there for some time, and lodged at the house of a tanner (Acts 9:32–43).

Now another circumstance also tended to the further propagation of Christianity, for a Roman military officer who had some acquaintance with the Old Testament Scriptures, but was not circumcised, was one day engaged in prayer in his house at Caesarea, when an angel appeared to him, and bid him send for Peter from Joppa to preach in his house. Before this the work of God had been wholly confined to the Jews, and Jewish prose-lytes, and even the apostles appeared to have had very contracted ideas of the Christian dispensation; but now God by a vision revealed to Peter that Christianity was to be spread into all nations. He accordingly went and preached at the house of Cor-nelius, at Caesarea, when several were converted, and baptized, and the foundation of a church laid in that city (Acts 10).

Some of the dispersed ministers, having fled to Antioch in Syria, began to preach to the Greeks in that city about the same time, and had good success; upon which the apostles sent Paul and Barnabas, who instructed and strengthened them, and a church was formed in that city also, which in a little time sent out several imminent preachers (Acts 11:19–26).

In the Acts of the Apostles we have an account of four of the principal journeys which Paul and his companions undertook. The first, in which he was accompanied by Barnabas, is recorded in the thirteenth and fourteenth chapters, and was the first attack on the heathen world. It was a journey into Asia Minor. On their way they passed over the land of Cyprus. No sooner had they entered on their undertaking than they met with great difficulty; for Mark, whom they had taken as their minister, deserted them, and returned to Jerusalem, where, it seems, he thought he should enjoy the greatest quiet. Paul and Barnabas however went forward; in every city they preached the word of the Lord, enter-ing into the Jewish synagogues and first preaching Christ to them, and then to the Gentiles. They were heard with great eagerness and candor by some, and rejected by others with obstinacy and wrath, and cruel persecution. On one occasion they had enough to do to restrain the people from worshipping them as gods, and soon after that Paul was stoned, dragged out of the city, and left for dead. Having penetrated as far as Derbe, they thought it proper to return by the way that they came, call-ing at every city where they had sown the good seed. They found in most, if not all these places, some who had embraced the gospel, and exhorted and strengthened them in the faith. They formed them into churches, and ordained them elders, and fasted and prayed with them; and so having commended them to the Lord on whom they had believed, returned to Antioch in Syria, from whence they first set out, and rehearsed to the church all that God had done with them, and how He had opened the door of faith to the Gentiles (Acts 13–14).

About this time a dispute arose in the churches concerning circumcision, and Paul and Barnabas were deputed to go up to Jerusalem, to consult the apostles and elders on the subject. The business being completed, they, accompanied with Judas and Silas, returned to Antioch with the general resolution, and continued there for a season, teaching and preaching the word of the Lord (Acts 15:1–35).

Paul now proposed to Barnabas, his fellow-laborer, that they might visit their brethren in the places where they had been already, and see how they did. To this Barnabas readily agreed, but a difference arising between them about taking with them John Mark, who had deserted them before, these two eminent servants of God were parted asunder, and never appear to have traveled together any more. They continued however each to serve in the cause of Christ, though they could not walk together. Barnabas took John, and sailed to Cyprus, his native island, and Paul took Silas, and went through Syria and Cilicia, to Derbe and Lystra, cities where he and Barnabas had preached in their first excursion (Acts 15:36-41). Here they found Timothy, a promising young man, whom they encouraged to engage in the ministry.

Paul being now at Lystra, which was the boundary of his first excursion, and having visited the churches already planted, and delivered to them the decrees of the apostles and elders relating to circumcision, seems to have felt his heart enlarged, and attempted to carry out the glorious work of preaching the gospel to the heathen to a greater extent. With Silas and Timothy in his second journey he took a western direction, passing through Phrygia, and the region of Galatia. Having preached the word with considerable success (Acts 18:23), he and his companions wished to have gone into the proconsular Asia, and afterwards tried to go into Bythinia; but being forbidden of the Holy Ghost, who seems to have had a special design of employing them elsewhere, passing by Mysia they came down to Troas on the sea coast. Here a vision appeared to Paul, in which he was invited to go over to Macedonia. Obedient to the heavenly vision, and greatly encouraged by it, they with all speed crossed the Aegean Sea, and passing through the island of Samothracia, landed at Neapolis, and went from thence to Philippi, the chief city of that part of Macedonia. It was here that Paul preached on a Sabbath day to a few women by a river side, and Lydia, a woman of Thyatira, was converted and baptized, and her household with her. It was here that a poor girl, who brought her employers considerable profit by foretelling future events, followed the apostles, had her spirit of divination ejected, on which account her masters were much irritated, and raised a tumult, the effect of which was that Paul and Silas were imprisoned. But even this was over-ruled for the success of the gospel, in that the keeper of the prison, and all his house, were thereby brought to believe in the Lord Jesus Christ, and were baptized (Acts 16).

From Philippi they passed through Amphipolis, Apollonia, Thessalonica (now Salonichi), Berea, Athens, and Corinth, preaching the gospel wherever they went. From hence Paul took ship and sailed to Syria, only giving a short call at Ephesus, determining to be at Jerusalem at the feast of the Passover; and having saluted the church, he came to Caesarea, and from thence to Antioch (Acts 17:1–18:22).

Here ended Paul's second journey, which was very extensive, and took up some years of his time. He and his companions met with their difficulties in it, but had likewise their encouragements. They were persecuted at Philippi, as already noticed, and generally found the Jews to be their most inveterate enemies. These would raise tumults, inflame the minds of the Gentiles against them and follow them from place to place, doing them all the mischief in their power. This was the case especially at Thessalonica, Berea, and Corinth. But amidst all their persecutions

God was with them, and strengthened them in various ways. At Berea they were candidly received, and their doctrine fairly tried by the Holy Scriptures; and "therefore," it is said "many of them believed" (Acts 17:12). At other places, though they affected to despise the apostle, yet some clave unto him. At Corinth opposition rose to a great height; but the Lord appeared to his servant in a vision, saying, "Be not afraid, but speak, and hold not thy peace, for I am with thee, and no man shall set on thee to hurt thee; for I have much people in this city" (Acts 18:9–10). And the promise was made abundantly good in the spirit displayed by Gallio, the proconsul, who turned a deaf ear to the accusations of the Jews, and nobly declined interfering in matters beside his province. Upon the whole a number of churches were planted during this journey, which for ages after shone as lights in the world.

When Paul had visited Antioch, and spent some time there, he prepared for a third journey into heathen countries, the account of which begins at Acts 18:23 and ends at Acts 21:17. At his first setting out he went over the whole country of Galatia and Phrygia in order, strengthening all the disciples; and passing through the upper coasts came to Ephesus. There for the space of three months he boldly preached in the Jewish synagogue, disputing and persuading the things concerning the kingdom of God. But when the hardened Jews had openly rejected the gospel, and spake evil of that way before the multitude, Paul openly separated the disciples from them, and assembled in the school of one Tyrannus. This, it is said, continued for the space of two years, "so that all who dwelt in" the proconsular "Asia heard the word of the Lord Jesus, both Jews and Greeks" (Acts 19:10). Certain magicians about this time were exposed, and others were converted, who burnt their books and confessed their deeds. So mightily grew the word of the Lord, and prevailed.

After this, an uproar having been raised by Demetrius the silversmith, Paul went into Macedonia, visited the churches planted in his former journey, and from thence passed into Greece. Having preached up and down for three months, he thought of sailing from thence directly to Syria; but in order to avoid the Jews, who laid wait for him near the sea coast, he took another course through Macedonia, and from thence to Troas, by the way of Philippi. There is no mention made in his former journey of his having preached at Troas; yet it seems he did, and a church was gathered, with whom the apostle at this time united in "breaking of bread" (Acts 20:7). It was here that he preached all night and raised Eutychus, who being overcome with sleep had fallen down and was taken up dead. From thence they set sail for Syria, and on their way called at Miletus, where Paul sent for the elders of the church at Ephesus, and delivered that most solemn and affectionate farewell, recorded in the twentieth chapter of the Acts of the Apostles. From hence they sailed for Tyre, where they tarried seven days and from thence proceeded to Jerusalem.

Paul's fourth and last journey (or rather voyage) was to Rome, where he went in the character of a prisoner. For while being at Jerusalem he was quickly apprehended by the Jews; but being rescued by Lysias, the chief captain, he was sent to Caesarea to take his trial. Here he made his defense before Felix and Drusilla, in such a way that the judge, instead of the prisoner, was made to tremble. Here also he made his defense before Festus, Agrippa, and Bernice, with such force of evidence that Agrippa was almost persuaded to be a Christian. But the malice of the Jews being insatiable, and Paul finding himself in danger of being delivered into their hands, was constrained to appeal unto Caesar. This was the occasion of his being sent to Rome, where he arrived after a long and dangerous voyage, and being shipwrecked on the island of Melita, where he wrought miracles, and Publius, the governor, was converted (Acts 21:17–28:10).

When he arrived at Rome he addressed his countrymen the Jews, some of whom believed; but when others rejected the gospel, he turned from them to the Gentiles, and for two whole years dwelt in his own hired house preaching the kingdom of God, and teaching those things which concern the Lord Jesus Christ, with all confidence, no man forbidding him (Acts 28:16–31).

Thus far the history of the Acts of the Apostles informs us of the success of the word in the primitive times; and history informs us of its being preached about this time in many other places. Peter speaks of a church at Babylon (1 Pet. 5:13); Paul proposed a journey to Spain (Rom. 15:24), and it is generally believed he went there and likewise came to France and Britain. Andrew preached to the Scythians, north of the Black Sea. John is said to have preached in India, and we know that he was at the Isle of Patmos, in the Archipelago. Philip is reported to have preached in upper Asia, Scythia, and Phrygia; Bartholomew in India, on this side of the Ganges, Phrygia, and Armenia; Matthew in Arabia, or Asiatic Ethiopia, and Parthia; Thomas in India, as far as the coast of Coromandel, and some say in the island of Ceylon; Simon, the Canaanite, in Egypt, Cyrene, Mauritania, Lybia, and other parts of Africa, and from thence to have come to Britain; and Jude is said to have been principally engaged in the lesser Asia and Greece. Their labors were evidently very extensive, and very successful; so that Pliny the Younger, who lived soon after the death of the apostles, in a letter to the emperor Trajan, observed that Christianity had spread not only through towns and cities but also through whole countries. Indeed before this, in the time of Nero, it was so prevalent that it was necessary to oppose it by an Imperial Edict, and accordingly the proconsuls, and other governors, were commissioned to destroy it.

Justin Martyr, who lived about the middle of the second century, in his dialogue with Trypho, observed that there was no part of mankind, whether Greeks or barbarians, or any others, by whatever name they were called, whether Samaritans, or the Scenites of Arabia Petrea, who lived in tents among their cattle, where supplications and thanksgivings are not offered up to the Father, and maker of all things, through the name of Jesus Christ. Irenaeus, who lived about the year 170, speaks of churches that were founded in Germany, Spain, France, the eastern countries, Lybia, and the middle of the world. Tertullian, who lived and wrote at Carthage in Africa, about twenty years afterwards, enumerating the countries where Christianity had penetrated, makes mention of the Parthians, Medes, Elamites, Mesopotamians, Armenians, Phrygians, Cappadocians, the inhabitants of Pontus, Asia, Pamphylia, Egypt, and the regions of Africa beyond Cyrene, the Romans, and Jews, formerly of Jerusalem, many of the Getuli, many borders of the Mauri, or Moors, in Mauritania; now Barbary, Morocco, etc., all the borders of Spain, many nations of the Gauls, and the places in Britain which were inaccessible to the Romans; the Dacians, Samaritans, Germans, Scythians, and the inhabitants of many hidden nations and provinces, and of many islands unknown to him, and which he could not enumerate. The labors of the ministers of the gospel in this early period were so remarkably blessed of God that the last-mentioned writer observed, in a letter to Scapula, that if he began a persecution the city of Carthage itself must be decimated thereby. Yes, and so abundant were they in the three first centuries, that ten years' constant and almost universal persecution under Diocletian could neither root out the Christians nor prejudice their cause.

After this they had great encouragement under several emperors, particularly Constantine and Theodosius, and a very great work of God was carried on; but the ease and affluence which in these times attended the church served to introduce a flood of corruption, which brought on by degrees the whole system of Popery, by means of which all appeared to be lost again; and Satan set up his kingdom of darkness, deceit, and human authority over conscience, through all the Christian world.

In the time of Constantine one Frumentius was sent to preach to the Indians, and met with great success. A young woman who was a Christian, being taken captive by the Iberians, or Giorgians, near the Caspian Sea, informed them of the truths of Christianity, and was so much regarded that they sent to Constantine for ministers to come and preach the word to them. About the same time some barbarous nations, having made irruptions into Thrace, carried away several Christians captive, who preached the gospel; by which means the inhabitants upon the Rhine, and the Danube, the Celtae, and some other parts of Gaul, were brought to embrace Christianity. About this time also James of Nisbia went into Persia to strengthen the Christians and preach to the heathens; and his success was so great that Adiabene was almost entirely Christian. About the year 372 one Moses, a monk, went to preach to the Saracens, who then lived in Arabia, where he had great success; and at this time the Goths, and other northern nations, had the kingdom of Christ further extended amongst them, but they were very soon corrupted with Arianism.

Soon after this the kingdom of Christ was further extended among the Scythian Nomades, beyond the Danube, and about the year 430 a people called the Burgundians received the gospel. Four years after that Palladius was sent to preach in Scotland, and the next year Patrick was sent from Scotland to preach to the Irish, who before his time were totally uncivilized and, some say, cannibals; he however was useful, and laid the foundations of several churches in Ireland. Soon after this, truth spread further among the Saracens, and in 522 Zathus king of the Colchians encouraged it, and many of that nation were converted to Christianity. About this time also the work was extended in Ireland by Finian, and in Scotland by Constantine and Columba; the latter of whom preached also to the Picts, and Brudaeus, their king, with several others, was converted. About 541 Adad, the king of Ethiopia, was converted by the preaching of Mansionarius; the Heruli beyond the Danube were now made obedient to the faith, and so were the Abfagi near the Caucasian Mountains.

But now popery, especially the compulsive part of it, was risen to such a height that the usual method of propagating the gospel, or rather what was so called, was to conquer pagan nations by force of arms, and then oblige them to submit to Christianity, after which bishoprics were erected and persons were sent to instruct the people. I shall just mention some of those who are said to have labored thus.

In 596, Austin, the monk, Melitus, Justus, Paulinus, and Ruffinian, labored in England, and in their way were very successful. Paulinus, who appears to have been one of the best of them, had great success in Northumberland; Birinnius preached to the West Saxons, and Felix to the East Angles. In 589 Amandus Gallus labored in Ghent, Chelenus in Artois, and

Gullus and Columbanus in Suabia. In 648, Egidius Gallus in Flanders, and the two Evaldi in Westphalia. In 684, Willifred, in the Isle of Wight. In 688, Chilianus, in upper Franconia. In 698, Boniface, or Winifred, among the Thuringians, near Erford, in Saxony, and Willibroad in West Friesland. Charlemagne conquered Hungary in the year 800, and obliged the inhabitants to profess Christianity, while Modestus likewise preached to the Venedi, at the source of the Save and Drave. In 833 Anigarius preached in Denmark, Gaudibert in Sweden, and about 861 Methodius and Cyril in Bohemia.

About the year 500, the Scythians overran Bulgaria, and Christianity was wiped out, but about 870 they were reconverted. Poland began to be brought over about the same time, and afterwards, about 960 or 990, the work was further extended amongst the Poles and Prussians. The work was begun in Norway in 960, and in Muscovy in 989, the Swedes propagated Christianity in Finland in 1168, Lithuania became Christian in 1386, Samitoga in 1439. The Spaniards forced popery upon the inhabitants of South America, and the Portuguese did the same in Asia. The Jesuits were sent into China in 1552. Xavier, whom they call the apostle of the Indians, labored in the East Indies and Japan from 1541 to 1552, and several missions of Capachins were sent to Africa in the seventeenth century. But blind zeal, gross superstition, and infamous cruelties, so marked the appearances of religion all this time, that the professors of Christianity needed conversion as much as the heathen world.

A few pious people had fled from the general corruption, and lived obscurely in the valleys of Piedmont and Savoy. They were like the seed of the church. Some of them now and then needed to travel into other parts, where they faithfully testified against the corruptions of the times. About 1369 Wickliffe began to preach the faith in England, and his preaching and writings were the means of the conversion of great numbers, many of whom became excellent preachers; and a work was begun which afterwards spread in England, Hungary, Bohemia, Germany, Switzerland, and many other places. John Huss and Jerome of Prague preached boldly and successfully in Bohemia and the adjacent parts. In the following century Luther, Calvin, Melancthon, Bucer, Martyr, and many others stood up against all the rest of the world; they preached, and prayed, and wrote; and nations agreed one after another to cast off the yoke of popery, and to embrace the doctrine of the gospel.

In England popish cruelty was followed by episcopal tyranny, which in the year 1620 obliged many pious people to leave their native land and settle in America; these were followed by others in 1629, who laid the foundations of several gospel churches which have increased amazingly since that time, and the Redeemer has fixed His throne in that country where but a little time ago Satan had universal dominion.

In 1632 Mr. Elliott of New England, a very pious and zealous minister, began to preach to the Indians, among whom he had great success; several churches of Indians were planted, and some preachers and schoolmasters were raised up amongst them; since which time others have labored amongst them with some good encouragement. About the year 1743 Mr. David Brainerd was sent as a missionary to some more Indians, where he preached, and prayed, and after some time an extraordinary work of conversion was wrought, and wonderful success attended his ministry. At this present time Mr. Kirkland and Mr. Sargeant are employed in the same good work, and God has considerably blessed their labors.

In 1706 the king of Denmark sent a Mr. Ziegenbalg and some others to Tranquebar, on the Coromandel coast in the East Indies. They were useful to the natives, so that many of the heathens were turned to the Lord. The Dutch East India Company likewise having extended their commerce built the city of Batavia, and a church was opened there; and the Lord's Supper was administered for the first time on the 3rd of January, 1621, by their minister James Hulzibos; from hence some ministers were sent to Amboyna, who were very successful. A seminary of learning was erected at Leyden, in which ministers and assistants were educated under the renowned Walaeus, and for some years a great number were sent to the East, at the company's expense, so that in a little time many thousands at Formosa, Malabar,

Ternate, Jaffanapatnam, in the town of Columbia, at Amboyna, Java, Banda, Macassar, and Malabar, embraced the religion of our Lord Jesus Christ. The work had decayed in some places, but they now have churches in Ceylon, Sumatra, Java, Amboyna, and some other of the Spice Islands, and at the Cape of Good Hope in Africa.

But none of the moderns have equaled the Moravian Brethren in this good work; they have sent missions to Greenland, Labrador, and several of the islands of the West Indies, which have been blessed for good. They have likewise sent to Abyssinia in Africa, but what success they have had I cannot tell.

The late Mr. Wesley lately made an effort in the West Indies, and some of their ministers are now laboring amongst the Caribbs and Negroes, and I have seen pleasing accounts of their success.

Containing a Survey of the Present State of the World

In this survey I shall consider the world as divided, according to its usual division, into four parts, Europe, Asia, Africa, and America, and take notice of the extent of the several countries, their population, civilization, and religion. The article of religion I shall divide into Christian, Jewish, Mahometan, and Pagan; and shall now and then hint at the particular sect of them that prevails in the places which I shall describe. The following tables will exhibit a more comprehensive view of what I propose, than anything I can offer on the subject.

EUROPE

Countries	EXTENT		Number of Inhabitants	Religion
	Length Miles	Breadth Miles		
Great Britain	680	300	12,000,000	Protestants, of many denominations
Ireland	285	160	2,000,000	Protestants, and Papists
France	600	500	24,000,000	Catholics, Deists, and Protestants
Spain	700	500	9,500,000	Papists
Portugal	300	100	2,000,000	Papists
Sweden, including Sweden proper, Gothland, Shonen, Lapland, Bothnia, and Finland	800	500	3,500,000	The Swedes are serious Lutherans, but most of the Laplanders are Pagans, and very superstitious
Isle of Gothland	80	23	5,000	
—Oefel	45	24	2,500	
—Oeland	84	9	1,000	
—Dago	26	23	1,000	
Isle of Aland	24	20	800	
—Hogland	9	5	100	
Denmark	240	114	360,000	Lutherans the of Helvetic Confession
Isle of Zeeland	60	60	284,000	Ditto
—Funen	38	32	144,000	Ditto
—Arroe	8	2	200	Ditto
—Iceland	435	185	60,000	Ditto
—Langeland	27	12	3,000	Ditto
—Laland	38	30	148,000	Ditto
—Falster	27	12	3,000	Ditto
—Mona	14	5	600	Ditto
—Alfen	15	6	600	Ditto

EUROPE

Countries	EXTENT		Number of Inhabitants	Religion
	Length Miles	Breadth Miles		
—Femeren	13	8	1,000	Ditto
Isle of Bornholm	20	12	2,000	Lutherans
Greenland	Undiscovered		7,000	Pagans, and Moravian Christians
Norway	750	170	724,000	Lutherans
24 Faro Isles			4,500	Ditto
Danish Lapland	285	172	100,000	Ditto, and Pagans
Poland	700	680	9,000,000	Papists, Lutherans, Calvinists, & Jews
Prussia[a]	400	160	2,500,000	Calvinists, Catholics, & Lutherans
Sardinia	135	57	600,000	Papists
Sicily	180	92	1,000,000	Ditto
Italy	660	120	20,000,000	Ditto
United Netherlands	150	150	2,000,000	Protestants of several denominations
Austrian Netherlands	200	200	2,500,000	Papists and Protestants
Switzerland	260	100	2,880,000	Papists and Protestants
The Grisons	100	62	800,000	Lutherans and Papists
The Abbacy of St. Gall	24	10	50,000	Ditto
Neufchatel	32	20	100,000	Calvinists
Valais	80	30	440,000	Papists
Piedmont	140	98	900,000	Ditto, and Protestants
Savoy	87	60	720,000	Ditto
Geneva, City			24,000	Calvinists

EUROPE

Countries	EXTENT		Number of Inhabitants	Religion
	Length Miles	Breadth Miles		
Bohemia	478	322	2,100,000	Papists and Moravians
Hungary	300	200	2,500,000	Papists
Germany	600	500	20,000,000	Ditto, and Protestants
Russia in Europe	1,500	1,100	22,000,000	Greek Church
Turkey in Europe	1,000	900	18,000,000	Greek Christians, Jews, & Mahometans
Budziac Tartary	300	60	1,200,000	Greek Christians, Jews, & Mahometans
Lesser Tartary	390	65	1,000,000	Ditto
Crim Tartary	145	80	500,000	Ditto
Isle of Tenedos	5	3	200	Mahometans
—Negropont	90	25	25,000	Ditto
—Lemnos	25	25	4,000	Ditto
—Paros	36 *in compass*		4,500	Greek Christians
—Lesbos, or Mitylene	160 *in compass*		30,000	Mahometans and Greeks
—Naxia	100 *in compass*		8,000	Greeks and Papists
—Scio, or Chios	112 *in compass*		113,000	Greek Chrisitans, Papists, & Mahometans
—Nio	40 *in compass*		1,000	Ditto
—Scyros	60 *in compass*		1,000	Ditto
—Mycone	36 *in compass*		3,000	Ditto
Isles of Samos	30	15	12,000	Mahometans
—Nicaria	70 *in compass*		3,000	Greek Christians
—Andros	120 *in compass*		4,000	Ditto
—Cyclades, *Delos the Chief*			700	Ditto

EUROPE

Countries	EXTENT		Number of Inhabitants	Religion
	Length Miles	*Breadth Miles*		
—Zia	40 *in compass*		8,000	Ditto
—Cerigo or Cytheraea	50 *in compass*		1,000	Ditto
—Santorin	36 *in compass*		10,000	Ditto, and Papists
—Policandra	8 *in compass*		400	Ditto
—Patmos	18 *in compass*		600	Ditto
—Sephanto	36 *in compass*		5,000	Greeks
—Claros	40 *in compass*		1,700	Mahometans
—Amorgo	36 *in compass*		4,000	Greek Christians
—Leros	18 *in compass*		800	Christians and Mahometans
Isle of Thermia	40 *in compass*		6,000	Greek Christians
—Stampalia	50 *in compass*		3,000	Ditto
—Salamis	50 *in compass*		1,000	Ditto
—Scarpanta	20 *in compass*		2,000	Ditto
—Cephalonia	130 *in compass*		50,000	Ditto
—Zant	50 *in compass*		30,000	Greek Christians
—Milo	60 *in compass*		40,000	Ditto
—Corfu	120 *in compass*		60,000	Ditto
—Candia, or Crete	200	60	400,000	Ditto, and Mahometans
—Coos, or Stanchia	70 *in compass*		12,800	Mahometans and Christians
—Rhodes	60	25	120,000	Ditto
—Cyprus	150	70	300,000	Mahometans

a. The rest of Prussian dominions being scatter about in several countries, are counted to those countries where they lie.

ASIA

Countries	EXTENT		Number of Inhabitants	Religion
	Length Miles	Breadth Miles		
Turkey in Asia *contains* Anatolia, Syria, Palestine, Diabekr, Turcomania, and Georgia	1,000	800	20,000,000	Mahametanism is most prevalent, but there are many Greek, Latin, Eutychian, and Armenian Christians
Arabia	1,300	1,200	16,000,000	Mahometans
Persia	1,280	1,140	20,000,000	Ditto, of the Sect of Ali
Great Tartary	4,000	1,200	40,000,000	Mahometans and Pagans
Siberia	2,800	960	7,500,000	Greek Christians and Pagans
Samojedia	2,000	870	1,900,000	Pagans
Kamtscatcha	540	236	900,000	Ditto
Nova Zembla	Undiscovered		thinly inhabit	Ditto
China	1,400	1,260	60,000,000	Ditto
Japan *contains* Niphon Isl.	900	360	10,000,000	Ditto
Isle of Ximo	210	200	8,000,000	Pagans
—Xicoco	117	104	1,800,000	Ditto
—Tsussima	39	34	40,000	Ditto
—Iki	20	17	6,000	Ditto
—Kubitessima	30	26	8,000	Ditto
—Matounsa	54	26	50,000	Ditto
—Fastistia	36i	34	30,000	Ditto
—Amacusa	27	24	6,000	Ditto
—Awasi	30	18	5,000	Ditto
—India, *beyond the Ganges*	2,000	1,000	50,000,000	Mahometans and Pagans
Indostan	2,0o00	1,500	110,000,000	Ditto
Tibet	1,200	480	10,000,000	Pagans

ASIA

Countries	EXTENT		Number of Inhabitants	Religion
	Length Miles	Breadth Miles		
Isle of Ceylon	250	200	2,000,000	Pagans, except the Dutch Christians
—Maldives	1,000 *in number*		100,000	Mahometans
—Sumatra	1,000	100	2,100,000	Ditto, and Pagans
—Java	580	100	2,700,000	Ditto
—Timor	240	54	300,000	Ditto, and a few Christians
—Borneo	800	700	8,000,000	Ditto
—Celebes	510	240	2,000,000	Ditto
—Boutam	75	30	80,000	Mahometans
—Carpentyn	30	3	2,000	Christian Protestants
—Ourature	18	6	3,000	Pagans
—Pullo Lout	60	36	10,000	Ditto

Besides the little Islands of *Manaar, Aripen, Caradivia, Pengandiva, Analativa, Nainandiva,* and *Nindundiva,* which are inhabited by Christian Protestants.
And *Banca, Madura, Bally, Lambeck, Flores, Solor, Leolana, Pantera, Miscomby* and several others, inhabited by Pagans and Mahometans.

The Moluccas are, —Banda	20	10	6,000	Pagans and Mahometans
—Buro	25	10	7,000	Ditto
—Amboyne	25	10	7,500	Christians;—the Dutch have 25 Ch.
—Ceram	210	45	250,000	Pagans and Mahometans
—Gillola	190	110	650,000	Ditto

The Philippine Islands are supposed to be about 11,000;—some of the chief are,

Isle of Mindanao	60	40	18,000	Pagans and Mahometans
—Bahol	24	12	6,000	Ditto
—Layta	48	27	10,000	Ditto
—Parragon	240	60	100,000	Ditto

ASIA

Countries	EXTENT		Number of Inhabitants	Religion
	Length Miles	Breadth Miles		
The Calmines are Sebu	60	24	10,000	Papists
—Mindora	60	36	12,000	Pagans and Mahometans
—Philippina	185	120	104,000	Ditto
—Negroes Isle	150	60	80,000	Papists
—Manilla			31,000	Ditto, and Pagans

The Ladrone Islands are inhabited by most uncivilized Pagans.

New Holland	2,500	2,000	12,000,000	Pagans;—1 or 2 Ministers are there
New Zeland[a]	960	180	1,120,000	Ditto
New Guinea	1,000	360	1,900,000	Ditto
New Britain	180	120	900,000	Ditto
New Ireland	180	60	700,000	Ditto
Orong Java	*A Cluster of Isles*			Ditto
New Caledonia	260	30	170,000	Ditto
New Hebrides				Ditto
Friendly Isles	20 *in number*			Ditto
Sandwich Isles	7 *in number*		400,000	Ditto
Society Isles	6 *in number*		800,000	Ditto
Kurile Isles	45 *in number*		50,000	Ditto
Pelew Isles				Pagans
Oonalashaka Isle	40	20	3,000	Ditto
The other South-Sea Islands				Ditto

a. *Two Islands*

AFRICA

Countries	EXTENT		Number of Inhabitants	Religion
	Length Miles	Breadth Miles		
Egypt	600	250	2,200,000	Mahometans and Jews
Nubia	940	600	3,000,000	Ditto
Barbary	1,800	500	3,500,000	Mahometans, Jews, and Christians
Biledulgerid	2,500	350	3,500,000	Mahometans, Christians, and Jews
Zaara, or the Desart	3,400	660	800,000	Ditto
Abyssinia	900	800	5,800,000	Armenian Christians
Abex	540	130	1,600,000	Christians and Pagans
Negroland	2,200	840	18,000,000	Pagans
Loango	410	300	1,500,000	Ditto
Congo	540	220	2,000,000	Ditto
Angola	360	250	1,400,000	Ditto
Benguela	430	180	1,600,000	Ditto
Mataman	450	240	1,500,000	Ditto
Ajan	900	300	2,500,000	Ditto
Zanguebar	1,400	350	3,000,000	Ditto
Monoemugi	900	660	2,000,000	Ditto
Sofala	480	300	1,000,000	Pagans
Terra de natal	600	350	2,000,000	Ditto
Cassraria, or the Hottentots Country	708	660	2,000,000	Ditto, & a few Christians at the Cape
Isle of Madagascar	1,000	220	2,000,000	Pagans and Mahometans
—St. Mary	54	9	5,000	French Papists
—Mascarin	39	30	17,000	Ditto

AFRICA

Countries	EXTENT		Number of Inhabitants	Religion
	Length Miles	Breadth Miles		
—St. Helena	21 *in compass*		1,000	English and French Christians
—Annabon	16	14	4,000	Portuguese Papists
—St. Thomas	25	23	9,000	Pagans
—Zocotora	80	54	10,000	Mahometans
—Comora Isles	5 *in number*		5,000	Ditto
—Mauritius	150 *in compass*		10,000	French Papists
Isle of Bourbon	90 *in compass*		15,000	French Papists
—Maderias	3 *in number*		10,000	Papists
—Cape Verd Isles	10 *in number*		20,000	Ditto
—Canaries	12 *in number*		30,000	Ditto
—Azores	9 *in number*		100,000	Ditto
—Maltha	15	8	1,200	Ditto

AMERICA

Countries	EXTENT		Number of Inhabitants	Religion
	Length Miles	Breadth Miles		
Brazil	2,900	900	14,000,000	Pagans and Papists
Paraguay	1,140	460	10,000,000	Pagans
Chile	1,200	500	2,000,000	Pagans and Papists
Peru	1,800	600	10,000,000	Pagans and Papists
Country of the Amazons	1,200	900	8,000,000	Pagans
Terra Firma	1,400	700	10,000,000	Pagans and Papists
Guiana	780	480	2,000,000	Ditto
Terra Magellancia	1,400	460	9,000,000	Pagans
Old Mexico	2,220	600	13,500,000	Ditto and Papists
New Mexico	2,000	1,000	14,000,000	Ditto

AMERICA

Countries	EXTENT		Number of Inhabitants	Religion
	Length Miles	*Breadth Miles*		
The States of America	1,000	600	3,700,000	Christians, of various denominations
Terra de Labrador, Nova Scotia, Louisiana, Canada, and all the country inland from Mexico to Hudson's Bay	1,680	600	8,000,000	Christians, of various denominations, but most of the North-American Indians are Pagans
California, and from thence along the western coast to 70 degrees south latitude, and so far inland as to meet the above article	2,820	1,380	9,000,000	Pagans
All to the North of 70 degrees	*unknown*			Pagan
Cape Breton	400	110	20,000	Christians
—Newfoundland	350	200	1,400	Protestants
—Cumberland's Isle	780	300	10,000	Pagans
—Madre de Dios	105	30	8,000	Ditto
—Terra del Fuego	120	36	5,000	Ditto
All of the Islands in the vicinity of Cape Horn				Pagans
The Bermudas extend	16	5	20,000	Half English, and Half Slaves
The Little Antilles are				
—Aruba	5	3	200	Dutch, and Pagan Negroes
—Curassoa	30	10	11,000	Ditto
—Bonaire	10	3	300	Ditto
—Magaritta	40	24	18,000	Spaniards, and Pagan Negroes
—St. Trinidad	90	60	100,000	Ditto

AMERICA

Countries	EXTENT		Number of Inhabitants	Religion
	Length Miles	Breadth Miles		
The Bahamas are				
—Bahama	50	16	16,000	Pagans
—Providence	28	11	6,000	Ditto

Besides Eluthera, Harbour, Lucayonegua, Andross, Cigateo, Guanaliana, Yumeta, Samana, Yuma, Mayaguana, Ynagua, Caieos, Traingula—Pagans

The Antilles are				
—Cuba	700	60	1,000,000	Papists
—Jamaica	140	60	400,000	English, and Pagan Negroes
—St. Domingo	450	150	1,000,000	French, Spaniards, and Negroes
—Porto Rico	100	49	300,000	Spaniards and Negroes
—Vache, or Cows I	18	2	1,000	Ditto

The Virgin Isles are 12 *in number,* of which Danes Island is the principal—Protestants

The Carribbees are				
—St. Cruz	30	10	13,500	Danish Protestants
—Anguilla	30	9	6,000	Protestants, and Negroes
—St. Martin	21	12	7,500	Ditto
—St. Bartholomew	6	4	720	Ditto
—Barbuda	20	12	7,500	Ditto
—Saba	5	4	1,500	Ditto
—Guardulope	45	38	50,000	Catholics and Pagan Negros
—Marigalante	15	12	5,400	Ditto
—Tobago	32	9	2,400	Ditto
—Desiada	12	6	1,500	Ditto
—Granada	30	15	13,500	English, and Pagan Negroes
—St. Lucia	23	12	5,000	Ditto, and Native Pagan Caribbs

AMERICA

Countries	EXTENT		Number of Inhabitants		Religion
	Length Miles	Breadth Miles	Whites	Negroes	
—St. Eustatia	6	4	5,000	15,000	Dutch, English, &c.
—St. Christopher	20	7	6,000	36,000	English
—Nevis	6	4	5,000	10,000	Ditto
—Antigua	20	20	7,000	30,000	Ditto
—Montserat	6	6	5,000	10,000	Ditto
—Martinico	60	30	20,000	50,000	French
—St. Vincent's	24	18	8,000	5,000	The 8,000 are Native Caribbs
—Barbadoes	21	14	50,000	100,000	English
—Dominica	28	13		40,000	Ditto, 2,000 of them Native Caribbs
—St. Thomas	15 *in compass*			8,000	Danish Protestants

This, as nearly as I can obtain information, is the state of the world; though in many countries, as Turkey, Arabia, Great Tartary, Africa, and America except the United States, and most of the Asiatic Islands, we have no accounts of the number of inhabitants that can be relied on. I have therefore only calculated the extent, and counted a certain number on an average per square mile; in some countries more, and in others less, according as circumstances determine. A few general remarks upon it will conclude this section.

First, the inhabitants of the world according to this calculation amount to about seven hundred and thirty-one millions; four hundred and twenty millions of whom are still in pagan darkness; an hundred and thirty millions of the followers of Mahomet; an hundred millions Catholics; forty-four millions Protestants; thirty millions of the Greek and Armenian churches, and perhaps seven millions of Jews. It must undoubtedly strike every thinking mind that a vast proportion of the sons of Adam remain in the most deplorable state of heathen darkness, without any means of knowing the true God, except what are afforded them by the works of nature; and utterly destitute of the knowledge of the gospel of Christ, or of any means of obtaining it. In many of these countries they have no written language, consequently no Bible, and are only led by the most childish customs and traditions. Such, for instance, are all the middle and back parts of North America, the inland parts of South America, the South Sea Islands, New Holland, New Zealand, New Guinea; and I may add Great Tartary, Siberia, Samojedia, and the other parts of Asia contiguous to the frozen sea; the greatest part of Africa, the island of Madagascar, and many places beside. In many of these parts also they are cannibals, feeding upon the flesh of their slain enemies with the greatest brutality and eagerness. The truth of this was ascertained beyond a doubt by the late eminent navigator, Cook, of the New Zealanders and some of the inhabitants of the western coast of America. Human sacrifices are also very frequently offered, so that scarce a week elapses without instances of this kind. They are in general poor, barbarous, naked pagans, as destitute of civilization as they are of true religion.

Secondly, barbarous as these poor heathens are, they appear to be as capable of knowledge as we are; and in many places, at least, have displayed uncommon genius and teachability; and I greatly question whether most of the barbarities practiced by them have not originated in some real or supposed affront, and are therefore more properly acts of self-defense than proofs of inhuman and bloodthirsty dispositions.

Thirdly, in other parts where they have a written language, as in the East Indies, China, Japan, etc., they know nothing of the gospel. The Jesuits indeed once made many converts to popery among the Chinese; but their highest aim seemed to be to obtain their good opinion; for though the converts professed themselves Christians, yet they were allowed to honor the image of Confucius their great lawgiver; and at length their ambitious intrigues brought upon them the displeasure of the government, which terminated in the suppression of the mission and almost, if not entirely, of the Christian name. It is also a melancholy fact that the vices of Europeans have been communicated wherever they themselves have been; so that the religious state of even heathens has been rendered worse by dealings with them!

Fourthly, a very great proportion of Asia and Africa, with some parts of Europe, are Mahometans; and those in Persia who are of the sect of Hali, are the most inveterate enemies to the Turks; and they in return abhor the Persians. The Africans are some of the most ignorant of all the Mahometans; especially the Arabs, who are scattered through all the northern parts of Africa, and live upon the depredations which they are continually making upon their neighbors.

Fifthly, in respect of those who bear the Christian name, a very great degree of ignorance and immorality abounds amongst them. There are Christians, so called, of the Greek and Armenian churches, in all the Mahometan countries; but they are, if possible, more ignorant and vicious than the Mahometans themselves. The Georgian Christians, who are near the Caspian Sea, maintain themselves by selling their neighbors, relations, and children, for slaves to the Turks and Persians. And it is remarked that if any of the Greeks of Anatolia turn Muslim, the Turks never set store by them, on account of their being so much noted for dissimulation and hypocrisy. It is well known that most of the members of the Greek church are very ignorant. Papists also are in general ignorant of divine things, and very vicious. Nor do the bulk of the Church of England much exceed them, either in knowledge or in holiness; and many errors, and much looseness of conduct, are to be found amongst dissenters of all denominations. The Lutherans of Denmark are much on a par with the churchmen in England; and the face of most Christian countries presents a dreadful scene of ignorance, hypocrisy, and profligacy. Various baneful and pernicious errors appear to gain ground in almost every part of Christendom; the truths of the gospel, and even the gospel itself, are attacked, and every method that the enemy can invest is employed to undermine the kingdom of our Lord Jesus Christ.

All these things are loud calls to Christians, and especially to ministers, to exert themselves to the utmost in their several spheres of action, and to try to enlarge them as much as possible.

The Practicability of Something Being Done, More Than What Is Done, for the Conversion of the Heathen

The impediments in the way of carrying the gospel among the heathen must arise, I think, from one or other of the following things: either their distance from us, their barbarous and savage manner of living, the danger of being killed by them, the difficulty of procuring the necessities of life, or the unintelligibleness of their languages.

First, as to their distance from us, whatever objections might have been made on that account before the invention of the mariner's compass, nothing can be alleged for it with any color of plausibility in the present age. Men can now sail with as much certainty through the Great South Sea as they can through the Mediterranean or any lesser sea. Yea, and Providence seems in a manner to invite us to the trial, as there are to our knowledge trading companies whose commerce lies in many of the places where these barbarians dwell. At one time or other ships are sent to visit places of more recent discovery, and to explore parts the most unknown; and every fresh account of their ignorance, or cruelty, should call forth our pity, and excite us to concur with Providence in seeking their eternal good. Scripture likewise seems to point out this method, "Surely the Isles shall wait for me; the ships of Tarshish first, to bring my sons from far, their silver, and their gold with them, unto the name of the Lord, thy God" (Isa. 60:9). This seems to imply that in the time of the glorious increase of the church in the latter days, of which the whole chapter is undoubtedly a prophecy, commerce shall subserve the spread of the gospel. The ships of Tarshish were trading vessels which made voyages for goods to various parts; this much therefore must be meant by it, that navigation, especially that which is commercial, shall be one great means of carrying on the work of God; and perhaps it may imply that there shall be a very considerable appropriation of wealth to that purpose.

Secondly, as to their uncivilized and barbarous way of living, this can be no objection to any except those whose love of ease renders them unwilling to expose themselves to inconveniences for the good of others.

It was no objection to the apostles and their successors, who went among the barbarous Germans and Gauls, and still more barbarous Britons! They did not wait for the ancient inhabitants of these countries to be civilized before they could be christianized, but went simply with the doctrine of the cross; and Tertullian could boast that "those parts of Britain that were proof against the Roman armies were conquered by the gospel of Christ." It was no objection to an Elliott, or a Brainerd, in later times. They went forth, and encountered every difficulty of the kind, and found that a cordial reception of the gospel produced those happy effects which the longest intercourse with Europeans could never accomplish without the gospel. It now is no objection to commercial men. It only requires that we should have as much love for the souls of our fellow-creatures and fellow-sinners as they have for the profits arising from a few otter skins, and all these difficulties would be easily surmounted.

After all, the uncivilized state of the heathen, instead of affording an objection against preaching the gospel to them, ought to furnish an argument for it. Can we as men, or as Christians, hear that ignorance and barbarism envelops a great part of our fellow creatures, whose souls are as immortal as ours and who are as capable as ourselves of adorning the gospel, and contributing by their preaching, writings, or practices to the glory of our Redeemer's name, and the good of the church? Can we hear that they are without the gospel, without government, without laws, and without arts and sciences, and not exert ourselves to introduce amongst them the sentiments of men, and of Christians? Would not the spread of the gospel be the most effectual means of their civilization? Would that not make them useful members of society? We know that such effects did in measure follow the aforementioned efforts of Elliott, Brainerd, and others amongst the American Indians; and if similar attempts were made in other parts of the world, and were followed with a divine blessing (which we have every reason to think they would), might we not expect to see able Divines, or read well-conducted treatises in the defense of the truth, even amongst those who at present seem to be scarcely human?

Thirdly, in respect to the danger of being killed by them, it is true that whoever goes must put his life in his hand, and not consult with flesh and blood; but do not the goodness of the cause, the duties incumbent on us as the creatures of God, and Christians, and the perishing state of our fellow men, loudly call upon us to venture all and use every warrantable exertion for their benefit? Paul and Barnabas, who "hazarded their lives for the name of the Lord Jesus Christ" (Acts 15:26), were not blamed as being rash but commended for so doing, while John Mark, who through timidity of mind deserted them in their perilous undertaking, was branded with censure. After all, as had been already observed, I greatly question whether most of the barbarities practiced by the savages upon those who have visited them have not originated in some real or supposed affront, and were therefore more properly acts of self-defense than proofs of ferocious dispositions. No wonder if the imprudence of sailors should prompt them to offend the simple savage, and the offense be resented; but Elliott, Brainerd, and the Moravian missionaries have been very seldom molested. Nay, in general the heathen have showed a willingness to hear the word; and have principally expressed their hatred of Christianity on account of the vices of nominal Christians.

Fourthly, as to the difficulty of procuring the necessities of life, this would not be so great as may appear at first sight; for though we would not procure European food, yet we might procure such as the natives of those countries which we visit subsist upon themselves. And this would only be passing through what we have virtually engaged in by entering on the ministerial office. A Christian minister is a person who is "not his own" (1 Cor. 6:19); he is the "servant" of God, and therefore ought to be wholly devoted to Him. By entering on that sacred office he solemnly undertakes to be always engaged as much as possible in the Lord's work, and not to choose his own pleasure or employment, or pursue the ministry as a something that is to subserve his own ends or interest, or as a kind of sideline. He engages to go where God pleases, and to do or endure what He sees fit to command or call him to in the exercise of His function. He virtually bids farewell to friends, pleasures, and comforts, and stands in readiness to endure the greatest sufferings in the work of the Lord, his Master. It is inconsistent for ministers to please themselves with thoughts of a numerous congregation, cordial friends, a civilized country, legal protection, affluence, splendor, or even an income that is sufficient. The slights and hatred of men, and even pretended friends, gloomy prisons, and tortures, the society of barbarians of uncouth speech, miserable accommodations in wretched wildernesses, hunger and thirst, nakedness, weariness, and diligence, hard work, and but little worldly encouragement, should rather be the objects of their expectation. Thus the apostles acted in primitive times and endured hardness as good soldiers of Jesus Christ; and though we live in a civilized country where Christianity is protected by law, and are not called to suffer these things while we continue here, yet I question whether all are justified in staying here, while so many are perishing without means of grace in other lands. I am sure that it is entirely contrary to the spirit of the gospel for its ministers to enter upon it from motives of self-interest or with great worldly expectations. On the contrary the commission is a sufficient call to them to venture all, and, like the primitive Christians, go everywhere preaching the gospel.

It might be necessary, however, for two, at least, to go together, and in general I should think it best that they should be married men. To prevent their time from being employed in procuring necessities, two or more other persons, with their wives and families, might also accompany them, who would be wholly employed in providing for them. In most countries it would be necessary for them to cultivate a little spot of ground just for their support, which would be a resource for them whenever their supplies failed. Not to mention the advantage they would reap from each other's company, it would take off the enormous expense which has always attended undertakings of this kind, for the first expense would be the whole; for though a large colony needs support for a considerable time, yet so small a number would, upon receiving the first crop, maintain themselves. They would have the advantage of choosing their situation, their wants would be few; the women, and even the children, would be necessary for domestic purposes; and a few articles of stock, as a cow or two, and a bull, and a few other cattle of both sexes, a very few utensils of husbandry, and some corn to show their land, would be sufficient. Those who attend the missionaries should understand husbandry, fishing, fowling, etc., and be provided with the necessary implements for these purposes. Indeed a variety of methods may be thought of, and when once the work is undertaken, many things will suggest themselves to us, of which we at present can form no idea.

Fifthly, as to learning their languages, the same means would be found necessary here as in trade between different nations. In some cases interpreters might be obtained, who might be employed for a time; and where these were not to be found, the missionaries must have patience, and mingle with the people, till they have learned so much of the language as to be able to communicate their ideas to them in it. It is well known to require no very extraordinary talents to learn, in the space of a year, or two at most, the language of any people upon earth, so much of it, at least, as to be able to convey any sentiments we wish to their understandings.

The missionaries must be men of great piety, prudence, courage, and forbearance; of undoubted orthodoxy in their sentiments, and must enter with all their hearts into the spirit of their mission; they must be willing to leave all the comforts of life behind them, and to encounter all the hardships of a torrid or a frigid climate, an uncomfortable manner of living, and every other inconvenience that can attend this undertaking. Clothing, a few knives, powder and shot, fishing tackle, and the articles of husbandry above mentioned, must be provided for them; and when arrived at the place of their destination, their first business must be to gain some acquaintance with the language of the natives (for which purpose two would be better than one), and by all lawful means to endeavor to cultivate a friendship with them, and as soon as possible let them know the errand for which they were sent. They must endeavor to convince them that it was their good alone which induced them to forsake their friends and all the comforts of their native country. They must be very careful not to resent injuries which may be offered to them, nor to think highly of themselves so as to despise the poor heathens, and by those means lay a foundation for their resentment or their rejection of the gospel. They must take every opportunity of doing them good, and laboring and traveling night and day they must instruct, exhort, and rebuke, with all long-suffering, and anxious desire for them, and, above all, must be instant in prayer for the outpouring of the Holy Spirit upon the people of their charge. Let but missionaries of the above description engage in the work and we shall see that it is not impracticable.

An Enquiry into the Duty of Christians in General, and What Means Ought to Be Used, in Order to Promote This Work

If the prophecies concerning the increase of Christ's kingdom be true, and if what has been argued concerning the commission given by Him to His disciples being obligatory on us be just, it must be inferred that all Christians ought heartily to concur with God in promoting His glorious designs, for "he that is joined to the Lord is one Spirit"
(1 Cor. 6:17).

One of the first and most important of those duties which are incumbent upon us is fervent and united prayer. However the influence of the Holy Spirit may be set at nought and run down by many, it will be found upon trial that all means which we can use will be ineffectual without it. If a temple is raised for God in the heathen world, it will not be "by might, nor by power," nor by the authority of the magistrate, or the eloquence of the orator; "but by my Spirit, saith the LORD of Hosts" (Zech. 4:6). We must therefore be in real earnest in supplicating his blessing upon our labors.

It is represented in the prophets that when there shall be "a great mourning in the land, as the mourning of Hadadrimmon in the valley of Megiddon, and every family shall mourn apart, and their wives apart," it shall all follow upon "a Spirit of grace, and supplication." And when these things shall take place it is promised that "there shall be a fountain opened for the house of David, and for the inhabitants of Jerusalem, for sin, and for uncleanness," and that "the idols shall be destroyed," and "the false prophets ashamed" of their profession (Zech. 12:10–13:4). This prophecy seems to teach that when there shall be a universal joining in fervent prayer, and all shall esteem Zion's welfare as their own, then upon the churches shall be shed copious influences of the Spirit, which like a purifying "fountain" shall cleanse the servants of the Lord. Nor shall this cleansing influence stop here; all old idolatrous prejudices shall be rooted out, and truth prevail so gloriously that false teachers shall be so ashamed as rather to wish to be classed with obscure herdsmen, or the meanest peasants, than bear the ignominy attendant upon their detection.

The most glorious works of grace that have ever taken place have been in answer to prayer; and it is in this way, we have the greatest reason to suppose, that the glorious outpouring of the Spirit, which we expect at last, will be bestowed.

With respect to our own immediate connections, we have within these few years been favored with some tokens for good, granted in answer to prayer, which should encourage us to persist and increase in that important duty. I trust our monthly prayer-meetings for the success of the gospel have not been in vain. It is true a want of importunity generally attends our prayers; yet unimportunate and feeble as they have been, it is to be believed that God has heard, and in a measure answered them. The churches that have engaged in the practice have in general since that time been evidently on the increase; some controversies which have long perplexed and divided the church are more clearly stated than ever; there are calls to preach the gospel in many places where it has not been usually published; yea, a glorious door is opened, and is likely to be opened wider and wider, by the spread of civil and religious liberty, accompanied also by a diminution of the spirit of popery; a noble effort has been made to abolish the inhuman Slave Trade, and though at present it has not been so successful as might be wished, yet it is to be hoped it will be persevered in till it is accomplished. In the meantime it is a satisfaction to consider that the late defeat of the abolition of the Slave Trade has proved the occasion of a praiseworthy effort to introduce a free settlement, at Sierra Leone on the coast of Africa; an effort which, if followed with a divine blessing, not only promises to pen a way for honorable commerce with that extensive country, and for the civilization of its inhabitants, but may prove the happy means of introducing amongst them the gospel of our Lord Jesus Christ.

These are events that ought not to be overlooked; they are not to be reckoned small things; and yet perhaps they are small compared with what might have been expected, if all had cordially entered into the spirit of the proposal, so as to have made the cause of Christ their own, or in other words to have been so solicitous about it as if their own advantage depended upon its success. If an holy solicitude had prevailed in all the assemblies of Christians on behalf of their Redeemer's kingdom, we might probably have seen before now not only an "open door" (2 Cor. 2:12) for the gospel, but "many running to and fro, and knowledge increased" (Dan. 12:4); or a diligent use of those means which Providence has put in our power accompanied with a greater than ordinary blessing from heaven.

Many can do nothing but pray, and prayer is perhaps the only thing in which Christians of all denominations can cordially and unreservedly unite; but in this we may all be one, and in this the strictest unanimity ought to prevail. Were the whole body thus animated by one soul, with what pleasure would Christians thus attend on all the duties of religion, and with what delight would their ministers attend on all the business of their calling.

We must not be contented however with praying without exerting ourselves in the use of means for the obtaining of those things we pray for. Were "the children of light" but "as wise in their generation as the children of this world" (Luke 16:8), they would stretch every nerve to gain so glorious a prize, nor ever imagine it was to be obtained in any other way.

When a trading company have obtained their charter they usually go to its utmost limits; and their stocks, their ships, their officers and men are so chosen and regulated as to be likely to answer their purpose; but they do not stop here, for encouraged by the prospect of success they use every effort, cast their bread upon the waters, cultivate friendship with everyone from whose information they expect the least advantage. They cross the widest and most tempestuous seas and encounter the most unfavorable climates; they introduce themselves into the most barbarous nations, and sometimes undergo the most affecting hardships; their minds continue in a state of anxiety, and suspense, and a longer delay than usual in the arrival of a vessel agitates them with a thousand changeful thoughts and foreboding apprehensions which continue till the rich returns are safe arrived in port. But why these fears? Whence all these disquietudes, and this labor? Is it not because their souls enter into the spirit of the project, and their happiness in a way depends on its success? Christians are a body whose truest interest lies in the exaltation of the Messiah's kingdom. Their charter is very extensive, their encouragements exceeding great, and the returns promised infinitely superior to all the gains of the most lucrative company. Let then everyone in his station consider himself as bound to act with all his might and in every possible way for God.

Suppose a company of serious Christians, ministers and private persons, were to form themselves into a society, and make a number of rules respecting the regulation of the plan, and the persons who are to be employed as missionaries, the means of defraying the expense, etc., etc. This society must consist of persons whose hearts are in the work, men of serious religion, and possessing a spirit of perseverance; there must be a determination not to admit any person who is not of this description, or to retain him longer than he answers to it.

From such a society a committee might be appointed, whose business it should be to procure all the information they could upon the subject, to receive contributions, to enquire into the characters, tempers, abilities and religious views of the missionaries, and also to provide them with the necessities for their undertakings.

They must also pay a great attention to the views of those who undertake this work; for want of this the missions to the Spice Islands, sent by the Dutch East India Company, were soon corrupted, many going more for the sake of settling in a place where temporal gain invited them, than of preaching to the poor Indians. This soon introduced a number of indolent or profligate persons, whose lives were a scandal to the doctrines which they preached; and by means of whom the gospel was ejected from Ternate in 1694, and Christianity fell into great disrepute in other places.

If there is any reason for me to hope that I shall have any influence upon any of my brethren and fellow Christians, probably it may be more especially amongst them of my own denomination. I would therefore propose that such a society and committee should be formed amongst the particular Baptist denomination.

I do not mean by this in any way to confine it to one denomination of Christians. I wish with all my heart that everyone who loves our Lord Jesus Christ in sincerity would in some way or other engage in it. But in the present divided state of Christendom it would be more likely for good to be done by each denomination engaging separately in the work than if they were to embark in it together. There is room enough for us all, without interfering with each other; and if no unfriendly interference took place, each denomination would bear good will to the other, and wish and pray for its success, considering it as upon the whole friendly to the great cause of true religion; but if all were intermingled, it is likely their private discords might throw a damp upon their spirits, and much retard their public usefulness.

In respect to contributions for defraying the expenses, money will doubtless be wanting; and suppose the rich were to use in this important undertaking a portion of that wealth over which God has made them stewards, perhaps there are few ways that would turn to a better account at last. Nor ought it to be confined to the rich; if persons of more moderate circumstances were to devote a portion, suppose a tenth, of their annual increase to the Lord, it would not only correspond with the practice of the Israelites, who lived under the Mosaic economy, but of the patriarchs Abraham, Isaac, and Jacob, before that dispensation commenced. Many of our most eminent forefathers amongst the Puritans followed that practice; and if that were but attended to now, there would not only be enough to support the ministry of the gospel at home, and to encourage village preaching in our respective neighborhoods, but to defray the expenses of carrying the gospel into the heathen world.

If congregations were to open subscriptions of one penny or more per week, according to their circumstances, and deposit it as a fund for the propagation of the gospel, much might be raised in this way. By such simple means they might soon have it in their power to introduce the preaching of the gospel into most of the villages in England; where, though men are placed whose business it should be to give light to those who sit in darkness, it is well known that they have it not. Where there was no person to open his house for the reception of the gospel, some other building might be procured for a small sum, and even then something considerable might be spared for the Baptist or other committees for propagating the gospel amongst the heathen.

Many persons have of late left off the use of West India sugar on account of the iniquitous manner in which it is obtained. Those families which have done so, and have not substituted anything else in its place, have not only cleansed their hands of blood, but have made a saving to their families, some of sixpence, and some of a shilling a week. If this or a part of this were appropriated to the uses previously mentioned, it would abundantly suffice. We have only to keep the end in view, and have our hearts thoroughly engaged in the pursuit of it, and means will not be very difficult.

We are exhorted "to lay up treasure in heaven, where neither moth nor rust doth corrupt, or thieves break through and steal" (Matt. 6:19). It is also declared that "whatsoever a man soweth, that shall he also reap" (Gal. 6:7). These Scriptures teach us that the enjoyments of the life to come bear a near relation to that which now is; a relation similar to that of the harvest, and the seed. It is true all the reward is of mere grace, but it is nevertheless encouraging; what a "treasure," what a "harvest" must wait such characters as Paul, and Elliott, and Brainerd, and others, who have given themselves wholly to the work of the Lord. What a heaven will it be to see the many myriads of poor heathens, of Britons among the rest, who by their labors have been brought to the knowledge of God. Surely a "crown of rejoicing" (1 Thess. 2:19) like this is worth aspiring to. Surely it is worthwhile to lay ourselves out with all our might in promoting the cause and kingdom of Christ.

Chapter Two

The Virginia Chronicle (1790)

JOHN LELAND

The first settlers in this state were emigrants from England, of the English church, just at a point of time when the Episcopalians were flushed with complete victory over all other religious persuasions; and having power in their hands, they soon discovered a degree of intolerance towards others. The oppressed Quakers, flying from persecution in England, cast their eyes on these colonies, as asylums of civil and religious liberty, but found them free for none but the reigning sects. Several acts of the Virginia Assembly, of 1659, 1662, 1693, made it penal in parents, to refuse to baptize their children; prohibited the unlawful assembling of Quakers, and made it penal for any master of a vessel to bring a Quaker into the colony; ordered those already here, and those who should come thereafter, to be imprisoned till they should abjure the country; provided a milder punishment for their first and second return, but death for the third; forbid all persons from suffering Quaker meetings in, or near their houses, entertaining them individually, or disposing of books that supported their tenets. It is a satirical saying, that every sect will oppress, when they have the power in their possession and the saying is too serious as well as satirical.

When we read of the sufferings of the Quakers, or any other society, we can hardly believe that those oppressed innocents would ever retaliate if it was in their power; much less that they would ever oppress those who had not oppressed them, but stubborn fact declares the contrary. I have pretty good authority that the Penn Quakers, in Pennsylvania, imprisoned and fined the Keibian Quakers in 1692 on account of some religious disputes. What contributes greatly towards this kind of oppression is the erroneous scheme of receiving all the natural offspring into the pales of the church. By this method, in general, a great majority of the church will be ignorant of the new birth and consequently of the nature of the gospel. And therefore, of course, appeal to the civil law, for protection, which naturally brings on oppression upon all nonconformists.

Notwithstanding the laws of Virginia were so severe against the Quakers, yet there is no account that any of them were put to death, and a remnant of them have continued in Virginia, down to this day, holding the same principles and pursuing the same manners of their brethren in the northern states and those in Europe.

Of the Slaves

The horrid work of bartering spirituous liquor for human souls, plundering the African coast, and kidnapping the people, brought the poor slaves into this state; and, notwithstanding their usage is much better here than in the West Indies, yet human nature, unbiased by education, shudders at the sight. They populate as fast as the whites do, and are rather more healthy.

The first republican assembly ever holden in Virginia passed an act utterly prohibiting the importation of any of them into the state. In some things, they are viewed as human creatures, and in others, only as property; their true state then is that of human property. The laws of Virginia protect their lives and limbs, but do not protect their skin and flesh. The marriage of slaves is a subject not known in our code of laws. What promises soever they make, their masters may and do part them at pleasure. If their marriages are as sacred as the marriages of freemen, the slaves are guilty of adultery when they part voluntarily, and the masters are guilty of a sin as great when they part them involuntarily; and yet, while they are property, it is not in the power of the masters to prevent their being forced apart, in numberless instances.

The marriage of a Hebrew servant with a Canaanitish slave, could be dispensed with at the servant's option, without sin. From this we should imagine, that there was little or no validity in the marriage of two slaves; but, if it is maintained that their marriages are equally binding with the marriages of the free-born, the inevitable parting of married slaves holds forth the idea of slavery in a still more aggravated point of view.

Liberty of conscience, in matters of religion, is the right of slaves, beyond contradiction; and yet, many masters and overseers will whip and torture the poor creatures for going to meeting, even at night, when the labor of the day is over. No longer ago than November, 1788, Mr. _____ made a motion in the assembly, for leave to bring in a bill, not only to prevent the assembling of slaves together, but to fine the masters for allowing it; but, to his great mortification, it was rejected with contempt.

No change is yet discernible among the negroes in Virginia, in point of color; but the children of the third and fourth generations retain as much of the jet, as their ancestors did, who were imported from Africa. The difference of climate, therefore, cannot be the cause of the difference of colors; and, as they live upon the same kind of food that the whites do, their diet cannot be the cause of a diversity of color, hair, or shape.

Letters were not much used, if any at all, before the days of Moses; consequently, 2,500 years elapsed without registers, which answers for our ignorance of the cause of the many colors, different shapes, and diversity of hues among the sons of grand-father Adam, and father Noah; and also apologizes for our uncertainty, how the many islands and continents were peopled, at first, with those animals that the ark unladen upon the mountains of Ararat.

From the blacks in Virginia, there have been few Albinos born. These Albinos proceed from black parents, but are in color like the tawny plastering of a wall, without any seams in their flesh, or much Cornelian. Their hair, in length and curl, is like that of blacks, but of a white color; their shape like blacks. Their eyes are sharp and tremulous, and cannot endure the light of the sun as well as others, but are better in the night. Some of their children are black, and others are Albino. I have seen a few of them and heard of others.

Romulus, the first king of Rome, placed the patricians in the senate and divided the plebians into tribes, but as for the slaves, they were not considered at all, which is true of the slaves in Virginia, as far as it respects incorporation, but not in every respect. Among us, they are tried before magistrates and courts, and their evidences are as valid, one against another, as the testimonies of the free-born are; but the concurring testimony of a thousand blacks against a white man is but a cypher in law. If a slave is ever so much abused by his master or overseer with unmerciful tasks, barbarous chastisement, etc., if his life and limbs are secure, nothing is done to the abuser. The slave has none to apply to for redress.

In our federal government, the slaves are treated with some more respect than they are in the state government. Although they have no vote in the choice of representatives to Congress, yet, according to the census established in the federal constitution, five of them number equal to three whites, which amounts to this, that a slave is possessed of three-fifths of a man, and two-fifths of a brute.

The state of slaves is truly pitiable, and that of the master, in some things, more so. Slaves drudge and toil for others and but seldom please them. Men seldom please themselves and others are almost sure to displease. When the mind is out of humor, it always seeks an object to accuse with the cause of its trouble: so Adam blamed Eve, and Eve the devil. Overseers commonly scold at slaves, let them do ill or well from the generally received opinion that negroes will not bear good usage; the slave grows heartless and sinks in despair, and, knowing that he labors for another, has nothing to stimulate him. The master finds that, without force, nothing will be done; and, therefore, without rage and lightning in his eyes, and a lash in his hand, can make him happy, he is sure to be miserable. If a hard hand and a meek heart are preferable to a soft hand and a turbulent, fretted, disappointed heart, the master would be better without them than with them.

The whole scene of slavery is pregnant with enormous evils. On the master's side, pride, haughtiness, domination, cruelty, deceit and indolence; and on the side of the slave, ignorance, servility, fraud, perfidy and despair. If these, and many other evils, attend it, why not liberate them at once? Would to Heaven this were done! The sweets of rural and social life will never be well enjoyed until it is the case. But the voice of reason (or perhaps the voice of covetousness) says it is not the work of a day; time is necessary to accomplish the important work: a political evil requires political measures to reform. Insurmountable difficulties arise to prevent their freedom. Can government free them? The laws have declared them property; as such, men have bought and enjoyed them. Is it not unconstitutional for government to take away the property of individuals? Can government ransom them? Their number is 276,923; if they should be valued at £30 in average, the sum would be £8,307,690, infinitely beyond what the commonwealth could pay to the holders of slaves for their ransom, unless they should be made to ransom themselves in discount; which would cast an intolerable burden upon those who, through conscience or poverty, have none of them in possession.

Some men have almost all their estates in slaves, while the estates of others are in lands; should the legislature, therefore, force one part of the community to give up their property, and leave the other part in full possession of all, would they not be justly accused of injustice?

Others, there are, who owe great sums of money; they were credited upon the value of their slaves; should their slaves be now emancipated by law the creditors would lose their just dues.

The custom of the country is such, that, without slaves, a man's children stand but a poor chance to marry in reputation. As futile as this may appear to a foreigner, I am well convinced, that now it is one of the great difficulties that prevent liberation of slaves among the common sort. To this I would add, that bad custom has so far prevailed, that it is looked upon rather mean for a free man to be employed in drudgery. Were they freed from their masters without being eligible to any post of honor and profit, it would only be another name for slavery; and, if they were eligible, it is not easy to say what governors, legislatures, and judges we should have. If they were walking at liberty, in every respect, I know not what past injuries might prompt them to do. And how much mixing of colors in marriage, and how many forcible debauches there might be, no mortal man can foretell.[1] But one thing is pretty certain, that fancy can hardly point out, how they could serve the whites worse than the whites now serve them. Something must be done! May Heaven point out that something, and may the people be obedient. If they are not brought out of bondage, in mercy, with the consent of their masters, I think that they will be, by judgment, against their consent.

It is the peculiarity of God to bring light out of darkness, good out of evil, order out of confusion, and make the wrath of man praise Him. The poor slaves, under all their hardships, discover as great inclination for religion as the free-born do. When they engage in the service of God, they spare no pains. It is nothing strange for them to walk twenty miles on Sunday morning to meeting and back again at night. They are remarkable for learning a tune soon and have very melodious voices.

They cannot read, and therefore, are more exposed to delusion than the whites are; but many of them give clear, rational accounts of a work of grace in their hearts, and evidence the same by their lives. When religion is lively, they are remarkably fond of meeting together, to sing, pray, and exhort, and sometimes preach, and seem to be unwearied in the exercises. They seem, in general, to put more confidence in their own color, than they do in the whites. When they attempt to preach, they seldom fail of being very zealous; their language is broken, but they understand each other and the whites may gain their ideas. A few of them have undertaken to administer baptism, but it generally ends in confusion. They commonly are more noisy, in time of preaching, than the whites, and are more subject to bodily exercise, and if they meet with any encouragement in these things, they often grow extravagant.

The Uniformity of Religion for 130 Years

Under the regal government, the Episcopal form of worship was established by law in Virginia. The ministers of that order, solemnly affirmed, that they gave their unfeigned assent and consent to the thirty-nine articles, and book of common prayer, and declared that they were inwardly moved by the Holy Ghost to enter upon the work of the ministry; this they avowed at their ordination, and being consecrated by a spiritual lord in England, they were proper subjects to fill the vacant, or new created parishes in Virginia. If it could be supposed, that they were avaricious salary-hunters, they surely had a tempting bait before them; like the people of old, who said, "put me, I pray thee, into the priest's office, that I may have bread to eat." But, as it is not my wish to inculcate slander, or raise a mean jealously in the minds of any, I shall attend to matter of fact. When an incumbent was inducted into a parish, he was entitled to a wealthy glebe, having all necessary houses built upon it, at the expense of the parish, which he held during good behavior. His fixed salary was 16,000 pounds of tobacco, which was stated at 16s and 8d per hundred, which made the sum of £133 6s and 8d, Virginia currency. He was also entitled to 20s, for every marriage that he solemnized in the mode of a license, and 5s for every one by publication. He had a further perquisite of 40s for every funeral sermon that he preached. His parishioners were under no legal bonds to have a funeral sermon preached for their deceased friends, but custom led all persons of reputation to request it.

Whether it was owing to their superabundant virtue, or the indolence of the people, or any other cause, it seldom so happened that they were dismissed from their parishes, after they were once inducted into them.

The king of Britain was the head of that church; every child that was baptized was a member of it, and no discipline was executed among them, but the civil law. The Quakers were few and peaceable, and, as there were none to oppose Episcopacy, it may be said that they enjoyed the full possession of the state until about 1740, without having any to call in question their doctrine and forms of worship.

Of the Presbyterians

That part of Virginia, between the Blue Ridge and the Alleghany, is peopled in part by emigrants from Pennsylvania, of Irish extraction and Presbyterian profession, who, before the middle of this century, set up their form of worship; but, being in the then frontiers of the state, were not troubled by government; but the rise and treatment of the Presbyterians below the Blue Ridge was as follows: A number of persons in the county of Hanover grew very uneasy in the state they were in; could not find that satisfaction under the preaching of Episcopal ministers which they desired, and had no opportunity of hearing any others; but, in the year 1743, a young gentleman from Scotland got a book of Mr. Whitefield's sermons, and one Mr. Samuel Morris read it, and received great benefit therefrom. He next invited his neighbors to come and hear the book read, and as the truth had great effect upon them, Mr. Morris was invited to meet the people at various places and read to them, which was much owned and blessed of God. But, for absenting from the church, they were cited to appear before the court to assign their reasons and declare what denomination they were of. As they were not acquainted with any dissenters but the Quakers; and as they had heard and read of Luther, the Reformer, they declared themselves Lutherans.

About this time, Mr. William Robinson, from a northern Presbytery, travelled through the back parts of Pennsylvania,

Maryland, Virginia, and North Carolina. On his return, he founded a Presbyterian congregation in the county of Luenburg, Virginia, and preached with great success in Amelia. The people in Hanover, hearing of him, sent a messenger desiring him to come into their Macedonia and help them. Accordingly, on July 6, 1743, he came and preached among them four days with remarkable success and directed them to pray and sing at their meetings as well as read. After him, came Mr. Roan, from the Presbytery of Newcastle, who was instrumental in spreading the work further around; but, for speaking a little freely of the degeneracy of the Episcopal clergy in Virginia, he was accused of speaking blasphemy. A vile wretch (like Jezebel's witnesses) deposed that he blasphemed God and the clergy, whereupon an indictment was drawn up; but he was returning to the northward when the trial came on, no witnesses appeared against him, so that the indictment fell through.

The people in Hanover then sent to the Synod of New York in 1745; the Synod drew an address to Sir William Gooch, governor of Virginia, and sent it by the Rev. Messrs. Tennant and Finley. The governor received them very politely, and gave them license to preach. After they left Virginia, Mr. Morris was several times presented to the court and fined for neglecting the church. Soon after came Messrs. William Tennant and Samuel Blair and after them, Mr. Whitefield, and preached among them four or five days. In the spring of the year 1747, came Mr. Samuel Davies, in a time of great need. A proclamation was set up at their meeting-house, obliging all the magistrates to suppress all itinerant preachers; but, Mr. Davies went to the governor and obtained a license to preach at four meeting-houses. He moved into Virginia in 1748, and preached there eleven years; he had seven meeting-houses, three of them were in Hanover and four in the counties of Henrico, Carolina, Goochland, and Louisa.

In 1759, he removed from Virginia to New Jersey, to be president over Nassau Hall College at Princeton; but the great and good man did not live long there, for he departed this life, February 1761.

About the time of the revival in Hanover, there was a great awakening in Augusta, under the ministry of Messrs. Dean and Byram, and something of a like work in Frederick. The Presbyterians are pretty numerous in Virginia; they have several academies in the state, and one college in Prince Edward, presided over by Mr. Smith, under whose ministry there has been a sweet revival of religion of late. Their doctrine and discipline are too well known to be repeated. They were all obliged to pay the Episcopal clergymen as much as if they had been Episcopalians, until the late Revolution; and, if their preachers solemnized the rites of matrimony, in the mode of license, the parish preacher claimed and recovered the fees, as though they had solemnized the rites themselves. The Presbyterians indulge, perhaps, in too much mirth at their houses, yet, it may be said in truth, that they have the best art of training up children in good manners of any society in the state.

Of the Methodists

The Methodists took their rise in England fifty or sixty years ago; but what concerns us at present is to consider their rise and spread in America and particularly in Virginia, which was as follows:

About 1764, Philip Embury, a local preacher from Ireland, came to New York and formed a society of his own countrymen and others. About the same time, Robert Strawbridge, another local preacher from Ireland, settled in Frederick county, in Maryland, and formed a few societies. In 1769, Richard Boardman and Joseph Pilmoor came to New York, who were the first regular Methodist preachers on the continent. In 1771, Francis Asbury and Richard Wright came over and many classes were formed and many ministers were raised up among them. From their first rise in America, until 1784, they called themselves the members of the Church of England, and went to the Episcopal ministers for baptism and the eucharist.

They never spread much in Virginia, till about 1775. Since that time, they have spread so much that they have a sprinkling all over the state, and, in some counties, are numerous. In 1784,

Rev. Thomas Coke came over from England, having authority from Mr. John Wesley (the first founder of the society) to organize the Methodists into a distinct church. Pursuant thereto, Mr. Francis Asbury was ordained superintendent, and a number of elders and deacons were consecrated for inferior services. Their number, on the continent, is above 43,000, and they have been the most fortunate in increasing their number of preachers of any society in Virginia. They deny the doctrine of predestination, according to the Calvinistic explanation; hold that Christ died for all Adam's progeny; believe that, after men are converted and sanctified, they may fall away and be finally damned; their doctrine, in fine, is Arminian, their magazine bears the name.

Their ministers are very constant preachers, and they exceed all societies in the state in spreading their books and written tenets among the people. They generally baptize by sprinkling, but their rules allow of pouring or immersion.[2]

Of the Tunkers

There are a few Tunkers and Mennonists in Virginia, and, as it is the design of this chronicle to treat all the religious sects in the state, I shall give an account of their first rise and peculiarities. First of the Tunkers.

The Germans sound the letter "t" like "d," for which reason they are called Dunkers, which name signifies Sops or Dippers. They first arose in Schwardznau in the year 1708. Seven religious neighbors, chiefly Presbyterians, consorted together to read the Bible and edify each other in the way that they had been brought up, having never heard that there was a Baptist in the world. However, being convinced of believers' baptism and congregational government, they desired Alexander Mack to baptize them, which he objected to, considering himself unbaptized; upon which they cast lots for an administrator.[3] Upon whom the lot fell has been cautiously concealed; but baptized they were in the river Eder, by Schwardzenau, and then formed themselves into a church, choosing Alexander Mack for their minister. As God prospered their labors and made them increase both in members and preachers, so Satan raised persecution against them. Some fled to Holland, and some to Creyfelt; and the mother church voluntarily removed to Frizland, and thence to America. In 1719, and in 1729, those of Holland and Creyfelt followed them. In Pennsylvania, Maryland, etc., there is a considerable number of them; and a few from those states have found their way into Virginia. They hold that Christ not only died for all Adam's race, but that He will finally restore all to glory. They practice trine-immersion in baptism; leading the candidate into the water, he kneels down, and the minister dips him, face downward, first in the name of the Father, then in the name of the Son, and then in the name of the Holy Ghost; which being done while he continues on his knees, the minister imposes hands upon his head, prays, and then leads them out. They also practice washing of feet, anointing the sick with oil and the holy kiss. They will neither swear, fight, nor keep slaves. They make little or no use of the civil law, and take no use for money. As Christians, they live mortified, self-denying lives; and, as citizens, they are patterns of peace; well-deserving their common title—harmless Tunkers.

Of the Mennonists

The Mennonists derive their name from Menno Simon. He was born in the year 1505—got into orders in 1528—continued a famous preacher and disputer till 1531. He then began to question the validity of many things in the Church of Rome, and among the rest, infant baptism; but neither the doctors of his order, nor those of the Protestant faith, gave him the satisfaction he wished for. He finally embraced believers' baptism, and continued preaching and planting churches in the low countries for thirty years, and died in peace, January 31, 1561.

Menno was dipped himself, and dipped others, and so did his successors, except when they were in prison, or were hindered from going to the water, and then pouring was practiced. What they used in Europe, only of necessity, is become the only mode practiced by them in America. They hold a profession of faith a prerequisite to baptism, which, in Virginia, is made by learning to answer a number of questions. The candidate being received, kneels down before the minister, and water is poured on his head; after which, follow imposition of hands and prayer. They believe the doctrine of universal provision, but not the doctrine of universal restitution; they are equally conscientious of swearing and bearing arms, with the Quakers and Tunkers. The only Virginia Baptist church that I know of in the state, that refuse to bear arms, or take an oath before a magistrate, is one in Shenandoah; the chiefest of whom are the natural descendants of the Mennonists. In worship and discipline, they are like other Baptists in the state; but some peculiarities of the Mennonists, keep them from uniting.

The Tunkers and Mennonists seem to be more consistent with themselves than the Quakers, in disusing the law as well as arms. Perhaps the reason is, because the two first have been small, persecuted societies, and have learned to bear affliction patiently, and have but little to do with mankind; but should they undertake to settle a colony themselves, as the Quakers did Pennsylvania, it is probable that they would see the necessity of civil law. Civil government is certainly a curse to mankind; but it is a necessary curse, in this fallen state, to prevent greater evils. It is yet a question, whether the good Quakers have a sufficient reason for using the law, and not appealing to arms. If an internal foe arises, and kills a man, they execute the law, and hang the murderer; but if external foes invade and kill and burn all before them, no means must be used to bring them to punishment. Is it bad reasoning to say that when innocency is injured, it appeals first to law for redress; but if it finds no redress at law, it finally appeals to arms? The law of a state is the compact of citizens in the state, and the law of nations in confederation, is the compact of bodies of men; and why the violators of one should be punished, and the breakers of the other pass with impunity, is not so easily answered. If all nations were true to their engagements, there would be no war in the world; so, if all the citizens in a state lived agreeable to the laws of it, there would be no punishment. If there was no sin in the world, there would be no laws needed. The more virtuous people are, the more liberal their laws should be; but the more vicious the people are, the more severe the laws must be, to restrain their unruly passions. Where rulers are more virtuous than the people, the more independent and important the rulers are, the better for the people; but where the people are more virtuous than the magistrates, magistrates should be dependent on, and responsible to the people. As it is generally seen that the people are more virtuous than those in power; consequently, a republican, responsible government is best. Great salaries given to officers, are as dangerous to the good of the community, as no salaries are. Great salaries stimulate avaricious men to make use of undue means to acquire those offices, while men of real merit feel a disgust to prey so much upon the industrious. Incompetent salaries, disable men of small fortunes from filling those offices their real merit entitles them to, and consequently fix government in the hands of the rich, who generally feel more for themselves, than they do for the poor. To fix salaries high enough and not too high, is the work of the wise; and to give power enough to men to do good, and yet have it so counterpoised that they can do no harm, is a line so difficult to be drawn, that it has never yet been done.

Of the Baptists

The Baptists took their rise in Virginia before the Methodists; but, as I purpose to treat more largely on the doctrine and forms of the Baptists, than I have done on other societies, I have reserved them for the last.

There were a few Baptists in Virginia before the year 1760, but they did not spread, so as to be taken notice of by the people, much less by the rulers, till after that date. About the year, 1764, they prevailed so much that, in the year following, they formed an Association called "the Ketocton Regular Baptist Association."[4] From 1764 to 1774, the Baptists spread over the greatest part of the state that was peopled. Several ministers of that order came from Pennsylvania and the Jerseys, and settled in the northern parts of the state, and others were raised up in the southern parts, who travelled about and preached like the old Baptist, John, "repent, for the kingdom of Heaven is at hand," and great numbers of the people went out unto them, and were baptized, confessing their sins. Many of the young converts caught the spirit of their teachers, and zealously engaged in the work. In a course of time, the fires from the northern preachers, and those in the south, met, like the two seas in St. Paul's shipwreck, in Orange County, 1767. Two or three ministers, from each side, assembled in conference, but did not so happily unite, as candor desired. A division took place. The northern members called themselves "Regular Baptists," and the southern members called themselves "Separate Baptists"; and, if some alienation of affection did not attend this division in some instances, it was because they were free from those temptations that have always mingled with religious divisions, and if there was not a little zeal discovered to proselyte, as well as convert the people, I have been wrongly informed.

The Regulars, adhered to a confession of faith, first published in London, 1689, and afterwards adopted by the Baptist Association of Philadelphia, in 1742; but the Separates had none but the Bible. Just upon the spot of ground where the division took place, the members knew something of the cause; but those who lived at a distance, were ignorant of the reason, and whenever they met, they loved each other as brethren, and much deplored that there should be a distinction or shyness among them. The Separates, who also formed an association, increased much the fastest, both in ministers and members; and occupied, by far, the greatest territory. The Regulars were orthodox Calvinists, and the work under them was solemn and rational; but the Separates were the most zealous, and the work among them was very noisy. The people would cry out, "fall down," and, for a time, lose the use of their limbs; which exercise made the bystanders marvel; some thought they were deceitful, others that they were bewitched, and many being convinced of all, would report that God was with them of a truth.

The Persecution of the Baptists. Soon after the Baptist ministers began to preach in Virginia, the novelty of their doctrine, the rarity of mechanics and planters preaching such strange things,[5] and the wonderful effect that their preaching had on the people called out multitudes to hear them—some out of curiosity, some in sincerity, and some in ill will.

Their doctrine, influence, and popularity, made them many enemies; especially among those who value themselves most for religion in the Episcopal mode. The usual alarm of the Church and State being in danger, was echoed through the colony; nor were the Episcopal clergymen so modest, but what they joined the alarm; like the silversmiths of old, crying "our craft is in danger of being set at naught." Magistrates began to issue their warrants, and sheriffs had their orders to take up the disturbers of the peace. The county of Spottsylvania took the lead, and others soon followed their example. Preaching, teaching, or exhorting, was what disturbed the peace. A like work disturbed the peace of Satan, when he cried out, "let us alone." Sometimes, when the preachers were brought before the courts, they escaped the prison by giving bonds and security, that they would not preach in the county in the term of one year; but most of them preferred the dungeon to such bonds. Not only ministers were imprisoned, but others, for only praying in their families, with a neighbor or two.

The act of toleration, passed in the first of William and Mary's reign, afforded the suffering brethren some relief. By applying to the general court, and subscribing to all the thirty-nine articles, saving the 34th, 35th, and 36th, together with one clause in the 20th, and part of the 27th, they obtained license to preach at certain stipulated places;[6] but, if they preached at any other places, they were exposed to be prosecuted.

Some of the prisoners would give bonds not to preach, and as soon as they were freed, would immediately preach as before. This was done when they had reason to believe that the court would never bring suit upon the bonds. I have never heard of but one such suit in the state, and that one was dismissed. The ministers would go singing from the court-house to the prison, where they had, sometimes, the liberty of the bounds, and at other times they had not. They used to preach to the people through the grates: to prevent which, some ill-disposed men would be at the expense of erecting a high wall around the prison; others, would employ half drunken strolls to beat a drum around the prison to prevent the people from hearing. Sometimes, matches and pepper-pods were burnt at the prison door, and many such afflictions the dear disciples went through. About thirty of the preachers were honored with a dungeon, and a few others beside. Some of them were imprisoned as often as four times, besides all the mobs and perils they went through. The dragon roared with hideous peals, but was not red—the Beast appeared formidable, but was not scarlet colored. Virginia soil has never been stained with vital blood for conscience sake. Heaven has restrained the wrath of man, and brought auspicious days at last. We now sit under our vines and fig trees and there is none to make us afraid.

The Reasons of Their Dissent. But why this schism? says an inquisitor. If the people were disposed to be more devotional than they had been before, why not be devout in the church in which they had been raised, without rending themselves off, and procuring so much evil unto themselves? This question may be answered in part by asking a similar one. Why did the Episcopal church rend off from the church of Rome in the Reformation? Why not continue in that church, and worship in her mode? What necessity for that schism, which occasioned so much war and persecution? If we are to credit Frederick, in his "Memoirs of the House of Brandenburg," the cause of the Reformation was, in England, the love of a woman—in Germany, the love of gain—in France, the love of novelty, or a song. But can the Church of England offer no other reason for her heretical schism, but the love of a woman? Undoubtedly she can: she has done it, and we approve of her reason; but after all, she is not so pure in her worship, but what we have many reasons for dissenting from her. Some of which are as follows:

1. No national church can, in its organization, be the Gospel Church. A national church takes in the whole nation, and no more; whereas, the Gospel Church, takes in no nation, but those who fear God and work righteousness in every nation. The notion of a Christian commonwealth, should be exploded for-ever, without there was a commonwealth of real Christians. Not only so, but if all the souls in a government were saints of God, should they be formed into a society by law, that society could not be a Gospel Church, but a creature of state.

2. The Church of England, in Virginia, has no discipline but the civil law. The crimes of their delinquent members are tried in a courthouse before the judges of the police, their censures are laid on at the whipping post, and their excommunications are administered at the gallows. In England, if a man cast contempt upon the spiritual court, the bishop delegates a grave priest, who, with his chancellor, excommunicate him. The man thus excommunicated, is by law, disabled from being a plaintiff or witness in any suit. But for heresy, incest or adultery, the bishop himself pronounces the exclusion. The outcast is not only denied the company of Christians, in spiritual duties, but also, in tem-poral concerns. He not only is disabled from being plaintiff or witness in any suit (and so deprived of the protection of the law), but if he continues forty days an excommunicant, a writ comes against him and he is cast into prison without bail, and there continues until he has paid the last mite. Mrs. Trask was judged a heretic, because she believed in the Jewish Sabbath, and for that, she was imprisoned sixteen years until she died; but a Gospel Church has nothing to do with corporeal punishments. If a member commits sin, the church is to exclude him, which is as far as church power extends. If the crime is cognizable by law, the culprit must bear what the law inflicts. In the Church of England, ecclesiastical and civil matters are so blended together, that I know not who can be blamed for dissenting from her.

3. The manner of initiating members into the Church of England is arbitrary and tyrannical. The subject (for a candidate I cannot call him) is taken by force, brought to the priest, bap-tized, and declared a member of the church. The little Christian

shows all the aversion he is capable of, by cries and struggles, but all to no purpose; ingrafted he is; and, when the child grows up, if he differs in judgment from his father and king, he is called a dissenter, because he is honest, and will not say that he believes what he does not believe; and, as such, in England, can fill no post of honor or profit. Here, let it be observed, that religion is a matter entirely between God and individuals. No man has a right to force another to join a church; nor do the legitimate powers of civil government extend so far as to disable, incapacitate, proscribe, or in any way distress, in person, property, liberty or life, any man who cannot believe and practice in the common road. A church of Christ, according to the Gospel, is a congregation of faithful persons, called out of the world by divine grace, who mutually agree to live together, and execute gospel discipline among them; which government is not national, parochial, or presbyterial, but congregational.

4. The Church of England has a human head. Henry VIII cast off the Pope's yoke, and was declared head of the church, 1533; which title, all the kings of England have borne since; but the Gospel Church acknowledges no head but King Jesus: He is lawgiver, king, and judge—is a jealous God, and will not give His glory unto another.

5. The preachers of that order, in Virginia, for the most part, not only plead for theatrical amusements, and what they call civil mirth, but their preaching is dry and barren, containing little else but morality. The great doctrines of universal depravity, redemption by the blood of Christ, regeneration, faith, repentance, and self-denial, are but seldom preached by them, and, when they meddle with them, it is in such a superficial manner as if they were nothing but things of course.

6. Their manner of visiting the sick, absolving sins, administering the Lord's Supper to newly married couples, burying the dead, sprinkling children with their gossips, promises, cross, etc., are no ways satisfactory, and, as they were handed to us through the force of law, we reject them in toto. These are some of the reasons we have for dissenting from the Episcopalians in Virginia, and though they may not be sufficient to justify our

conduct, in the opinion of others, yet they have weight with us.[7]

Three Great Principles. There are three grand, leading principles which divide the Christian world: I say leading principles— for each of them is subdivided into a number of peculiarities; these three, I shall call fate, free-will, and restitution.

Fate. Those who believe this doctrine, say, that God eternally ordained whatsoever comes to pass: that if the minutest action should be done that God did not appoint, it would not only prove a world of chance, but create an uneasiness in the Divine mind; that providence and grace are stewards, to see that all God's decrees are fulfilled. Sometimes a distinction is made between God's absolute and permissive decrees; that God absolutely decreed the good, and permissively decreed the evil. Other times it is stated thus: that upon the principle of God's knowing all things, everything comes to pass of necessity. With this sentiment, most commonly, is connected the doctrine of particular redemption: that Jesus Christ undertook for a certain number of Adam's progeny, and for them alone He died; that those for whom He died, shall be called, by irresistible grace, to the knowledge of the truth and be saved; that if one of these, whom He chose and redeemed, should miss of Heaven, His will would be frustrated, and His blood lost. And as this, at first view, seems to excuse the non-elect for not believing in the Mediator, it is sometimes said that Jesus died virtually for all, but intentionally for a few. Others who disdain such pitiful shifts, say, that the want of the faith of God's elect is no sin; that justice cannot require a man to have a more divine life than Adam possessed in Eden; that if we, as rational creatures, do not believe as much as Adam could have believed in innocency, when revealed to us, that we are guilty of the sin of unbelief; but that the law cannot require us to believe in a Mediator, and therefore, the want of that faith is not a sin. Those who adhere to this principle are called: Fatalists, Predestinarians, Calvinists, Supralapfarians, etc.

Free-Will. Those who adopt this principle affirm that God eternally decreed to establish the freedom of the human will. That if men are necessary agents, the very idea of virtue and vice is destroyed; that the more angels and men are exalted in their creation, in the state of free agency, the greater was the probability of their falling; that sin could never have entered into the world, upon any other footing; that if man does what he cannot avoid, it is no rebellion in the creature; that God never offers violence to the human will in the process of grace; that Christ has fulfilled the law, which all were under—bore the curse for all—spilt His blood for all—makes known His grace to all—gives to each a talent—bids all improve—and finally, that if men are damned, it will not be for the want of a Savior; but for refusing to obey Him, damned for unbelief, and that those who are damned will have their torment augmented for refusing an offered Savior. Some, who adhere to this doctrine, believe that when men are once born again, that they can never perish, and others believe, that there is no state so secure in this world, but what men may fall from it into eternal damnation. The advocates for the above sentiment are called Arminians, Free-Willers, Universalists, Provisionists, etc.

Restitution. Those who espouse this sentiment declare that God eternally designed to save all men; that He made them to enjoy Him for ever, and that He will not be frustrated—that Christ died for all and will not lose His blood—that if more souls are lost than saved, Satan will have the greatest triumph, and sin have a more boundless reign than grace—than if ever one soul should be miserable, world without end, the sting of death and the victory of the grave would never be destroyed—that Jesus will reign till all His foes, even the last enemy, shall be rooted up—that He will reconcile all things unto Himself, and make all things new—that every creature in heaven, in earth, and under the earth, shall join in the celestial doxology. But those who hold this doctrine are equally perplexed and divided with those who believe the two before-mentioned principles.

Some of them extend the doctrine to fallen angels, others confine it to the human race—some believe there will be no punishment after death, others conclude that torment will be inflicted in Hades upon rebellious souls, even until the resurrection of the body; and others think that they will not all be restored till the expiration of several periodical eternities. Those who avow this doctrine are called Universalists, Hell-Redemptioners, etc.

Whether it is a blessing or a curse to mankind, it is a certain truth, that the theoretic principles of men, have but little effect upon their lives. I know men of all the before-written doctrines that equally seem to strive to glorify God in the way which they conceive will do it the most effectually. It is no novelty in the world for men of different sentiments to stigmatize the doctrines of each other, with being pregnant with dangerous consequences; but it is not the doctrine or system that a man believes that makes him either a good or bad man, but the spirit he is governed by. It is a saying among lovers that "love will triumph over reason," and it is as true, that the disposition of the heart will prevail over the system of the head.

The third principle, mentioned above, has few, if any, vouchers among the Baptists in Virginia; but the two first spoken of, divide counties, churches, and families, which, about the year 1775, raised a great dispute in Virginia, and finally split the Separate Baptists, which division continued several years; but, after both parties had contested till their courage grew cool, they ceased their hostilities, grounded their arms, and formed a compromise upon the middle ground, of "think and let think"; and ceded to each other its territory and liberty.

I am acquainted with men of all these principles, who are equally assured they are right. No doubt they are right in their own conceits, and they may be all right in their aims; but I am assured they are not all right in their systems; and far enough from being right, when they bitterly condemn each other.

Of Marriage. It is a question, not easily answered, whether marriage was appointed by the Divine Parent, merely for the propagation of the human species or for the education of children. Whether one or the other or both were reasons of the institution, it certainly was appointed by God, honored by Jesus, and declared to be honorable unto all by St. Paul. What lies before me at present is to consider the mode of marriage in Virginia before the late revolution, and the alterations that have since taken place.

Under the regal government, the rites of matrimony were solemnized two ways. The first, and most reputable way, was this:
From the clerk's office, in the county where the bride lived, a
license was issued to the bridegroom, which cost twenty shillings, which was a perquisite of the governor; and fifty pounds of
tobacco for the fee of the clerk, which raised the price to a
guinea. This license was delivered to the clergyman on the wedding day for his security; and for solemnizing the rites, he was
entitled to twenty shillings. This way of getting wives was too
expensive for the poor, and, there, another mode was prescribed
by law, as an alternative. The clergyman published the banns of
marriage on three holy days, for which he was entitled to eighteen pence, and for joining such couples together he was entitled
to five shillings. The Presbyterian ministers sometimes solemnized the rites; but if it was by a license, the parish preacher
claimed and recovered his fee, as though he had solemnized the
rites himself. After the declaration of independence, in 1780, an
act passed the general assembly to authorize as many as four
ministers in each county, of each denomination, to solemnize the
rites; but the act was so partial that some would not qualify, others took what indulgence the act gave, and still petitioned for
equal liberty. The Episcopal clergymen were allowed to join in
people together in any part of the state, while others were cir-
cumscribed by county bounds. In 1784, this partiality was
removed and all ministers were set on a level. By presenting credentials of their ordination and a recommendation of their good
character in the society where they are members, and also giving
bond and security to the court of the county where they reside,
they receive testimonials, signed by the senior magistrate, to join
together any persons who legally apply in any part of the state.
Publication is now abolished. From the county in which the
bride resides, a license is issued out of the clerk's office, which
costs the groom fifteen pence; this license is given to the
preacher for his security; and for joining them together he is
entitled to five shillings. The preacher is under bonds to certify
the clerk, from whom the license came, of the solemnization;
and the clerk, for registering the certificate, is entitled to fifteen

pence more: so that it costs but seven shillings and six pence to get a wife in these days.

The Declension among the Baptists. A review of text beginning on page 72 informs us what persecution the Baptist preachers were subject to, which continued in some counties unto the Revolution. Upon the declaration of independence, and the establishment of a republican form of government, it is not to be wondered at that the Baptists so heartily and uniformly engaged in the cause of the country against the king. The change suited their political principles, promised religious liberty, and a freedom from ministerial tax; nor have they been disappointed in their expectations. In 1776, the salaries of the Episcopal clergymen were suspended, which was so confirmed in 1779 that no legal force has ever been used since to support any preachers in the state. But as they gained this piece of freedom, so the cares of war, the spirit of trade, and moving to the western waters, seemed to bring on a general declension. The ways of Zion mourned. They obtained their hearts' desire (freedom) but had leanness in their souls. Some of the old watchmen stumbled and fell, iniquity did abound, and the love of many waxed cold. But the declension was not so total, but what God showed Himself gracious in some places; His blessings, like small showers in the drought of summer, were scattered abroad. Delegates from the churches assembled in association once or twice in each year; but so much of the time was taken up in confiding what means had best be used to obtain and preserve equal liberty with other societies, that many of the churches were discouraged in sending delegates. Many of the ministers removed from their churches to Kentucky, and left their scattered flocks like a cottage in the vineyard, like a lodge in a garden of cucumbers. In this point of view was the Baptist Society in Virginia, at the close of the war, and the return of auspicious peace.

October, 1788, was the last General Association the Separate Baptists ever had. They divided into four or five districts; but to maintain a friendly correspondence, and be helpers to each other in a political way, they established a General Committee, to be composed of delegates sent from each distinct Association, to meet annually. Not more than four delegates from one Association are entitled to seats. This committee give their opinion on all queries sent to them from any of the Associations, originate all petitions to be laid before the legislature of the state, and consider the good of the whole society. It may be here noted that the General Committee, as well as the Associations, exercise no lordship over the churches—all they attempt is advice, which is generally received by the churches in a cordial manner. Should they attempt anything more, without legal authority, they would appear ridiculous; and with legal authority, they would grow tyrannical. Of this Committee, the regular Baptist Association became a member.

In 1784, the Episcopal Society was legally incorporated, and such exertions were made for a general assessment, to oblige all the citizens in the state to pay some preacher, that a bill for that purpose passed two readings; but the final determination of the bill was postponed until November, 1785; when the time came, the Presbyterians, Baptists, Quakers, Methodists, Deists, and covetous, made such an effort against the bill that it fell through.[8] In 1786, the act, incorporating the Episcopal Society, was repealed; but in 1788, their trustees were legalized to manage the property, which is the state of things at this time.

Several attempts were made, at different times, to unite the Regular and Separate Associations together, but all proved in vain, until August, 1787, when they united upon the principle of receiving the confession of faith, before mentioned, as containing the great essential doctrines of the gospel, yet, not in so strict a sense, that all are obliged to believe everything therein contained.[9] At the same time, it was agreed, that the appellations, Regular and Separate, should be buried in oblivion, and that in future they should be called "the United Baptist Churches of Christ in Virginia."

The Great Work. The first part of the last head gives an account of the declension of religion among the Baptists, which continued until 1785. In the summer of that year, the glorious work of God broke out on the banks of James River and from thence has spread almost over the state. In treating of this great revival, I shall not write as a divine, a philosopher, or an opposer, but solely as an historian.

In the greatest part of the meetings, when religion is low among the people, there is no unusual appearance among them; a grave countenance, a solemn sigh, or a silent tear, is as much as is seen or heard, and sometimes a great degree of inattention and carelessness: but in times of reviving it is quite otherwise, in most places. It is no thing strange to see a great part of the congregation fall prostrate upon the floor or ground; many of whom, entirely lose the use of their limbs for a season. Sometimes numbers of them are crying out at once, some of them in great distress, using such language as this: "God, be merciful to me a sinner—Lord, save me or I must perish—what shall I do to be saved?" etc. Other breaking out in such rapturous expressions as these: "Bless the Lord, O my soul! O, sweet Jesus, how I love thee!—Let everything that hath breath praise the Lord!—O, sinners! Come, taste, and see how good the Lord is!", etc.

I have seen such exercise and heard such melody for several hours together. At Association and great meetings, I have seen numbers of ministers and exhorters improving their gifts at the same time. Such a heavenly confusion among the preachers, and such a celestial discord among the people, destroy all articulation, so that the understanding is not edified; but the awful echo, sounding in the ears, and the objects in great distress, and great raptures before the eyes, raise great emotion in the heart. Some of the ministers rather oppose this work, others call it a little in question, and some fan it with all their might. Whether it be celestial or terrestrial, or a complication of both, it is observed by the candid that more souls get first awakened at such meetings, than at any meetings whatever, who afterwards give clear, rational accounts of a divine change of heart. This exercise is not confined to the newly convicted, and newly converted, but persons who have been professors a number of years, at such lively meetings, not only jump up, strike their hands together, and shout aloud, but will embrace one another, and fall to the floor. I have never known the rules of decency broken so far as for persons of different sexes, thus to embrace and fall at meetings. It is not to be understood that this exercise is seen in all parts of the state, at times when God is working on the minds of the people. No, under the preaching of the same man, in different neighborhoods and counties, the same work, in substance, has different exterior effects.

At such times of revival, it is wonderful to hear the sweet singing among the people, when they make melody in their hearts and voices to the Lord. In the last great ingathering, in some places, singing was more blessed among the people than the preaching was. What Mr. Jonathan Edwards thought might be expedient in some future day, has been true in Virginia. Bands go singing to meeting, and singing home. At meeting, as soon as preaching is over, it is common to sing a number of spiritual songs; sometimes several songs are sounding at the same time, in different parts of the congregation. I have travelled through neighborhoods and counties at times of refreshing, and the spiritual songs in the fields, in the shops, and houses, have made the heavens ring with melody over my head; but, as soon as the work is over, there is no more of it heard. Dr. Watts is the general standard for the Baptists in Virginia; but they are not confined to him; any spiritual composition answers their purpose. A number of hymns originate in Virginia, although there is no established poet in the state. Some Virginia songs have more divinity in them, than poetry or grammar; and some that I have heard have but little of either.

Candidates generally make confession of their faith before the whole assembly present; but, sometimes there are so many to offer, that the church divides into several bodies, each of which acts for the whole, and receives by the right hand of fellowship. At times appointed for baptism, the people generally go singing to the water side, in grand procession: I have heard many souls declare they first were convicted, or first found pardon going to, at, or coming from the water. If those who practice infant baptism can say as much, it is no wonder they are so fond of it. Forty, fifty, and sixty have often been baptized in a day, at one place, in Virginia, and sometimes as many as seventy-five. There are some ministers now living in Virginia, who have baptized more than 2,000 persons. It is said that St. Austin baptized 10,000 in the dead of winter in the river Swale, in England, in the year 595. I have seen ice cut more than a foot thick, and people baptized in the water, and yet I have never heard of any person taking cold or any kind of sickness in so doing. And strange it is that Mr. Wesley should recommend cold bathing for such a vast number of disorders, and yet be so backward to administer it for the best purpose, viz., to fulfil righteousness.

The Number of Baptists. There are in Virginia, at this time, about 150 ordained preachers of the Baptist denomination, and a number besides who exercise a public gift; but in the late great additions that have been made to the churches, there are but few who have engaged in the work of the ministry. Whether it is because the old preachers standing in the way, or whether it is because the people do not pray the Lord of the harvest to thrust out laborers, or whether it is not rather a judgment of God upon the people for neglecting those who are already in the work, not communicating to them in all good things,[10] I cannot say; but so it is, that but few appear to be advancing, to supply the places of the old ones, upon their decease.

There are also about 202 churches. The exact number of members I cannot ascertain. Between Potomac and James rivers, are 9,000; and as there is about the same number of preachers and churches, between James river and North Carolina, together with some good account, I judge there are as many as 9,000 south of James river. Upon the western waters, in Kentucky, there are thirty-one churches, divided into three Associations. In one of them, there were 1,000 members, May, 1789. In another, there is about the same number; but, lest I should swell my numbers high, I will add the little Association at the falls of Ohio containing five churches, to make the round number of 2,000 in Kentucky; and, as there are a few Baptists between Alleghany and Kentucky, I conclude the sum of 20,000 is a moderate estimate. These churches are classed into eleven Associations, nine of which correspond in the General Committee. For the ease of the eye, they are stated in the following table:

1	General Committee
11	Associations
202	Churches
150	Ministers,[11]
20,000	Members

The number of communicants compose but a small part of those who commonly attend Baptist worship. It will not appear extravagant, to those who are generally acquainted in the state, to say that, taking one part of the state with another, there are more people who attend the Baptist worship than any kind of worship in the state.

Of Dress. Upon the first rise of the Baptists in Virginia, they were very strict in their dress. Men cut off their hair, like Cromwell's round-headed chaplains, and women cast away all their superfluities; so that they were distinguished from others, merely by their decoration. Where all were of one mind, no evil ensued; but where some did not choose to dock and strip, and churches made it a matter of discipline, it made great confusion for no standard could be found in the Bible to measure their garments by. No doubt, dressing, as well as eating and drinking, can be carried to excess; but it appears to be a matter between God and individuals; for, whenever churches take it up, the last evil is worse than the first. This principle prevailed until the war broke out, at which time the Baptist mode took the lead. Those who went into the army cut off their hair, and those who stayed at home were obliged to dress in home-spun. Since the return of peace, and the opening of the ports, the uniformity between the Baptists and others, in point of clothing, still exists; notwithstanding the great work of conversion there has been in the state, but very little is said about rending garments; those who behave well, wear what they please, and meet with no reproof.

The Excess of Civil Power Exploded. The principle that civil rulers have nothing to do with religion in their official capacities, is as much interwoven in the Baptist plan, as Phydias's name was in the shield. The legitimate powers of government extend only to punish men for working ill to their neighbors, and no way affect the rights of conscience. The nation of Israel received their civil and religious laws from Jehovah, which were binding on them and no other; and with the extirpation of that nation, were abolished. For a Christian commonwealth to be established upon the same claim, is very presumptuous, without they have the same charter from Heaven. Because the nation of Israel had a divine grant of the land of Canaan, and orders to enslave the heathen, some suppose Christians have an equal right to take away the land of the Indians, and make slaves of the negroes. Wretched religion that pleads for cruelty and injustice. In this point of view, the Pope offered England to the king of Spain, provided he would conquer it; after England became Protestant, and in the same view of things, on May 4, 1493, the year after America was discovered, he proposed to give away the heathen lands to his Christian subjects. If Christian nations were nations of Christians, these things would not be so. The very tendency of religious establishments by human law is to make some hypocrites, and the rest fools; they are calculated to destroy those very virtues that religion is designed to build up; to encourage fraud and violence over the earth. It is error alone, that stands in need of government to support it; truth can and will do better without: so ignorance calls in anger in a debate, good sense scorns it. Religion, in its purest ages, made its way in the world, not only without the aid of the law, but against all the laws of haughty monarchs, and all the maxims of the schools. The pretended friendship of legal protection, and learned assistance, proves often in the end like the friendship of Joab to Amasa.

Government should protect every man in thinking and speaking freely, and see that one does not abuse another. The liberty I contend for is more than toleration. The very idea of toleration is despicable; it supposes that some have a pre-eminence above the rest to grant indulgence; whereas, all should be equally free, Jews, Turks, Pagans, and Christians. Test oaths and establish creeds, should be avoided as the worst of evils. A general assessment (forcing all to pay some preacher) amounts to an establishment; if government says I must pay somebody, it must next describe that somebody, his doctrine, and place of abode. That moment a minister is so fixed as to receive a stipend by legal force, that moment he ceases to be a gospel ambassador, and becomes a minister of state. This emolument is a temptation too great for avaricious men to withstand. This doctrine turns the gospel into merchandise, and sinks religion upon a level with other things.

As it is not the province of civil government to establish forms of religion, and force a maintenance for the preachers, so it does not belong to that power to establish fixed holy days for divine worship. That the Jewish seventh-day Sabbath was of divine appointment, is unquestionable; but that the Christian first-day Sabbath is of equal injunction, is more doubtful. If Jesus appointed the day to be observed, He did it as the head of the church, and not as the king of nations; or if the apostles enjoined it, they did it in the capacity of Christian teachers, and not as human legislators. As the appointment of such days is no part of human legislation, so the breach of the Sabbath (so called) is no part of civil jurisdiction. I am not an enemy to holy days (the duties of religion cannot well be performed without fixed times), but these times should be fixed by the mutual agreement of religious societies, according to the Word of God, and not by civil authority. I see no clause in the federal constitution, or the constitution of Virginia, to empower either the federal or Virginia legislature to make any Sabbatical laws.

Under this head, I shall also take notice of one thing, which appears to me unconstitutional, inconsistent with religious liberty, and unnecessary in itself; I mean the paying of the chaplains of the civil and military departments out of the public treasury. The king of Great Britain has annual 48 chaplains in ordinary, besides a number extraordinary; his army also abounds with chaplains. This, I confess, is consistent with the British form of government, where religion is a principle, and the church a creature of the state; but why should these plans of proud, covetous priests, ever be adopted in America? If legislatures choose to have a chaplain, for Heaven's sake, let them pay him by contributions, and not out of the public chest. In some of the states, a part of each day, during the session of assembly, is taken up in attending prayers; and they may well afford it, for they are paid for their time; but whether they would pray as long if they were not under pay, is a question; and whether the chaplain would pray as long for them if the public chest was like Osiron's purse, is another.

For chaplains to go into the army is about as good economy as it was for Israel to carry the ark of God to battle: instead of reclaiming the people, they generally are corrupted themselves, as the ark fell into the hands of the Philistines.[12] The words of David are applicable here: "Carry back the ark into the city." But what I aim chiefly at, is paying of them by law. The very language of the proceeding is this: "If you will pay me well for preaching and praying, I will do them, otherwise I will not." Such golden sermons and silver prayers are of no great value.

Washing of Feet and Dry Christening. Washing of feet is practiced by some of the Baptists, disused by others, and rejected by the third class, which breaks no friendship among them, each one acting according to his persuasion. Baptism and the Lord's supper, are neither of them used for the good of the body; but the first is significant, and the last commemorative. The question is, whether washing of feet is to be performed for the good of the body, or as a sacred rite? If for the good of the body, it should be done when, and only when, the feet are sore and filthy; but if as a sacred rite, people should do as they now do, viz., wash their feet clean before they meet together for the purpose of washing feet. A person being taken upon surprise at a washing feet meeting, made this confession: "If I had known that you would have washed feet tonight, I would have washed mine clean before I came from home."

Some of the preachers practice what is satirically called dry christening, and others do not. The thing referred to is this: when a woman is safely delivered in child-bearing, and raised to health enough to go to meeting, she brings her child to the minister, who either takes it in his arms, or puts his hands upon it, and thanks God for His mercy, and invokes a blessing on the child; at which time the child is named.

The Baptists believe that those who preach the gospel should live of it: that a preacher is as much entitled to a reward for his labor, as the reaper in the field is to his hire. It is a gross innovation from truth, to view the wages of a minister in the light of alms. That religion that opens the heart, unties the purse-strings. When souls are caught in the net of the gospel (like the fish that Peter caught) they have a piece of money in their mouths. If people will not give the preacher his due, they and their money must perish together.

Finally, the Baptists hold it their duty to obey magistrates, to be subject to the law of the land, to pay their taxes, and pray for all in authority. They are not scrupulous of taking an oath of God upon them to testify the truth before a magistrate or court; but reject profane swearing. Their religion also allows them to bear arms in defense of their life, liberty, and property, and also to be friendly to those who differ with them in judgment, believing a cynic to be as bad as a sycophant.

The Virginia Baptists Compared with the German. From this account of the Virginia Baptists, they appear to be a very different sect from the German Anabaptists. The grand error of those rioters, was founding both dominion and property in grace; which is the error of the Church of Rome, and the Church of England unto this day; and, indeed, the error of all established churches that incapacitate a man from holding his office and property, without he will submit to a religious test. The confusion in Germany was not of the religious kind, but the struggles of the people to get clear of the oppression of the princes. Their leader taught them, that if they would acknowledge their mission, they should be free from taxes, rents, and subjection; the prospect of which drew multitudes of them, until, like the followers of Theudas and Judas, they were all dispersed. If the German fanatics were really Baptists, yet it is as cruel to impute their errors, by wholesale, to the Virginia Baptists, as it would be to impute all the cruelty of the Church of Rome to those societies in Virginia that practice infant baptism. I have two histories of the German insurgents before me, one of which appears to be a scorpidium, written with the head of an asp, dipped in gall, the other is more mild. If these histories may be depended upon, neither Nicholas Stork nor Thomas Muncer, were Anabaptists; Melchoir Hoffman and John Bechold were. They were called Anabaptists, because they repeated baptism; but they did not dip but sprinkle, so that the whole uproar belongs to other societies, and not to the Baptists. A late author, Rev. Mr. Pattilloe, in giving an account of the rise of other societies, says, "the Baptists made their appearance in Germany, soon after the Reformation began." Has the good Mr. Pattilloe got this by rote, hearing of it so often? Or has the judicious pen of Mr. Smith helped him out in a dead lift? Or can the gentleman demonstrate his assertion and implication by real facts? Should I affirm that the Presbyterians made their appearance in London in the reign of James I, on the fifth of November, 1605, in the gun powder plot, it might perhaps raise the bristles of his meek heart; and this I might affirm with as much propriety as he could affirm what he has. The names Papist and Presbyterian are as much alike as Baptist and Anabaptist, and their modes of baptism far more uniform. I admire Mr. Pattilloe's writing in general; I was a subscriber for his book, and think my dollar well exchanged; but, let the Rev. Gentleman remember, that the Baptists can produce sacred proof for their appearance in Judea, about 1,500 years before those tumults in Germany, and if he can produce more antiquated proof of the Presbyterians, then let him triumph; otherwise, be peaceable, as becomes him.

Some Remarks

A retrospective view of this chronicle informs us that the number of religious sects in Virginia, is seven, viz., Episcopalians, Quakers, Presbyterians, Methodists, Tunkers, Mennonists, and Baptists. There are a few Jews, but they have no synagogue, nor is there any chapel for Papists. If men had virtue enough, it would be pleasing to see all of one mind; but in these lethargic days, if there is not a little difference among men, they sink into stupidity. It is happy for Virginia, in a political point of view, that there are several societies, nearly of a size; should one attempt to oppress another, all the rest would unite to prevent it. And the same may be said of the United States; more than 20 religious societies are in them, which render it almost impossible for one order to oppress all the others. This is a greater security for religious liberty than all that can be written on paper. If two or three of the most popular societies in the Union should unite together, the other societies would have cause to fear, from the consideration, that the many generally oppress the few; but if things in future, emerge as they have heretofore, we have more reason to believe, that the present societies will split and subdivide, than we have to believe, that parties, now at variance, will ever unite. O, Virginia! O, America!—a people favored of the Lord!—may the goodness of God excite our obedience. There are yet remaining some vestiges of religious oppression, but they are chiefly theoretical. It may be said that in substance, the different societies enjoy equal liberty of thinking, speaking, and worshipping, and equal protection by law. Perhaps there is not a constitutional evil in the states, that has a more plausible pretext, than the proscription of gospel ministers; I say in the states, for most of them have proscribed them from seats of legislation, etc. The federal government is free in this point: to have one branch of the legislature composed of clergymen, as is the case in some European powers, is not seemly—to have them entitled to seats of legislation, on account of their ecclesiastical dignity, like the bishops in England, is absurd. But to declare them ineligible, when their neighbors prefer them to any others, is depriving them of the liberty of free citizens, and those who prefer them, the freedom of choice.

If the office of a preacher were lucrative, there would be some propriety in his ineligibility; but as the office is not lucrative, the proscription is cruel. To make the best of it, it is but doing evil, that good may come: denying them the liberty of citizens, lest they should degrade their sacred office. Things should be so fixed in government, that there should be neither degrading checks, nor alluring baits to the ministry; but as the proscription, mentioned above, is a check, so there are some baits, in the states, to the sacred work. In some of the states, the property of preachers is free from tax. In Virginia, their persons are exempt from bearing arms. Though this is an indulgence that I feel, yet it is not consistent with my theory of politics. It may be further observed, that an exemption from bearing arms is, but a legal indulgence, but the ineligibility is constitutional proscription, and no legal reward is sufficient for a constitutional prohibition. The first may be altered by the caprice of the legislature, the last cannot be exchanged, without an appeal to the whole mass of constituent power.

The Rights and Bonds of Conscience

The subject of religious liberty, has been so canvassed for 14 years, and has so far prevailed, that in Virginia, a politician can no more be popular with the possession of it, than a preacher who denies the doctrine of the new birth; yet many, who make this profession, behave in their families, as if they did not believe what they profess. For a man to contend for religious liberty on the court house green and deny his wife, children, and servants the liberty of conscience at home is a paradox not easily reconciled. If a head of a family could answer for all his house in the day of judgment, there would be a degree of justice in his controlling them in the mode of worship and joining society; but answer for them he cannot; each one must give an account of himself to God, and none but cruel tyrants will prevent their wives, children or servants, either directly or indirectly, from worshipping God according to the dictates of their consciences, and joining the society they choose; for as religion does not destroy either civil or domestic government, so neither of them extend their rightful influence into the empire of conscience.

The rights of conscience are so sacred, that no mortal can justly circumscribe them, and yet the conscience is so defiled by sin, as well as the other powers of the soul, that it may lead men into error. The word conscience, signifies common science; a court of judicature, erected by God in every human breast: and, as courts of justice often give wrong judgment, for want of good information, so it happens with conscience. The author of our religion said, "the time will come, when he that killeth you will think that he doeth God service." And Paul verily thought that he ought to do many things against the Lord Jesus. So that conscience is not the rule of life, but the Word of God. Though conscience should be free from human control, yet it should be in strict subordination to the law of God.

Thoughts on Systems

That devil, who transforms himself into an angel of light, is often preaching from these words; "contend earnestly for the faith once delivered to the saints." Whenever men are self-conceited enough to believe themselves infallible in judgment, and take their own opinions for tests of orthodoxy, they conclude they are doing God service, in vindicating His truth; while they are only contending for their particular tenets. By this gross mistake, the Christian world is filled with polemical divinity. I very much question, whether there was ever more sophistry used among the old philosophers, than there has been among divines. I never saw a defense of a religious system, but what a great part of it was designed to explain away the apparent meaning of plain texts of scripture. System writers generally adopt a few principles, which, they say, are certain truths, and all reasoning against those principles they strive to make sophistry, and all texts that seem to withstand their scheme, they endeavor to explain away; sometimes by mending the translation of the Bible. I have never yet known an instance of a man's altering the translation of a text that expressed his own sentiment, as it is translated.

When men are run hard to support their plan, they will appeal from scripture to the reason of things; and when reason fails them, they will fly back again to scripture; and when both disappear, they will have recourse to the unsearchable ways of God. There is no doubt in my mind, that the God of order acts consistently with Himself; but it is a grand doubt, whether divine materials ever did, or ever will, submit to human standards. And, I think it much safer for a man to own his ignorance, and stand open to conviction, than to be too positive in asserting things that he himself may doubt of in his cool retired hours.

Notes

1. If we were slaves in Africa, how should we reprobate such reasoning as would rob us of our liberty. It is a question, whether men had not better lose all their property, than deprive an individual of his birth-right blessing—freedom. If a political system is such that common justice cannot be administered without innovation, the sooner such a system is destroyed, the better for the people.

2. Baptism, by some, is made everything; by some, anything; and, by others, nothing. The Episcopalians make it everything; they say that the water is blest to the mystical washing away of sin; that, by it, children are regenerated, and engrafted into the body of Christ, which is everything we need. The Methodists make it anything; either sprinkling, pouring or immersion. No matter how it is done, if it is done. Can it be supposed that Jesus, who was faithful in all His house, in the character of a Son, should be less definite in His orders than Moses was, who was only a servant? See (says the Hebrew prophet) that thou makest the tabernacle, in all things, according to the pattern shown to thee in the Mount; and is the pattern of Jesus of no more use than to be made anything of? That which is to be done but once in a man's life should be well done. Are the words of St. Paul inapplicable here? "One baptism."

The Quakers make it nothing; but when they regard the Word of God more, and the word of Barclay less, they will then find baptism, not only to be a command, but the first command, after repentance and faith.

If baptism is everything, Simon, the witch, is gone to heaven, and the thief dropt from the cross to hell. If it is anything, we may say of it, as Mr. Wesley does of praying time, "any time is no time." And if it is nothing, why is the noun, with its verb and participle, recorded almost one hundred times in the New Testament? If men can be perfect or obedient in all things, without it, what means this bleating of the Scriptures which I hear?

3. This mode was used in the ordination of Matthias to the apostleship; and, like every other account in the New Testament, is a precedent without a second. As no two instances of ordination are uniform, can it be a piece of licentiousness to treat the subject, as to its mode, with a degree of indifference? In Virginia, Episcopal, Presbyterial, and Congregational ordinations are all contended for. Imposition and non-imposition of hands are equally pleaded for; but, after all, a commission from Heaven, to preach and baptize, is the great quintessence.

4. Ketocton is the name of a water-course in Loudoun County, that empties into the Potomac. Most of the Baptist churches now in Virginia, take their names of distinction from the waters where they are.

5. To this day there are not more than three or four Baptist ministers in Virginia who have received the diploma of M.A., which is additional proof that the work has been of God and not of man.

6. There are other parts of the thirty-nine articles, equally exceptionable with those parts excepted. If a creed of faith, established by law, was ever so short, and ever so true; if I believed the whole of it with all my heart—should I subscribe to it before a magistrate in order to get indulgence, preferment, or even protection—I should be guilty of a species of idolatry, by acknowledging a power, that the Head of the Church, Jesus Christ, has never appointed. In this point of view, who can look over the constitutions of government adopted in most of the United States with real sorrow? They require a religious test to qualify an officer of state. All the good such tests do is to keep from office the best of men; villains make no scruple of any test. The Virginia Constitution is free from this stain. If a man merits the confidence of his neighbors, in Virginia—let him worship one God, twenty gods, or no God—be he Jew, Turk, Pagan, or Infidel, he is eligible to any office in the state.

7. What is here said of the Church of England, respects them before the late Revolution. Since the independence of the state, a great number of those who still prefer Episcopacy, have the most noble ideas of religious liberty, and are so far from wishing to oppress those who differ with them in judgment as any men in the state. Experience proves, that while each man believes what he chooses, and practices as he pleases, although they differ widely in sentiment, yet they love each other better than they do when they are all obliged to believe and worship in one way. The only way to live in peace and enjoy ourselves as freemen, is to think and speak freely, worship as we please, and be protected by law in our persons, property, and liberty.

8. Before this, the Methodists petitioned for a continuation of the established religion of the state; but being organized a distinct church, they vigorously opposed the assessment; and at the same time petitioned the legislature for a general liberation of the slaves. Although the petition was rejected, as being impracticable, yet it shows their resolution to bring to pass a noble work.

9. A union seemed so necessary and desirable, that those who were somewhat scrupulous of a confession of faith, other than the Bible, were willing to sacrifice their peculiarities, and those who were strenuous for the confession of faith, agreed to a partial reception of it. "United we stand, divided we fall," overcome, at that time, all objections; but had they united without any confession of faith, as they did in Georgia, perhaps it would have been better. In kingdoms and states, where a system of religion is established by law, with the indulgence of toleration to non-conformists of restricted sentiments, it becomes necessary for such nonconformists to publish a confession of their

faith, to convince the rulers that they do not exceed the bounds of toleration; but in a government like that of Virginia, where all men believe and worship as they please—where the only punishment inflicted on the enthusiastical, is pity—what need of a confession of faith? Why this Virgin Mary between the souls of men and the Scriptures? Had a system of religion been essential to salvation, or even to the happiness of the saints, would not Jesus, who was faithful in all His house, have left us one? If He has, it is accessible to all. If He has not, why should a man be called a heretic because he cannot believe what he cannot believe, though he believes the Bible with all his heart? Confessions of faith often check any further pursuit after truth, confine the mind into a particular way of reasoning, and give rise to frequent separations. To plead for their utility, because they have been common, is as good sense, as to plead for a state establishment of religion, for the same reason; and both are as bad reasoning, as to plead for sin, because it is everywhere. It is sometimes said that heretics are always averse to confessions of faith. I wish I could say as much of tyrants. But after all, if a confession of faith, upon the whole, may be advantageous, the greatest care should be taken not to sacradize or make a petty Bible of it.

10. Gospel preachers are generally like the ass seen by Agelastus, loaded with figs, and feeding upon thistles.

11. In England, are two archbishops, and twenty-six bishops. In Ireland are four archbishops, and nineteen bishops. In Scotland, one general assembly, thirteen provincial synods, and sixty-eight presbyters.

12. A sheriff being sent to bring a Tartar to court, was a long time detained; when solicited to make his return, he replied, "the Tartar will not come." "Come without him then," said the judge. "Yes sir," said the sheriff; "but the Tartar will not let me."

Chapter Three

Selections from
Manual of Theology (1857)

JOHN L. DAGG

Doctrine Concerning the Will and Works of God:
"Duty of Delighting in the Will and
Works of God"

If any one supposes the religion consists merely of self-denial and painful austerities, and that it is filled with gloom and melancholy, to the exclusion of all happiness, he greatly mistakes its true character. False religions, and false views of the true religion, may be liable to this charge; but the religion which has God for its author, and which leads the soul to God, is full of peace and joy. It renders us cheerful amidst the trials of life, contented with all the allotments of Divine Providence, happy in the exercises of piety and devotion, and joyful in the hope of an endless felicity. Heaven is near in prospect; and while on the way to that world of perfect and eternal bliss, we are permitted, in some measure, to anticipate its joys, being, even here, blessed with all spiritual blessings in heavenly places in Christ Jesus. We are enabled, not only to pursue our pilgrimage to the good land with content and cheerfulness, but even to "delight ourselves in the Lord." Our happiness is not merely the absence of grief and pain, but it is positive delight.

The delight which attends other religious exercises should be felt in the investigation of religious truth, and should stimulate to diligence and perseverance. Divine truth is not only sanctifying, but it is also beautifying. To the ancient saints it was sweeter than honey and the honeycomb; and the early Christians, in "believing" the trust as it is in Jesus, "rejoiced with joy unspeakable and full of glory." If we loved the truth as we ought, we should experience equal delight in receiving it; and the careful investigation of it would be a source of pure and abiding pleasure. It would not suffice to employ our intellectual powers in the discussion of perplexing questions appertaining to religion, but we should find a rich feast in the truth that may be known and read by all. The man who indulges his skeptical doubts, and suffers Himself to be detained by questions to no profit, is like one who, when a bountiful feast is spread before Him, instead of enjoying the offered food, employs Himself in examining a supposed flaw in the dish in which it is served. The glorious truths which are plainly revealed concerning God, and the things of God, are sufficient to enable everyone to delight himself in the Lord.

We have before seen that love to God lies at the foundation of true religion. Love, considered as simple benevolence, has for its object the production of happiness, and not the receiving of it. But, by the wise arrangements of infinite goodness, the producing of happiness blesses him that gives as well as him that receives. It is even "more blessed to give than to receive." But when God is the object of our love, as we cannot increase His happiness, we delight in it as already perfect; and all the outflowing of our love to Him, finding the measure of His bliss already full, returns back on ourselves, filling us also with the fullness of God. God is love; and to love God with all the heart is to have the heart filled, to the full measure of its capacity, with the blessedness of the divine nature. This is the fullness of delight.

In the existence and attributes of God a sufficient foundation is laid for the claim of supreme love to Him; but, for the active exercise of the holy affection, God must be viewed not merely as existing, but as acting. To produce delight in Him, His perfections must be manifested. So we enjoy the objects of our earthly love by their presence with us, and the display of those qualities which attract our hearts. Heaven is full of bliss, because its inhabitants not only love God, but see the full manifestations of His glory. To enjoy God on earth, we must contemplate Him in such manifestations of Himself as He has been pleased to make to us who dwell on His footstool. These we may discover in the declarations of His will, and in His works, which are the execution of His will. In a contemplation of these, the pious heart finds a source of pure, elevating delight.

When the Son of God consented to appear in human nature for the salvation of man, He said: "I delight to do thy will, O my God." If the same mind were in us that was in Christ Jesus, we, too, would delight in the will of God. We should be able to say with David, "I will delight myself in thy commandments"; and with Paul, "I delight in the law of God." We should yield obedience to every precept, not reluctantly, but cheerfully; not cheerfully only, but with joy and delight. It would be to us meat and drink to do the will of God, as it was to our blessed Lord. Our religious enjoyment would consist not merely in receiving good from God, but in rendering active service to Him; like the happy spirits before the throne, who serve God day and night, and delight in His service. Not only should we delight to render personal service to our Sovereign, but we should desire His will to be done by all others, and should rejoice in His universal dominion. "The Lord reigneth, let the earth rejoice."

As the ancient saints delighted in the will and government of God, so they delighted in His works. They saw in them the manifestations of His wisdom, power, and goodness; and they delighted to meditate on them. His glory, displayed in the heavens, and His handiwork, visible in earth, they contemplated with holy pleasure. They rejoice to remember, "It is He that made us"; and, in approaching Him with religious worship, they were accustomed to address Him as the Creator of all things: "Lord, thou art God, which hast made heaven and earth, and the sea, and all that in them is."

The goodness displayed in God's works awakens gratitude in the pious man. While he enjoys the gift, he recognizes the hand which bestows it; and each blessing is rendered more dear, because conferred by Him whom he supremely loves. He sees in creation a vast store house of enjoyment, and blesses the author of it. He receives from the providence of God the innumerable benefits which are every day bestowed, and He blesses the kind bestower. God is in every mercy, and His heart, in enjoying it, goes out ever to God, with incessant praise and thanksgiving.

The trial of our delight in God is experienced when affliction comes. The pious man feels that this, too, is from the hand of God. So thought all the saints, of whose religious exercises the Bible gives us an account. They bowed under affliction in the spirit of resignation to God, as the author of the affliction. So Job, "The Lord gave, and the Lord hath taken away; blessed be the name of the Lord." So David, "I was dumb, I opened not my mouth; because thou didst it." So Eli, "It is the Lord; let Him do what seemeth Him good." So Paul's companions, "We ceased, saying, the will of the Lord be done." The ancient saints believed in an overruling Providence, and they received all afflictions as ordered by Him, in every particular; and on this faith the resignation was founded by which their eminent piety was distinguished. To the flesh, the affliction was not joyous, but grievous, and, therefore, they could not delight in it, when considered in itself; but, when enduring it with keenest anguish, they could still say, with Job, "Blessed be the name of the Lord." They firmly believed that the dispensation was wisely and kindly ordered, and that God would bring good out of the evil; and, however oppressed with suffering, and filled with present sorrow, they still trusted in God; and delight in Him alleviated their misery, and mingled with their sorrows.

Let love to God burn in our hearts while we contemplate His existence and attributes. Let delight in Him rise to the highest rapture of which earthly minds are susceptible, while we study His will and works. The grand work of redemption, into which the angels especially desire to look, and which is the chief theme of the song of the glorified, is fitted to produce higher ecstasy; but even the themes of creation and providence may fill us with delight, if we approach them as we ought. When the foundations of the earth were laid, the morning stars sang together, and all the sons of God shouted for joy; and angels now delight to be the ministers of God's providence. Let us, with like devotion to Almighty God, delight in His will and works.

Doctrine Concerning Divine Grace: "Duty of Gratitude for Divine Grace"

As love is the affection which should arise in our hearts, from a view of God's character, so gratitude is the affection which should be produced, by a view of the benefits that He confers. The stream of His benefits flows incessantly so that our cup is ever full. To receive the benefits thoughtlessly, like the brutes that perish, and to enjoy them without thanksgiving to Him from whom they come, is demonstration complete of human depravity. Such demonstration is given daily and hourly in the conduct of mankind, and by it God is offended and His wrath provoked. The unthankful man is the evil man, and the enemy of God. Hence, when we are called on to love our enemies, the example proposed for our imitation is the bestowment of God's providential blessing on the unthankful.

Love your enemies, and do good, and lend, hoping for nothing again, and your reward shall be great, and ye shall be the children of the Highest; for He is kind unto the unthankful and to the evil.

We are bound to thank God for the blessings of providence so incessantly and so richly bestowed; but far higher obligations to gratitude, arise from the grace that bringeth salvation. This grace includes God's gift of His Son, a gift so great that no name for it can be found. "God so loved the world, that He gave His only begotten Son, that whosoever believeth in Him should not perish, but have everlasting life." The love of the Son, which demands our gratitude, is not less unmeasured, than the love of the Father: whence Paul labored to explore "the height, the length, the breadth and the depth of the love of Christ, which passeth knowledge." And our gratitude is not complete till we acknowledge and celebrate also, the love of the Spirit, by whom believers are fitted for the enjoyment of God, and brought into fellowship with Him.

In exercising and cultivating our gratitude for the blessings of salvation, we must distinctly recognize that they come from God, and that they are intentionally bestowed. When we trace them to their source, the infinite love of the triune God; and when we receive them, as conferred according to His eternal counsel, we are prepared while we enjoy the benefit, to return thanks to its Author, and to exclaim with liveliest emotion, "Bless the Lord, O my soul, and forget not all His benefits."

That our gratitude to God may be proportional to the blessing received, we should count His mercies over, and survey their magnitude. Unmeasurable! Unspeakable! Passing knowledge!— yet we should labor to know them; and as we make progress in this spiritual knowledge, our gratitude should swell and fill the enlarged capacity of the mind.

In order to the full exercise of gratitude to God it is necessary to be thoroughly impressed with the conviction that the blessings received are wholly undeserved, and proceed entirely from the mere mercy and grace of God. When we feel that we are less than the least of all God's mercies, that our only desert is hell, and that if salvation is bestowed on us, it will be of His own good pleasure; we are prepared to give thanks for the unspeakable gift, and to say, "Not unto us, O Lord, not unto us, but unto thy name give glory."

(Material from: Rev. John L. Dagg, *Autobiography of Rev. John L. Dagg, D.D.* (Harrisonburg, Va.: Gano Books, 1982).

Chapter Four

"Three Changes in Theological Institutions" (July 31, 1856)

James Petigru Boyce

(An inaugural address delivered before the board of trustees of Furman University, July 31, 1856)

I congratulate myself that I address tonight a body of men pledged to the interests of theological education and that I do it in the existence of our present relations and in the discharge of the duty assigned me. Otherwise, it might appear from the sentiments I shall utter that I am opposed to the thorough training and education of the Christian ministry. The circumstances, however, under which we have gathered together this evening indicate at once the deep interest felt by you and by myself in the cause of theological education and that, whatever sentiments may be spoken by me or heard with approbation by you, we hold the education of the ministry a matter of the first importance to the churches of Christ.

Indeed, did we think otherwise, we could no longer justly stand forth as exponents in any sense of the opinions upon this subject which prevail in our denomination. The Baptists are unmistakably the friends of education and the advocates of an educated ministry. Their twenty-four colleges and ten departments or institutions for theological instruction in this country furnish sufficient testimony to the fact that they feel the value of education and the importance, under God, of the means it affords for the better performance of the work of the ministry. And rather would I that my tongue should cleave to the roof of my mouth than that I should say anything tonight which might justly be construed into dissent from an opinion so truly in accordance with the Word of God and the enlightened sentiments of the age.

So far am I from entertaining such opinions that I would see the means of theological education increased, I would have the facilities for pursuing its studies opened to all who would embrace them, I would lead the strong men of our ministry to feel that no position is equal in responsibility or usefulness to that of one devoted to this cause, and I would spread among our churches such an earnest desire for educated ministers as would make them willing so to increase the support of the ministry as to enable those without means to anticipate the support they will receive and feel free to borrow the means by which their education may be completed.

I cannot perceive, however, how the most earnest desire for thorough theological education is inconsistent in any degree with the advocacy of the changes I propose. How can any scheme be regarded as unfavorable to that education, which, while it abates not the attainments urged upon all so far as practicable, seeks to provide such instruction as will increase the education of each individual and take the mass now uneducated and make them capable and efficient workmen for God?

The truth is that the time has come at last when the sophistry of the objection here supposed will be easily detected. The mind of the whole denomination has been awakened to the want of success under which we have suffered in our past efforts, and the best intellects and hearts in all our Southern bounds are directed in the causes of our failure and to the means by which success may be attained.

In the efforts to establish the common theological institution, proposed as a remedy for the evil, I heartily concur. I do not think that the demand for theological education calls at present for more than one institution. The experiments to be made in finally securing the best ends will be experiments for the common good and should be at the common expense. It is only by such a combination that we can procure the best and ablest instructors afforded by our denomination throughout the world. And it is, thus, only that the scheme adopted will attract sufficient notice and sympathy to test beyond doubt its value as a remedy for existing evils and as a means of developing additional changes for the improvements of theological instruction.

The recollection of past efforts to create union among us upon this subject leads many, however, to suppose that the present one will end in disappointment. I confess that many indications favor this opinion. If they be verified, and this attempt at united efforts fail, nothing will remain for us but the hope that some one of our present institutions may be able, single handed, to make the experiment for the whole and to establish the true principles of theological education.

Indeed, gentlemen, since the common institution would only have greater facilities and since the introduction of these changes, perhaps to the full extent at present necessary, will come within our power, why may we not make the experiment at once? The organization of the proposed institution will take time, especially if the location of one of our present colleges be not selected. During that time it will be incumbent upon you to provide for the instruction of the ministry. While such a time may not give opportunity for the fairest trial, especially under the circumstances of isolation in which the university stands, as the institution of a single state, yet it may be more than adequate to prove the entire practicability of the plan and to secure the honor of its inception. And more than this—should it prove successful, the knowledge of the fact will be to the denomination at large a most powerful motive for selecting this location for the common institution.

It is on this account that in performing the duty assigned me, I find myself irresistibly forced from other subjects which might have been appropriate and led to suggest to you "Three Changes in Theological Institutions," which would enable them to fulfill more adequately at least, if not completely, the hopes of their founders. These changes are intended to meet evils which, in one case by the many, in the others by the few, have been already experienced, and they are suggested as furnishing ample remedies for the existing evils.

The first evil to which I would apply a remedy is one which has been universally experienced—which, more than anything else, has shaken the faith of many in the value of theological institutions, has originated the opposition which they have at any time awakened, and has caused the mourning and sorrow of those who, having laid their foundations, still continue to cluster around them. I refer to the failure of the theological institution to call forth an abundant ministry for the churches and supply to it adequate instruction.

Whatever other purposes may have been intended to be accomplished, there can be no doubt that this has been the primary object of all our educational efforts. The university, over the interests of which you are called to preside, must for one at least be regarded as the growth of this single idea. From the very beginning of Baptist efforts for education in this state to the present moment, this has always been the mainspring of our movements. Looking back upon that band of worthies in whose minds first originated the idea of the Furman Academy and inquiring of them, and of you, gentlemen, who now hold and exercise the sacred trusts of its guardians, the objects of all the efforts put forth, I hear but one overwhelming response—that we may have an abundance of able, sound, and faithful men to proclaim the gospel of Christ, and "to feed the flocks over which the Holy Ghost shall make them overseers." The university is the offspring of prayers to the Lord of the harvest that He would send forth laborers into His harvest. It is the method our best wisdom has devised to make, through the aid of His grace, of those whom He sends in answer to our prayers, "workmen that need not to be ashamed rightly dividing the word of truth."

It is mournful that we are forced so inevitably to the conclusion that these prayers have not yet been answered and that these purposes not yet fulfilled. The theological seminary has not been a popular institution. But few have sought its advantages. But few have been nurtured by the influences sent forth from it. And while our denomination has continued to increase, and our principles have annually been spreading more widely, it has been sensibly felt that whatever ministerial increase has accompanied has been not only disproportionate to that of our membership but has owed its origin in not respect to the influence of theological education.

And this seems to be the general law in the denomination. The complaint is not peculiar to our institution. It seems to exist everywhere, despite all the efforts to counteract it which have been put forth; and not to be confined to Baptists, but to be the lamentation of all. You will see it in the organs of all the prominent denominations, and the cause of it is the subject of earnest inquiry.

The whitened harvest, the awakened activity of the churches, the favorable reception given to the Word of God, have never been more signally manifested. Never have been heard more piercing cries for the gospel than those with which Ethiopia accompanies her outstretched hands; never have been felt deeper longings for the coming of the kingdom of God than are uttered by praying hearts throughout Christendom; never has sin appeared to develop more fearful evils; never has "hydra headed error" so fully or so variously exalted herself; neither has God ever multiplied to so gracious an extent the means which He gives the church as an aid to the ministry not to diminish its labors, but to make them fourfold more abundant and an hundred-fold more valuable. The world seems ready, lying at the very door of the Christian church, yet calling for laborious efforts to gather it in. Oh! Were there ever a time when we would expect that God would answer the prayers of His churches and overflood the land and the world with a ministry adequate to uphold His cause in every locality, it should seem to be now—now, when the wealth of the churches is sufficient to send the gospel to every creature, now, when, in the art of printing, the church has again received the gift of tongues; now, when the workings of God Himself indicate His readiness to beget a nation in a day; now, when the multiplication a thousand-fold of the laborers will still leave an abundant work for each; but now, alas! Now, when our churches at home are not adequately supplied; when dark and destitute places are found in the most favored portions of our own land; when the heathen are at our very doors, and the cry is help, and there is no help because there are not laborers enough to meet the wants immediately around us.

There are serious questions presented to us here. To what are these things due? Have we not disregarded the laws which the providence and Word of God have laid down for us? And does He not now chastise us by suffering our schemes to work out their natural results, that we, being left to ourselves, may see our folly and return to Him and to His ways as the only means of strength!

In ascribing this evil for the most part to our theological institutions, I would not appear unmindful of other circumstances upon which an increase of the ministry in our churches depends. Never would I consent to lift my voice upon such a subject as this without a distinct recognition of the sovereignty of God working His own will and calling forth, according to that will, that many or the few with whose aid He will secure the blessing. Never could I proceed upon any assumption that would seem to take for granted that there is not the utmost need of more special awakening to devotion and piety in our churches and a more fervent utterance of prayer for the increase of the laborers. Neither would I have it supposed that all that the theological institution can effect will be fully adequate to our wants while our pastors neglect to search out and encourage the useful gifts which God has bestowed upon the members of their churches or the churches themselves neglect the law of God which provides an adequate support for the ministry. But while due prominence is given to all of these circumstances, it yet appears that the chief cause is to be found in our departure from the way which God has marked out for us and our failure to make provision for the education of such a ministry as He designs to send forth and honor.

Permit me to ask what has been the prominent idea at the basis of theological education in this country? To arrive at it we have only to notice the requisitions necessary for entrance upon a course of study. Have they not been almost universally that the student should have passed through a regular college course or made attainments equivalent thereto? And have not even the exceptional cases been rare instances in which the faculty or board have, under peculiar circumstances, assumed the responsibility of a deviation from the ordinary course?

The idea, which is prominent as the basis of this action, is that the work of the ministry should be entrusted only to those who have been classically educated—an assumption which singularly enough is made for no other profession. It is in vain to say that such is not the theory or the practice of our denomination. It is the theory and the practice of by far the larger portion of those who have controlled our institutions and have succeeded in engrafting this idea upon them, contrary to the spirit which prevails among the churches. They have done this without doubt in the exercise of their best judgment, but have failed because they neglected the better plan pointed out by the providence and Word of God.

The practical operation of this theory has tended in two ways to diminish the ranks of our valuable ministry. It has restrained many from entering upon the work and has prevented the arrangement of such a course of study as would have enabled those who have entered upon it to fit themselves in a short time for valuable service. The consequences have been that the number of those who have felt themselves called of God to the ministry has been disproportioned to the wants of the churches; and of that number but a very small proportion have entered it with a proper preparation for even common usefulness. And only by energy and zeal, awakened by their devotion to the work, have they been able to succeed in their labors, and to do for themselves the work, the greater part of which the theological school should have accomplished for them.

In His Word and in His providence, God seems to have plainly indicated the principle upon which the instruction of the ministry should be based. It is not that every man should be made a scholar, an adept in philology, an able interpreter of the Bible in its original languages, acquainted with all the sciences upon the various facts and theories of which God's Word is attacked and must be defended, and versed in all the systems of true and false philosophy. Indeed, some must understand these in order to encounter the enemies which attack the very foundations of religion. But while the privilege of becoming such shall be freely offered to all, and every student shall be encouraged to obtain all the advantages that education can afford, the opportunity should be given to those who cannot or will not make thorough scholastic preparation to obtain that adequate knowledge of the truths of the Scriptures systematically arranged and of the laws which govern the interpretation of the text in the English version, which constitutes all that is actually necessary to enable them to preach the gospel, to build up the churches on their most holy faith, and to instruct them in the practice of the duties incumbent upon them.

The scriptural qualifications of the ministry do, indeed, involve the idea of knowledge, but that knowledge is not of the sciences not of philosophy nor of the languages, but of God and of His plan of salvation. He who has not this knowledge, though he be learned in all the learning of the schools, is incapable of preaching the Word of God. But he who knows it, not superficially, not merely in those plain and simple declarations known to every believing reader, but in the power, as revealed in its precious and sanctifying doctrines, is fitted to bring forth out of his treasury things new and old, and is a workman that needeth not to be ashamed, although he may speak to his hearers in uncouth words or in manifest ignorance of all the sciences. The one belongs to the class of educated ministers, the other to the ministry of educated men, and the two things are essentially different.

The one may be a Bunyan, unlearned withal, and in many respects ignorant, rough and rugged of speech, with none of the graces of the orator or the refinement of the rhetorician, but so filled with the grace abounding to the chief of sinners, so learned in the Scriptures quoted at every point for the support of the truth he speaks, and discoursing such sweet and godly doctrine, that he is manifest as one taught so truly in the gospel that the most learned scholars may sit silently at his feet and learn the wonders of the Word of God. The other may be a Parker, with all the grace and polish of the finished scholar, poring forth the purest and most powerful English, able to illustrate and defend his cause by contributions from every storehouse of knowledge, presenting attractions in his oratory which induce his educated audience to receive or to overlook his blasphemous doctrines, yet so destitute of the knowledge of true Christianity and of a genuine experience of the influences of the Holy Ghost, that he denies the plainest doctrines of the Bible, saps the very foundation of all revealed truth, and manifests so profound an ignorance of the Book he undertakes to expound and the religion of which he calls himself a Minister that the humblest Christian among our very servants shall rise up in condemnation against him in the great day of accounts.

Who is the minister here—the man of the schools or the man of the Scriptures? Who bears the insignia of an ambassador for Christ? Whom does God own? Whom would the church hear? In whose power would she put forth her strength? And yet these instances, though extreme, will serve to show what may be the ministry of the educated man and what that of the illiterate man, the educated minister. The perfection of the ministry, it is gladly admitted, would consist in the just combination of the two; but it is not the business of the church to establish a perfect, but an adequate ministry—and it is only of the latter that we may hope for an abundant supply. The qualification God lays down is the only one He permits us to demand, and the instruction of our theological schools must be based upon such a plan as shall afford this amount of education to those who actually constitute the mass of our ministry and who cannot obtain more.

The providential dispensation of God, in the administration of the affairs of His church, fully illustrate the truth of this principle, so plainly in accordance with His Word. That the education of the schools is of great advantage to the minister truly trained in the word of truth has been illustrated by the labors of Paul, Augustine, Calvin, Beza, Davies, Edwards, and a host of others who have stood forth in their different ages the most prominent of all the ministry of their day and the most efficient workmen in the cause of Christ. While in the eleven apostles, in the mass of the ministry of that day, and of all other times and places, God has manifested that He will work out the greater proportion of His purposes by men of no previous training and educated only in the mysteries of that truth which is in Christ Jesus.

Never has He illustrated that principle more fully than in connection with the progress of the principles of our own denomination. We have had our men of might and power who have shown the advantages of scholastic education as a basis, but we have also seen the great instruments of our progress to have been the labors of a much humbler class. Trace our history back, either through the centuries that have long passed away or in the workings of God during the last hundred years, and it will be seen that the mass of the vineyard laborers have been from the ranks of fishermen and tax gatherers, cobblers and tinkers, weavers and ploughmen, to whom God has not disdained to impart gifts, and whom He has qualified as His ambassadors by the presence of that Spirit by which, and not by might, wisdom or power, is the work of the Lord accomplished.

The Baptists of America, especially, should be the last to forget this method of working on the part of their Master and the first to retrace any steps which would seem to indicate such forgetfulness. It has been signally manifested in the establishment of their faith and principles. The names which have been identified with our growth have been those of men of no collegiate education, of no learning or rhetorical eloquence, of no instruction even in schools of theology. Hervey, Gano, Bennet, Semple, Broadus, Armstrong, Mercer, who were these? Men of education, of collegiate training, of theological schools? Nay, indeed. All praise to those who did possess any of these advantages. They were burning and shining lights. They hid neither talents nor opportunities, but devoted them to the cause they love, and accomplished much in its behalf. They maintained positions which perhaps none others could have occupied. But their number was not sufficient for the work of the Lord, and He gave a multitude of others—men who were found in labors oft, in wearisome toils by day and by night, in heat or in cold, facing dangers of every kind, enduring private and public persecution, travelling through swamp and forest to carry the glad tidings of salvation to the lost and perishing of our country. And the Baptists can neither forget them nor the principle taught us in their labors, by the providence of God. Whatever may be the course of those who have the training of their ministry, these ideas have sunk so deeply into the minds of the denomination that they can never be eradicated. And the day will yet come, perhaps has already come, when the churches will rise in their strength and demand that our theological institutions make educational provisions for the mass of their ministry.

I have spoken of our ministry in the past as composed of men whose success illustrates the theory of the need only of theological education. And yet it is apparent that they enjoyed none of the advantages for that purpose which are connected with the present arrangements for study. In the absence of these, however, they did attain to the amount of theological education which is essential. This was accomplished through excessive labor exercised by minds, capable of mighty efforts, and drawn forth under circumstances favorable to their development.

When we look attentively at the record they have left us, or contemplate those of them whom God's mercy to us permits yet to linger with us, we perceive that they were not the uneducated ministers commonly supposed. It is true, as has been said, that they had not the learning of the schools. A few books of theology—perhaps a single commentary—formed, with their Bibles, their whole apparatus of instruction and measured the extent of their reading. But of these books they were wont to make themselves masters. By a course of incessant study, accompanied by examinations of the Word of God, they were so thoroughly imbued with the processes and results of the best thoughts of their authors that they became, for all practical purposes, almost the same men. And if, by any course of training, substantially of the same kind, our theological schools can restore to us such a mass ministry as was then enjoyed, the days of our progress and prosperity will be realized to have but just begun. And we shall go forward, by the help of the Lord, to possess the whole land which lieth before us. If by any means to these can be added at least five-fold the number of those now educated in the regular course of theology, I doubt not but it will be felt that the most sanguine hopes they have ever excited will be more than fulfilled.

I believe, gentlemen, that it can be done; and more than this, that in the attempt to do it, we shall accomplish an abundantly greater work. Let us abandon the false principle which has so long controlled us and adopt the one which God points out to us by His Word and His providence and from the very supplies God now gives to us may be wrought out precisely such a ministry. Those who have entered upon the work will be rendered fully capable to perform its duties, and numbers besides will be called forth to it who have heretofore been restrained by insurmountable obstacles.

Let such a change be made in the theological department as shall provide an English course of study for those who have only been able to attain a plain English education. Let that course comprise the evidences of Christianity, systematic and polemic theology, the rules of interpretation applied to the English version; some knowledge of the principles of rhetoric, extensive practice in the development from texts of subjects and skeletons of sermons, whatever amount of composition may be expedient, and full instruction in the nature of pastoral duties—let the studies of this course be so pursued as to train the mind to habits of reflection and analysis, to awaken it to conceptions of the truths of Scripture, to fill it with arguments from the Word of God in support of its doctrines, and to give it facility in constructing and presenting such arguments—and the work will be accomplished.

Experience alone can determine the length of time such a course should occupy. It should be so arranged for two years, however, that the better prepared and the more diligent may be able to pass over it in one. Doubtless this would be done by the vast majority, at least of those of riper years.

By the means proposed, the theological school will meet the wants of a large class of those who now enter the ministry without the advantages of such instruction—a class equally with their more learned associates burning with earnest zeal for the glory of God and deep convictions of the value of immortal souls, one possessed of natural gifts, capable even with limited knowledge of enchaining the attention, affecting the hearts and enlightening the minds of many who surround them. A class composed, however, of those who, with few exceptions, soon find themselves exhausted of their materials, forced to repeat the same topics in the same way, and finally to aim at nothing but continuous exhortation, bearing constantly upon the same point, or as is oftentimes the case, destitute of any point at all. In their present condition, these ministers are of comparatively little value to the churches, having no capacity to feed them with the Word of God, affording no attractions to bring a congregation to the house of God, and no power to set before them such an exposition of the Word of God as may, through the influences of His Spirit, awaken them to penitence and lead to faith in the Lord Jesus Christ. What the same men might become were they better instructed is apparent from the results attained by men of the same previous education, who, possessed of more leisure or of a greater natural taste for study, have so improved themselves as to occupy positions of greater respectability and usefulness.

The class of men whose cause I now plead before you is of all those which furnish material for our ministry, that which most needs the theological training I would ask for it. Every argument for theological schools bears directly in favor of its interests. Are such schools founded that our ministry may not be ignorant of the truth? Which class of that ministry is more ignorant than this? Is the object of their endowment that such education may be cheapened? Who are generally in more straitened circumstances? Is it designed to produce an abundant, able, faithful and practical ministry? Where are the materials more abundant? Whence, for the amount of labor expended, will come more copious harvests? So that it appears that whatever may be our obligations to other classes, or the advantages to be gained in their education, the mere statement of them impresses upon us our duty and the yet greater advantages to be gained by the education of that class which should comprise two-thirds at least of those who receive a theological education.

The men who go from college walls untaught in theology have yet a training and an amount of knowledge of incalculable benefit. They can do something to make up their deficiencies. But what chance is there for these others? They know not how to begin to study. Let one of them take up the Scriptures, and he finds himself embarrassed in the midst of statements which the church, for centuries after the apostles, had not fully harmonized—statements which constitute the facts of theology, from which, in like manner with other sciences, by processes of induction and comparison, the absolute truth must be established. If, to escape the difficulty, he turns to a textbook of theology, he is puzzled at once by technicalities so easily understood by those better instructed, that this technical character is totally unperceived. If he turns in this dilemma to our seminaries, he finds no encouragement to enter.

A man of age, perhaps of family, he is called upon to spend years of study in the literary and scientific departments before he is allowed to suppose that he can profitably pursue theology. Straitened, perhaps, in his circumstances and unwilling to partake of the bounty of others, he is told that he must study during a number of years, during which his expenses would probably exhaust five-fold his little store. With a mind capable of understanding and perceiving the truth, and of expressing judicious opinions upon any subject, the facts of which he comprehends, he is told that he must pass through a course of study, the chief value of which is to train the mind, and which will only benefit him by the amount of knowledge it will incidentally convey. I can readily imagine the despair with which that man would be filled who, impelled by a conviction that it is his duty to preach the gospel, contemplates under these circumstances the provisions which the friends of an educated ministry have made for him. We know not how many affected by that sentiment are at this moment longing to enter upon preparation for a work which they feel God has entrusted only to those who, because of their knowledge of His Word, have an essential element of aptness to teach. Be it yours, gentlemen, to reanimate their drooping hopes by opening up before them the means of attaining this qualification.

The adoption of the true principle will not only tend, however, to secure for us this education in the masses, which we need, but will also increase five-fold the number of those who will receive a thorough theological education. It will do this by the change of policy to which it will lead in reference to another class of our candidates for the ministry.

We have among us a number of men who have enjoyed all the advantages of college life, but who have not been able, or willing, to spend the additional years needed for theological study. These are possessed of far greater advantages than those of the other class, men of polished education, of well trained minds, capable of extensive usefulness to the cause of Christ, but their deficiencies are plainly apparent and readily traceable to the lack of a theological education. They are educated men, but not educated ministers, for, while familiar with all the sciences which form parts of the college curriculum, they are ignorant for the most part of that very science which lies at the foundation of all their ministerial labors. The labors of their pastoral charges prevent such study of the Word of God, either exegetically or systematically, as will enable them to become masters of its contents. Having entered upon the work of the ministry, however, they are forced to press forward, encountering difficulties at every step—fearing to touch upon many doctrines of Scripture, lest they misstate them—and frequently guilty of such misstatements, even in the presentation of the simpler topics they attempt, because they fail to recognize the important connections which exist among all the truths of God.

A few, indeed, possessed of giant minds capable of the most accurate investigation and filled with indomitable energy in the pursuit of what they feel to be needful, overcome every obstacle and attain to knowledge often superior to that of others whose training has been more advantageous. But the vast majority find themselves burdened with a weight which they cannot remove and by which they feel that their energies are almost destroyed.

It is needless to say of these that the churches do not grow under their ministry; that, not having partaken of strong meat, they cannot impart it. Their hearers pass on from Sabbath to Sabbath, awakened, indeed, to practical duties, made in many respects efficient in cooperating with Christ's people, but not built up to this condition on their most holy faith, but upon other motives which, however good, are really insufficient for the best progress, at least of their own spiritual natures. Such is not the position of the ministry which four-fifths of our educated men should occupy. They will tell you themselves, gentlemen, that this should not be the case. If due to their own precipitancy, they will attach blame to themselves, but if it result from the exclusiveness of theological schools, their declaration is equivalent to testimony in favor of its removal, and of the admission of all who are capable of pursuing the regular course to participate in its advantages. The disturbances felt about unsettled doctrines, the inability experienced to declare the whole counsel of God, the doctrinal mistakes realized as frequently committed, have long since convinced them that all of their other education is of but little value compared with that knowledge of theology which they have lost in its acquisition.

The theory of the theological school should doubtless be to urge upon every one to take full courses in both departments; but when this is not possible, it should give to those who are forced to select between them the opportunity of omitting the collegiate and entering at once upon the theological course. I see not how anyone can rationally question that many, if not all of those who are fitted for the sophomore, or even the freshman class in college, are prepared, so far as knowledge of books or languages is concerned, to enter with very great, though not with the utmost profit, upon the study of theology. The amount of Greek and Latin acquired, is ample for this purpose. The study of Hebrew and Chaldee are commenced in the theological course, while that which is really the main object for the younger men in the collegiate course, the training and forming of the mind so far as at all practicable, will for the old students have been already accomplished, or for them and for the younger ones may be compensated in great part by the more thorough training in the studies of the seminary, necessary to all who would acquire such knowledge of theology as will make them fully acquainted with its truths.

Since this is the case, why compel this class to spend their time in studies which, however valuable in themselves, have but a secondary importance, compared with those they are made to supercede? If there be any who will pursue the studies of both departments, their number will never be diminished by the adoption of the plan proposed. If it will, better that this be so than that so many others neglect theology. But we may confidently believe that the results will only be to take from the collegiate course those who would neglect the other and cause them to spend the same number of years in the study of that which has an immediate bearing upon their work. It is simply a choice as to certain men between a thorough literary and a thorough theological course. The former may make a man more refined and intelligent, better able to sustain a position of influence with the world, and more capable of illustrating, by a wide range of science, the truth he may have arrived at. The latter will improve his Christian graces, will impart to him the whole range of revealed truth, will make him the instructor of his people, truly the man of God prepared in all things to give to each one his portion in due season.

The bare announcement of the changes proposed in the application of our principle will show that but little additional provision will be needed to put it into operation. The same course of systematic theology will be sufficient for all classes—the advantages possessed by those more highly educated, enabling them simply to add to the textbook or lectures, the examination of Turretine, of some other prescribed author. In the study of Scripture interpretation, it may be necessary to make two divisions, though experience will probably prove the practicability even of united these. There will be needed for all classes the same instruction in the evidences of Christianity, the pastoral theology, in the analysis of texts, the construction of skeletons, and the composition of essays and sermons; and in all of these the classes may be united. So that, really, we will only so far revolutionize the institution, as to add numbers to the classes, and permit some of those whom we add, to take up those studies only which the plain English education will enable them to pursue profitably. All the inconvenience which may accrue therefrom will be gladly endured by all for the benefit of the masses, and because of the mutual love and esteem which, by their throwing together, will be fostered between the most highly educated and the plainest of our ministry.

Is it too much, gentlemen, to ask that this experiment may be tried? Does it not seem practicable? Are not the fruits it would produce, if brought to a successful issue, an ample inducement to us to venture upon an experiment so likely to succeed, and which, if unsuccessful, can so easily be abandoned? And would not that trial seem to put the institution upon the basis of that principle which God has established, and which we may therefore expect him to bless by sending forth, as the Lord of the harvest, an abundance of laborers into the harvest?

In adopting this change, we are so far from saying that education is unnecessary that we proclaim its absolute necessity. We undertake, however, to point out what education it is that is, thus, essential and we provide the means by which adequate theological instruction may be given to the four-fifths of our ministry who now enjoy no means of instruction. We look with confidence for the blessing of God upon this plan, not because we believe that He favors an ignorant ministry, but because we know that He requires that His ministry be instructed, and by His Word and His providence He has pointed out the nature of the learning He demands. We believe that the plan proposed is based upon these indications; and that His refusal to send forth laborers has been chastisement inflicted upon us that we may be brought back to His own plans, which we have abandoned for those of men.

I proceed now to speak more briefly of a second change needed in our theological institutions, by which it is to be hoped they will be enabled to produce scholars adequate to the exigencies of our own denomination and to the common cause of Christianity. It is singularly enough the case that, while they have abandoned the education of the masses for the thorough training of the few, God has not permitted them to accomplish the very object made most prominent in their pretensions. It is not to be concealed that upon this point a dissatisfaction exists which, though not so general, has taken deep root in the minds of our better educated laymen and ministers.

I refer not now to the charge that there has been want of practical training by which those who have taken a theological course. This evil, which I believe may be justly urged against the instruction of every theological institution in our country, is to be attributed to the fact that the professors place the means of instruction in the hands of their students without exercising over their pursuit of those studies the superintendence which is needed. The remedy for this evil is the adoption of that method of instruction which should have marked the previous collegiate course. The studies should be so pursued as to call forth and improve all the powers of analysis and synthesis in the consideration of the subjects presented. Then the student must have practice in the quick production of his thoughts, as well as in deriving the appropriate subject from his text, and in forming skeletons of discourses. Thus, he will not only be fully acquainted with the truth but also able to present it readily and appropriately upon all occasions. If this course be pursued, and the student be encouraged at the same time to engage in every practical work, such as instructing in Sabbath Schools and Bible classes, conducting social meetings in destitute places, preaching where the only ambition will be to present the truth plainly and simply, the complaints about the lack of efficient and practical training in theological students will no longer be heard.

Neither do I allude to the inability of our institutions to compel the attendance of those immediately about them who seek the highest attainments. To remove this, the department must also secure a sufficient number of ablest men, the course must be extended to three years, so as to furnish time for the pursuit of the widest range of study, and the practical training already referred to being then adopted, the superior advantages afforded would soon manifest themselves in the character of the scholarship and the ministry it would send forth. Under such training, the same material would be made doubly as efficient as under that of any of our present institutions.

The dissatisfaction to which I refer, has been awakened by the inadequate extent to which all theological institutions have pursued their studies, and the consequent lack among us of the scholarship which prevails in some countries abroad. It has been felt as a sore evil, that we have been dependent in great part upon the criticism of Germany for all the more learned investigations in biblical criticism and exegesis, and that in the study of the development of the doctrine of the church, as well as of its outward progress, we have been compelled to depend upon works in which much of error has been mingled with truth, owing to the defective standpoint occupied by their authors.

And although the disadvantages of American scholars have been realized as arising from the want of adequate theological libraries, as well as from the inaccessible nature of much other material, it has been felt that it has also been in great part due to the limited extent to which the study of theological science has been pursued among us. We have been much dependent upon others and unable to push forward investigations for ourselves and even so inadequately acquainted with the valuable results of others who have accomplished the work for us. Only a few perhaps have participated in this sentiment, but the evil which awakens it is not, therefore, the less momentous.

It is an evil which may be regarded as pervading the whole field of American religious scholarship, and the remedy should be sought alike by all denominations. It is a matter of the deepest interest to all, that we should be placed in a position of independence in this matter, and that our rising ministry should be trained under the scholarship of the Anglo Saxon mind, which, from its nature, as well as from the circumstances which surround it, is eminently fitted to weigh evidence and to decide as to its appropriateness and its proper limitations. But the obligation resting on the Baptist denomination is far higher than this. It extends not merely to matters of detail, but to those of vital interest. The history of religious literature, and of Christian scholarship, has been a history of Baptist wrongs. We have been overlooked, ridiculed and defamed. Critics have committed the grossest perversions, violated the plainest rules of criticism, and omitted points which could not have been developed without benefit to us. Historians who have professed to write the history of the church, have either utterly ignored the presence of those of our faith or classed them among fanatics and heretics or, if forced to acknowledge the prevalence of our principles and practice among the earliest churches, have adopted such false theories as to church power, and the development and growth of the truth and principles of Scripture, that by all, save their most discerning readers, our pretensions to an early origin and a continuous existence, have been rejected.

The Baptists in the past have been entirely too indifferent to the position they, thus, occupy. They have depended too much upon the known strength of their principles and the ease with which from Scripture they could defend them. They have, therefore, neglected many of those means which extensive learning affords and which have been used to great advantage in support of other opinions. It is needless to say, gentlemen, that we can no longer consent to occupy this position. We owe a change to ourselves—as Christians, bound to show an adequate reason for the differences between us and others—as men of even moderate scholarship, that it may appear that we have not made the gross errors in philology and criticism, which we must have made if we be not right—as the successors of a glorious spiritual ancestry illustrated by heroic martyrdom, by the profession of noble principles, by the maintenance of true doctrine—as the Church of Christ, which He has ever preserved as the witness of His truth, by which He has illustrated His wonderful ways, and shown that His promises are sure and steadfast. Nay, we owe it to Christ Himself, whose truth we hold so distinctively as to separate us from all others of His believing people.

But the question arises, how can we avoid it? The amplest course now afforded, gives to students but slight preparation for entrance upon such duties. Our ministry receives no such support as warrants the purchase of more than moderate libraries. The labors of most of our pastoral charges are sufficient fully to occupy the time of those upon whom they are devoted. And how shall we avoid it?

It is a ray of hope to us, gentlemen, that even under these disadvantageous circumstances, some are taking steps to this end.

There are men of such indomitable energy, so fertile of resources and so full of faith, that no work seems too great to undertake and no difficulties too serious to overcome. And some of these are already among us, and justice shall not altogether be long refused us. But the men of whom I speak are too rare, and the obligation which we owe, too great for us to be thus content. We must provide facilities to these and necessities to others if we would yet occupy our true position.

It is scarcely necessary to remark that any plan which can be devised must be based upon the presence in the institution of a good theological library—one which shall not only be filled with the gathered lore of the past but also endowed with the means of annual increase. Without this, no institution can pursue extensive courses of study or contribute anything directly to the advancement of learning. The professor is cut off from valuable and necessary books and the student hindered from making even the least important investigations in the course of study he is pursuing.

The plan I propose to you supposes the possession of such a library; and this, even if it be such, is its only peculiar item of expense. It has occurred to me that an additional course of study might be provided for those who may be graduates of theological institutions. This course might extend over one or two years, according to the amount of study the student may propose to accomplish. In it the study of the Oriental languages might be extended subjects for investigation and give a more ample acquaintance with the original text and with the laws of its interpretation. The textbooks or lectures studied in systematic and polemic theology could be compared with kindred books, the theories of opponents examined in their own writings, and notes taken for future use from rare and costly books. These and similar studies which should be laid down in a well-digested course would bestow accurate scholarship, train the student in the methods of original investigation, give him confidence in the results previously attained, and open to him resources from which he might draw extensively in interpreting the Scriptures and in setting forth the truths they contain. The result would be that a band of scholars would go forth from almost every one of whom we might expect valuable contributions to our theological literature.

It is to be expected that but few would take advantage of this course. Such would certainly be the case at first. The only result would be that but little additional provision will be needed. Two additional recitations a week for each of three or four professors would be more than adequate. And though such students should not be more than a twentieth part of those graduated, though not more than one each year, will not their value to the denomination more than counter balance the little additional attention which will, thus, be given?

Were the production of this kind of scholars the only advantage to be gained, we might readily rest upon this the advocacy of this change. But there are others connected with it which may still further commend it by an apparently more practical tendency. I have mentioned the Arabic as one of its studies. The knowledge of that language would be of obvious value to those who go forth as missionaries to Central Africa. Mohammedanism is there the only form of religion, which is violently opposed to the truth, and the language of the Koran is a medium of common intercourse. This, however, would be but trifling, as compared with those common to all our missionaries, who may be instructed in such a course. The results of past missionary efforts, appear to indicate that we, like the apostles, must adopt the system of home laborers, if we would evangelize the world. We must get natives to proclaim the glad tidings of salvation. The men whom we send forth to missionary stations must then be qualified to instruct the native preachers in all the elements of theological education. They will not only have to put the Bible into their hands as a textbook, but they will have to prepare, in the native language, or translate into it such books of theology, as shall give them adequate instruction. There are but few of those who take the ordinary course that are capable of this. Theology is not a science so easily understood, and a mistake about which is of such slight importance, that the instructor in it dares attempt his work without ample investigation. In the course of missionary labors, many years must, therefore, elapse before opportunity can be gained for such research; and if this be afforded, the missionary, with his few books, limited time, and weighty responsibilities, will still feel the great importance of the advantages gained from this course and will be grateful to that institution which has placed it within his reach. And while from this class we would furnish such instruction abroad, would it not be to them also that our institutions at home would chiefly look for their professors? And though there were no others to take advantage of its additional instruction, would not the impetus given to these, the love of learning which would be begotten, the ready preparation to enter at once upon any field to which they might be called, and the number from which we might select the most competent, be ample inducements to lay down this additional course?

I have striven, gentlemen, merely to suggest the benefits to be derived. Multiply and develop them for yourselves, and realize the results. I cannot see how any conception can arise which will prove extravagant. Learning will abound among us. The world will be subdued to Christ. The principles dear to our hearts will universally prevail.

The change which I would in the last place propose is not intended to meet an evil existing in our theological institutions so much as one which is found in the denomination at large, and which may at some future time injuriously affect this educational interest. It is the adoption of a declaration of doctrine to be required of those who assume the various professorships.

The most superficial observer must perceive that in our day the sound doctrine of our churches is much imperiled. Campbellism, though checked in every direction in which it attempted to develop itself, has left no little of its leaven among us and exerts no inconsiderable influence. The distinctive principles of Arminianism have also been engrafted upon many of our churches; and even some of our ministry have not hesitated publicly to avow them. That sentiment, the invariable precursor, or accompaniment of all heresy—that the doctrines of theology are matters of mere speculation, and its distinctions only logomachines and technicalities, has obtained at least a limited prevalence. And the doctrinal sentiments of a large portion of the ministry and membership of the churches are seen to be either very much unsettled or radically wrong.

Sad will be the day for this university should such sentiments ever obtain prevalence in your board or receive the sanction of any of your theological professors. And yet that this is not impossible is evident from the history of others similarly situated. The day has already come when it has been made matter of congratulation in a Baptist journal of high standing that at the examination of perhaps the best endowed and most flourishing Baptist theological seminary in America the technical terms of theology were no longer heard.

A crisis in Baptist doctrine is evidently approaching, and those of us who still cling to the doctrines which formerly distinguished us have the important duty to perform of earnestly contending for the faith once delivered to the saints. Gentlemen, God will call us to judgment if we neglect it.

The evil is one which calls for the adoption of a remedy by every church and every minister among us. It demands that every doctrine of Scripture be determined and expressed and that all should see to it; the churches which call and the Presbyteries which ordain, that those set apart to preach the Word be men "whose faith the Churches may follow," "who take heed to themselves and the doctrine," and "are not as many who corrupt the Word of God."[1]

Peculiar obligations rest, however, upon those to whom are entrusted the education of the rising ministry. God in His mercy preserve the instructors from the crime of teaching a single error, however unimportant, and grant unto all our boards the grace necessary for faithfulness to the trusts developed upon them, that false doctrine, however trifling, may receive no countenance.

It is with a single man that error usually commences; when such a man has influence or position, it is impossible to estimate the evil that will attend it. Ecclesiastical history is full of warning upon this subject. Scarcely a single heresy has ever blighted the church which has not owed its existence, or its development, to that one man of power and ability whose name has always been associated with its doctrines. And yet seldom has an opinion been thus advanced, which has not subsequently had its advocate in every age, and which in some ages has not extensively prevailed.

The history of our own denomination in this country furnishes an illustration. Playing upon the prejudices of the weak and ignorant among our people, decrying creeds as an infringement upon the rights of conscience, making a deep impression by his extensive learning and great abilities, Alexander Campbell threatened at one time the total destruction of our faith. Had he occupied a chair in one of our theological institutions, that destruction might have been completed. There would have been time to disseminate widely and fix deeply his principles before it became necessary to avow them publicly; and when this necessity arrived, it would have been attended by the support of the vast majority of our best educated ministers. Who can estimate the evil which would then have ensued!

The danger which threatened in this instance may assail us again. Another such, and yet another, may arise and, favored by better circumstances, may instill false principles into the minds of his pupils, and sending them forth to occupy the prominent pulpits of the land, may influence all our churches, and the fair fabric of our faith may be entirely demolished.

This it is that should make us tremble when we think of our theological institutions. If there be an instrument of our denominational prosperity which we should guard at every point, it is this. The doctrinal sentiments of the faculty are of far greater importance than the proper investment and expenditure of its funds, and the trusts devolved upon those who watch over its interests should in that respect, if in any, be sacredly guarded.

For all the purposes aimed at, no other test can be equally effective with that confession of faith acknowledged in the Charleston Baptist Association—the doctrines of which had almost universal prevalence in this state at the time of the foundation of the institution. Let that then be adopted, and let subscription to it on the part of each theological professor be required as an assurance of his entire agreement with its views of doctrine and of his determination to teach fully the truth which it expresses and nothing contrary to its declarations.

It seems to me, gentlemen, that you owe this to yourselves, to your professors, and to the denomination at large; to yourselves, because your position as trustees makes you responsible for the doctrinal opinions of your professors, and the whole history of creeds has proved the difficulty without them of convicting errorists of perversion of the Word of God—to your professors, that their doctrinal sentiments may be known and approved by all, that no charges of heresy may be brought against them; that none shall whisper of peculiar notions which they hold, but that in refutation of all charges they may point to this formulary as one which they hold "ex animo," and teach in its true import— and to the denomination at large, that they may know in what truths the rising ministry are instructed, may exercise full sympathy with the necessities of the institution, and look with confidence and affection to the pastors who come forth from it.

But some one will object that Scripture authorizes no such test in our churches; and that as Christians, who claim even in matters of church government to be guided merely by Scripture example and precept, the Baptists cannot consistently introduce it. Let the objection be admitted. It would operate only against the use of such tests in a church and not in any voluntary society or combination into which we enter of our own accord. The theological school is not a matter of scriptural regulation, as is the church; and in arranging its laws, we have only to see to it that the principles upon which they are based do not violate those of the Scriptures. They may be matters of mere expediency. The church being a scriptural institution, receives its laws and its forms from the commands or examples contained in the New Testament; but the theological institution receives such laws as human wisdom can best devise, to carry out the laudable designs of its founders.

But I cannot grant that such a test is without due warrant from Scripture, even in the church. The very duties which God enjoins upon the churches plainly suppose the application of every principle involved in the establishment of creeds. They are directed to contend earnestly against error and for the faith once delivered to the saints. They are to mark them which cause divisions and offenses contrary to the doctrine which they have learned. They are to cut off them which trouble them by the proclamation of false doctrine. A man that is an heretic after the first and second admonitions is to be rejected. They are commendable when they try false prophets and pseudo-apostles, and blameworthy whenever teachers of false doctrine are found among them. So far, indeed, did the apostles enjoin the trial and reprobation of men guilty of false doctrine, that the Christian, even in his private capacity, is told that in receiving such an one into his house, or in bidding him Godspeed, he becomes a partaker of his evil deeds.

The obligations, thus, imposed upon Christians involve the decision of what is truth, not merely that they may believe it, but that they may repudiate those that reject it. They compel every man to establish his own standard of biblical doctrine and by it to judge others. He does not obey the apostolic injunction by receiving men simply because they profess to adopt the same canon of Scripture, but by requiring assent also to the particular truths which he knows to be taught therein. It is not whether they believe the Bible, but whether believing it they deduce from it such doctrine as shows, according to the judgment of the Christian, that they have been so taught by the Spirit of God as to be guided into the knowledge of all truth.

The adoption of an abstract of doctrine is but the means taken by the church to meet these obligations. Perceiving the probability that at some time such questions must arise, she acts beforehand, when her judgment is perfectly cool, when there are no outward circumstances to warp it, and when she can patiently examine the Word of God, and know if these things be so. The time of trial is not the time for legislation. Too many evil passions are then awakened, too many unfounded prejudices then excited, to allow that freedom from bias necessary to justice, as well to the purity of the church of Christ, as to the orthodoxy of the member arraigned before it. Matters of doctrine must be arranged beforehand, when God can be approached in prayer, when His Word can be diligently studied, and when the mind is ready to receive the conclusions to which prayer and study may lead.

This development of their necessity leads us naturally to believe that doctrinal confessions were applied to this purpose in the apostolic churches. Accordingly, we find that the germ of them as used for a two-fold purpose, the declaration of faith and the testing of its existence in others, seems traceable to the apostles and even to Christ Himself. It is remarkable that it has been so frequently overlooked that, upon almost every approach to Him for the performance of a cure, Christ demanded that public confession of His ability to do so, which involved the confession of His messiahship and divine authority, and manifested the individual approaching Him to be one of those who had taught by the Spirit. That was a memorable illustration of the same principle, when, after inquiring the views of others, He made a direct appeal to His own disciples, and said: "But whom say ye that I am?" and when Peter answered, "Thou are the Christ, the Son of the living God," in commendation of that declaration, He pronounced him blessed and taught by his Father in heaven. This commendation was given to an express confession of faith. The act of baptism also, enjoined by Christ as the initiative rite of His church, is an act which involves in the very formulary which accompanies it, profession of doctrinal belief.

The idea of a profession of the name and doctrine of Christ, originated by these, and doubtless by many unrecorded circumstances, had in the times of the apostles universally spread. It was then that the confession of doctrine became more particularly the test of pretension to the name of Christian and to the authority of teacher of the Word of God. The gospel which Paul preached, by which is meant the doctrine he had taught them, was to be such a test that he who should speak otherwise was to be regarded as preaching another gospel and was to be accursed. The apostle John, in his first general epistle, charges the churches to try the spirits, whether they be of God, and encourages them to that duty by calling to their remembrance their past victories over error. The confession of that particular doctrine then chiefly denied by the heretics who abounded was the test to be applied. Here it is evident that a general declaration of belief in the truth of the Scriptures, or the authority of the apostles, was not to be deemed sufficient, but a declaration to be made in the form of words which puts a particular interpretation upon the Scriptures. "That Jesus Christ is come in the flesh," was required by apostolic command of every teacher of the churches. The allusion made by the author of the Book of Revelation to the relations borne to heretics by the churches to which he wrote, confirms us still more in the opinion that the churches of that day were accustomed to receive a declaration of doctrine, to judge of its purity, to exclude for any defect therein, and that this was done with reference to certain doctrinal sentiments avowed, and not to any denial of a general belief of Scripture.

The same two-fold use of creeds may be traced historically through the fathers of the first three centuries. It is apparent that these formularies of doctrinal confession continued to exist, that they were used at the baptism of Christians, that they were applied to the doctrine of error, that they were of various extent, comprising several doctrines of Christianity, that the doctrines added to those which were fundamental were such as were opposed to the peculiar heresies of the section of country which used them, that they were gradually increased as questions about doctrines multiplied in the churches, and that they were not in the same language, betokening their separate origin in the particular churches which used them. Their use in these centuries, however, is simply valuable as showing the growth and development of a Christian practice already established. It shows the value attached to them by the more immediate successors of the apostles, and as evidencing, by the providence of God, that He intended them, like all other blessings conferred upon the churches, to be continued in use to the remotest ages.

By the Baptists of all ages, creeds have been almost universally used and invariably in this two-fold way. To some of other denominations, it has seemed that we have been without them because the principle of liberty of conscience which we have at the same time maintained has forbidden the laying of civil disabilities upon those who have differed from us. We have appeared to them, therefore, to put them forth only as declarative of our principles. It is to be regretted that many Baptists in our own day have given countenance to this opinion by misstatements of our practice. And it would, therefore, have been to me tonight a pleasant labor to pass over the history of our denomination in the past in proof of the position we have undoubtedly occupied. But I could not have done this without sacrificing a stronger desire to present to your consideration questions of greater practical utility.

Suffice it to state that we have simply maintained that civil disabilities are not the means of punishing the offending members of the church of Christ. We have looked to the Scriptures for the rule to govern us in such matters, and we have adopted the truly apostolic plan by which we have accomplished all at which they aimed. The truth of God, which we have held, has been plainly declared. A confession of faith in Christ, and in at least the prominent doctrines of Christianity, has been required of the candidate for baptism. By the principles, thus, set forth, we have judged the heretical among us and, wherever they agreed not with us, have excommunicated them from our churches and our fellowship. The ideas which we have held of the spiritual nature of the kingdom of Christ have developed the principle of liberty of conscience and debarred us from the infliction of bodily punishment or the subjection of any civil disability. But the same views of the spirituality of the church have impressed upon us the necessity of excluding those who have violated the simplicity which is in Christ.

It is, therefore, gentlemen, in perfect consistency with the position of Baptists, as well as of Bible Christians, that the test of doctrine I have suggested to you should be adopted. It is based upon principles and practices sanctioned by the authority of Scripture and by the usage of our people. In so doing, you will be acting simply in accordance with propriety and righteousness. You will infringe the rights of no man, and you will secure the rights of those who have established here an instrumentality for the production of a sound ministry. It is no hardship to those who teach here to be called upon to sign the declaration of their principles, for there are fields of usefulness open elsewhere to every man, and none need accept your call who cannot conscientiously sign your formulary. And while all this is true, you will receive by this an assurance that the trust committed to you by the founders is fulfilling in accordance with their wishes, that the ministry that go forth have here learned to distinguish truth from error, and to embrace the former, and that the same precious truths of the Bible which were so dear to the hearts of its founders, and which I trust are equally dear to yours, will be propagated in our churches, giving to them vigor and strength and causing them to flourish by the godly sentiments and emotions they will awaken within them. May God impress you deeply with the responsibility under which you must act in reference to it!

These, gentlemen, are the changes I would propose in theological institutions. To you I submit them as unto wise men; judge ye what I say. I feel confident that I need not ask you to consider them in a spirit of candid inquiry. The very subject with which they are connected commends them to your attention. With such men I feel that appeals are superfluous, and that changes, the scripturalness, practicability and importance of which seems so manifest, will be made the subject of earnest prayer to God for guidance, and will secure your approval and adoption, if that guidance be vouchsafed.

I may be permitted to say, however, that we have reached a crisis in theological education. Some change has become necessary. The dissatisfaction which prevails in the denomination, taking various forms in different individuals, is indicative of the common sentiment that our past efforts have been a failure. Had we labored alone in this cause, I might have believed this due to the want of a sufficiently elevated institution. But the failures of other denominations at whose institutions are pursued as extensive courses of study as can be compressed into three years, and who have in charge of theological education men of preeminent abilities and scholarship, show that the evil rests not entirely here. While, therefore, we seek a change by aiming to establish a common institution, let us see to it that our changes there and elsewhere are not confined to the extended facilities for scholarship we afford. As I have shown you, there are vital interests which in that case would be neglected—interests of ten-fold more importance than the single one the institution would secure.

The changes I propose to you, neglect not these interests, nor the extensive scholarship at which others aim. They present facilities to all of our ministry. They give to everyone those facilities he most needs. They offer inducements to secure the utmost progress possible. While they hold forth the possession of adequate scholarship as alone necessary, they contend for the possession of all knowledge as important. They urge upon the student such a consecration of every power to Christ as leads to the attainment of the highest possible learning. They provide the means by which the most extensive acquirements may be attained. They point out work before our thinking and reading men, the accomplishment of which will be of inestimable value of our denomination. They furnish the means for the proper education of our missionaries, giving them the knowledge requisite to establish schools of theology for the native preachers, and to instruct them in the truth at a period when a single error may result in irreparable injury to the progress of pure Christianity. And all of this is to be accomplished, if at any, at the most trifling additional expense, either of time, talent or labor.

The principles upon which these changes are based are undoubtedly scriptural. Indeed, in the first case, and in the last, they are not simply based upon scriptural authority, but upon its injunctions and commands. So far, therefore, we seem to have no liberty to reject them.

The details by which they are to be carried out, it is acknowledged, rest simply upon their applicability to these principles, and the simple manner in which they seek their development. Any improvement here will be hailed as matter of additional advantage, and as cause for great rejoicing. It will be perceived that the great peculiarity of the plans proposed is, that they contemplate gathering all our students into a single institution. The courses of study are all to be pursued conjointly. The several classes of young men are to be thrown together in the pursuit of their respective studies. It is for this, as opposed to any other method, that I would strenuously contend.

The object is not the centralization of power in a single institution, for I believe the adoption of these changes will make many seminaries necessary. I advocate a single one now because the demand for more than one does not exist. But it is that our young men may be brought into closer contact with each other.

Various prejudices are arising in our denomination among the various classes of the ministry. This would be my scheme to remove them. The young men should be so mingled together as to cause each class to recognize the value of the others, and thus truly to break down entirely any classification. Those who take the plain English course will see the value of learning in the increased facilities for study it affords to their more favored companions. Those who have this learning will see that many of the other class are their superiors in piety, in devotion to God, in readiness to sacrifice for His cause, in willingness to be counted as nothing, so that Christ may be preached. The recognition of such facts will be mutually beneficial. The less educated ministers will feel that they have the confidence and affection of their brethren; the better educated will know the esteem with which they are regarded, and the bonds of mutual love will yearly grow stronger until we shall see a ministry of different gifts, possessed of extensive attainments, thrown into entirely different positions in the field, yet laboring conjointly, mutually aiding and supporting one another in advancing the kingdom of Christ, in preaching His glorious gospel, in calling forth laborers into His field, and in fostering those influences which shall tend to the education of a sound and practical and able ministry.

On the other hand, let these institutions be separated, and the fate of our theological education is sealed. Jealousies and suspicions will be constantly awakened. The inadequacy of the one and the learning and fancied arrogance of the other will be made the subject of mutual crimination. In some of our churches, prejudices will be excited against our largest and, on that account, our most useful class of ministers. In others, the value of learning will be despised. It will be thought that the mere knowledge of the English Scriptures is alone necessary. Ideas contrary to education of any kind will begin to awaken, and unless the excitement of mutual jealousies, motives most unworthy, should sustain them, the instruction given in either kind of institution will have to be abandoned.

Said I not truly then that we have reached a crisis in theological education? A change is demanded and will certainly be made. But through indiscretion, it may be so made as to lead to the destruction of all our hopes, to the removal of all our present advantages, and to the substitution in their place only of such means of education as shall be mutually subversive. Let us avoid this change, and adopt such an one as shall confine all classes to a single institution. If more than one be found necessary, let them all be conformed to this model. Let thorough training for each class be provided in them; and let us take advantage of the bonds which so strongly bind together fellow students to make the theological institution the means of begetting union, sympathy and love among our widely scattered ministry.

It seems to me, gentlemen, that the opportunity you have to show that this is possible involves you in deep responsibility. The denomination will look to you to meet it. It will feel the momentous interests involved, the dangers which threaten, the advantages which may be gained, and the importance at the juncture of trying an experiment which may be a guide to all future efforts. Let me ask you, gentlemen, to meet all such just expectation by candidly examining the necessity of the changes to which I have referred and the adequacy of the remedies proposed. It is to your wisdom that I have submitted them. To your candor, to your love of truth, to your sense of the value of theological education, I commend them; and should you judge that thus the increase, the knowledge, the power and the soundness of our ministry will be best advanced, I ask you to adopt them.

---

1. It is not my design here to urge that the same abstract of faith be applied in like manner to members of churches, to ministers and to theological professors. It is right that the doctrine held by every church should be distinctly declared but Scripture and experience teach that many members are as yet babes in Christ and, therefore, not prepared to express that knowledge of the doctrine of the word to be expected of those who are teachers thereof. The apostolic rule in such cases is plain—"him that is weak in the faith receive ye, but not to doubtful disputations" (Rom. 14:1). If, therefore, an applicant for membership gives evidence of a change of heart and is so far convinced of the truth of these peculiarities which mark us as a denomination as to desire to unite with us, he should be admitted—it being admitted that he is not to disturb the church about any different opinion he may entertain until by thorough examination of the Scriptures he has satisfied himself that the church is in error.

While, however, this is all that should be required of a member of the church, we should ask of one of its ministers such an agreement to its expressed doctrine as should be even more than substantial. The points of difference here allowable are very trivial, being such as will not in any respect interfere in his ministrations with that fullness of agreement of Scripture truth, through which he is enabled to preach the Word of God without danger of misleading his people in any particular.

But of him who is to teach the ministry, who is to be the medium through which the fountain of Scripture truth is to flow to them—whose opinions more than those of any living man, are to mold their conceptions of the doctrines of the Bible, it is manifest that much more is requisite. No difference, however slight, no peculiar sentiments, however speculative, is here allowable. His agreement with the standard should be exact. His declaration of it should be based upon no mental reservation, upon no private understanding with those who immediately invest him into office; but the articles to be taught having been fully and distinctly laid down, he should be able to say from his knowledge of the Word of God that he knows these articles to be an exact summary of the truth therein contained. If the summary of truth established be incorrect, it is the duty of the board to change it, if such change be within their power; if not, let an appeal be made to those who have the power, and if there be none such, then far better is it that the whole endowment be thrown aside than that the principle be adopted that the professor sign any abstract of doctrine with which he does not agree and in accordance with which he does not intend to teach. No professor should be allowed to enter upon such duties as are there undertaken, with the understanding that he is at liberty to modify the truth, which he has been placed there to inculcate.

I have added this note that my meaning upon this point may not be misconceived. The same principle of Scripture lies at the foundation of the requirements here proposed for members of churches, ministers and theological professors; and it is to that principle that I refer above. But its application is confined to the necessity of the case. In the church the great essential to membership is that a genuine work of grace be evidenced. Hence we apply a test sufficient to secure this. In the ministry, it is essential, however, that the Word of God be preached in its purity and power. Hence must a minister be not only a converted man, but one acquainted even more than substantially with the system of truth taught in the Bible. But the theological professor is to teach ministers, to place the truth, and all the errors connected with it in such a manner before his pupils, that they shall arrive at the truth without danger of any mixture of error therewith. He cannot do this if he has any erroneous tendencies, and hence his opinions must be expressly affirmed to be upon every point in accordance with the truth we believe to be taught in the Scriptures. What is here laid down as the application of the principle referred to above, is essential respectively in each of the relations sustained to us, to give that confidence in the individual which will secure to him our Christian sympathy, support and fellowship.

Chapter Five

"Circular Letter on Confessions of Faith"

S. M. NOEL

To the churches composing the Franklin Association:

Behold how good and how pleasant it is for brethren to dwell together in unity! Standing fast in one spirit, with one mind, speaking the same thing—of one accord, of one heart, and of one soul—acknowledging one Lord, possessing one faith, practicing one baptism, speaking the truth in love, growing up into Him in all things which is the head even Christ, making one body, not one in name or theory only, but one in their religious allegiance, one in their views of the plan of salvation; animated and encouraged by the same hope while observing and practicing the same duties. Such is the unity and symmetry of the Church of Jesus Christ as described by the pen of inspiration.

In this annual address we propose to consider this question: Is it lawful and expedient to adhere to a creed in the admission of members into the fellowship of the church and particularly in the admission of candidates into office?

Creeds formed or enforced by the civil authority are usurpations, leading to persecution and to despotism; while those formed by voluntary associations of Christians, enforced by no higher penalty or sanction than exclusion from membership in the society, are not really lawful, but necessary, in the present state of the religious world. To deny to any religious society the privilege of expressing their views of the Bible in their own words and phrases, and of denying admission to those who reject their views, is a violent interference with the rights of conscience—it is tyranny. It is to subjugate the many with all their interest, right, and happiness, to the dictation of one or a few—the very essence of tyranny.

By a creed we mean an epitome, or summary exhibition of what the Scriptures teach. Are we to admit members into the church and into office, are we to license and ordain preachers without enquiring for their creed? Shall we ask them no question in regard to principles or doctrines? Shall we receive license and ordain candidates, upon a general profession of faith in Christ requiring of them this only, that they agree to take the Bible for their guide? Can we do this and still expect to preserve the unity, purity, and peace of the church?

There are but two methods of admitting members into church and into office. It must be done either with or without respect to a creed. We cannot conceive any third method. If the church rejects a candidate because he holds Sabellian, Arian, or Socinian principles, she then has respect to a creed. She insists upon her own interpretations of the Bible, upon fundamental points. She does not deny him the liberty of interpreting the Bible for himself; this would be tyranny. But while he condemns and reviles her views of the Bible, she claims to herself the right of denying to him her fellowship. She tells him that her interpretations of the Bible, touching doctrines considered cardinal, are settled. In other words, that her creed is fixed, and that his hostility to these well settled principles disqualifies him for membership in her body. If this be an unwarrantable exercise of power, the result is inevitable, that the church is constrained to receive into her bosom, and cherish with her fellowship, those whom she must esteem her worst enemies; the enemies of truth. Yet without respect to a creed, she is reduced to the cruel necessity of harboring under her wings, the vilest heresies that now disgrace the Christian name. Can she do this and incur no guilt? Can she do this and yet preserve her unity, purity, and harmony? Can a church, a New Testament church, keeping the unity of the Spirit, in the bond of peace and love, be found in that miserable Babel composed of Trinitarians, Unitarians, Hutchinsonians, Universal Restorationists, Rellyan Universalists, Destrovetionists, Swedenborgians, Mystics, Dunkers, Jumpers, Shakers, and all others who profess to take the Bible for their guide? Is there communion between light and darkness, fellowship between righteousness and unrighteousness, concord between Christ and Belial?

If the modern adversaries of all creeds and confessions should say that they will not go thus far, that they will not admit into the church, and much less into the ministry, or rather the bishops office, one holding Socinian principles, they evidently yield the question. They admit that in the present state of things, it is both lawful and expedient to have a creed. They cease to oppose the principle of requiring subscription to a creed; or they merely oppose in theory what they adopt in practice. For if they can make one article to exclude a Socinian, they may make another to exclude the Arian, and a third to exclude the Pelagian, and a fourth to exclude the Armenian, etc., and adding article to article, until they get as many as they conceive the exigencies of the church requires. We have not forgotten that one of our own churches not long ago, in her wrath against all creeds protested against the Confession of Faith, with its thirty-four articles, but shortly afterwards made one for herself and published it. A memorable instance of anti-creed inconsistency, of which she herself became quickly convinced, and honestly retraced her steps, but not without injury. It is one thing to oppose the principle of requiring a subscription to a summary of leading principles. It is quite a different thing to oppose the principles contained in that summary. And those who would refuse membership or office to a Socinian or Universalist, do, by their act, admit the necessity of a creed; and in reviling this principle they revile themselves. If they regard consistency and truth, they will no longer denounce what they are pleased to term "an odious array of creeds and confessions." They will no longer be found associated with Latitudenarians and Heretics, who have been the implacable foes of confessions in every age of the church, from her infancy to this day. They will cease to despise a remedy, merely because it has not healed every malady, cured every disorder. For the same reason they might pour contempt upon the Holy Bible. They will cease to fight against Scripture, sense, and reason, against the experience of the church of God, in all ages, which speaks volumes upon this subject. Before the adversaries of creeds can boast of having gained anything in this controversy, it devolves upon them to do what we apprehend cannot easily be done; they must exhibit some method, scriptural and practicable, of excluding corruption from the church, without a creed. It is in vain to say that the Bible is sufficient for that purpose; for these corruptions grow out of false and spurious interpretations of the Bible. And according to their plan, each one is allowed to interpret for himself; to place his own constructions upon the Scriptures. It denies to the church the right to interfere in these "matters of conscience." Their church can only concern with the actions or morals, not with the faith or principles of its members and Bishops. Whether they be sound or unsound in the faith is a question upon their plan, reserved for the Day of Judgment. In such a church there surely will be found unity and purity, worthy of all admiration and great harmony too, flowing from that charity which throws her mantle over multitudes of errors, great and small.

We do not propose to enquire how long or how short a church covenant or creed shall be. Nor will we examine now into the merits or defects of any existing summary of faith. These questions do not enter into the present controversy. Is it lawful and expedient for a church to adopt any articles of faith, whatever, as a test of union and a fence against corruption? This is the enquiry to which the attention of the Christian world has been recently summoned, and to which we respond.

We are not concerned to enquire, whether this creed should be written or unwritten; whether it should be registered only in the minds of the members, or for greater certainty, recorded. Our practice convinces that we are not disposed to leave a matter so essential, to the well being of a church, to the uncertain recollections, to the vague and ever varying impressions of individuals. A nuncupative creed is not calculated to quiet disturbances or to exclude corruption. If we use a religious test at all we should be honest and independent enough to avow it and to exhibit its principles in our pulpit ministrations, as a tribute to truth and candor, which every Christian church owes to other churches and to the world around her.

Our confessions are human productions: they may all require revision and be susceptible of amendment, but to erase them from our books, our memory, and our practice, is to make a tremendous leap, a leap into chaos, into the awful vortex of Unitarianism.

It has been said that to adopt a creed as a religious test "is to supersede the Bible, and to make a human composition instead of it, a standard of faith. That when we do this, we offer a public indignity to the sacred volume, as we virtually declared either that it is not infallible or not sufficient." In reply to this, we use the language of a distinguished divine, who in a few words has exposed its fallacy and swept it from the arena of ecclesiastical controversy.

> The whole argument which this objection presents is founded on a false assumption. No Protestant ever professed to regard his creed, considered as a human composition, as of equal authority with the Scriptures, and far less as of paramount authority. Every principle of this kind is with one voice disclaimed by all the creeds and defenses of creeds that have appeared in ancient or modern times, so far as we are informed. And whether, notwithstanding this, the constant repetition of the charge ought to be considered as fair argument or gross calumny, the impartial will judge. A church creed professes to be deduced from the Scriptures, and to refer to the Scriptures, for the whole of its authority.

Of course when any one subscribes to it, he is so far from dishonoring the Bible, that he does public homage to it. He simply declares by a solemn act how he understands the Bible, in other words, what doctrines he considers it as containing. In short, the language of an orthodox believer, in subscribing his ecclesiastical creed, is simply of the following import:

While the Socinian professes to believe the Bible and to understand it as teaching the mere humanity of Christ; while the Arian professes to receive the same Bible, and to find in it the Savior represented as the most exalted of all creatures, but still a creature: while the Pelagian and Semi-Pelagian, make a similar profession of their general belief in the Scriptures and interpret them as teaching a doctrine far more favorable to human nature and far less honorable to the grace of God than they appear to me really to teach, I beg the privilege of declaring for myself that while I believe with all my heart that the Bible is the word of God, the only perfect rule of faith and manners and the only ultimate test in all controversies; it plainly teaches as I read and believe the deplorable and total depravity of human nature; the essential divinity of the Savior; a trinity of persons in the Godhead; justification by the imputed righteousness of Christ; and regeneration and sanctification by the Holy Spirit, as indispensable to prepare the soul for Heaven. These I believe to be the radical truths which God hath revealed in His Word; and while they are denied by some and fettered away or perverted by others who profess to believe that blessed word, I am verily persuaded, they are the fundamental principles of the plan of salvation.

Is there in all this language anything dishonorable to the Bible; anything that tends to supersede its authority or to introduce a rule or a tribunal of paramount authority? Is there not on the contrary, in the whole language and spirit of such a declaration, an acknowledgment of God's Word, as of ultimate and supreme authority; and an expression of belief in certain doctrines, simply and only because they are believed to be revealed in that word? If this be dishonoring the Scriptures or setting up a standard above them, there is an end of all meaning, either of words or actions.

But still we are asked, "If the Scriptures are not plain and easy to be understood, can we make them plainer than the author has done? Why hold a candle to the sun?" This objection amounts to nothing, while the fact remains undisputed that thousands who profess to receive the Scriptures, by their false and spurious glosses, do virtually deny the radical doctrines contained therein. The lamentable fact that the enemy (even now) comes in like a flood, and it devolves upon every religious society who would bear witness to the truth, the imperious duty of lifting up a standard for truth.

Let those who oppose the use of creeds answer these questions: Has the Head of the church made no qualifications necessary for the admission of members into the church? Has He made no qualifications necessary for admission into office? Has He established no tribunal on earth to judge of these qualifications? Is an Arian, Socinian, or Universalist qualified for either membership or office? Can it be said they are not without respect to a creed? Strip the point in issue of all the tawdry guise which the ingenuity of modern times has cast over it and there is scarcely room for controversy.

The common sense of every man revolts at the idea of assembling in the same church and around the same board, everything that now bears the name of Christian; many bear it, who consider the worship of Christ abominable idolatry; whom an Apostle would pronounce accursed; whom he would not suffer you to receive into your houses or bid Godspeed. Even in his day there are some who preach another Gospel and there are many such yet. Are you to welcome these into your communion? Has the Spirit of inspiration anywhere suggested that the church of Jesus Christ is made up of this mixed assemblage, this heterogeneous group of conflicting elements? Is this the body of Christ fitly joined together and compacted? And what becomes of those heresies, which the Apostle pronounced damnable? Must these too be embraced and cherished in your fellowship and affections? Must those who maintain the true Gospel walk together in church fellowship with those who are accursed for preaching another gospel and who espouse damnable heresies? Is this the New Testament plan? If you say (as doubtless you will) that it is not, that such a society would not be the church of Christ, the result is this: "If there be any divine warrant for a church (in this day) there is a divine warrant for a creed as a test of union, a bond of fellowship, a fence against error, and a shield against that spirit of restless innovation which esteems every novelty an improvement." What shall be its dimensions, its height or depth, its length or breadth, is not now the topic of enquiry. But one thing is certain. It should be large enough to meet the exigencies of the church by preserving her while in the wilderness, exposed to trials, in peace, purity and loyalty. And it should be small enough to find a lodgment in the heart of the weakest lamb, sound in the faith.

When we cease to "hold fast, our form of sound words," we cease to strive together for the faith of the Gospel; we cease to contend "earnestly for the faith once delivered to the saints, the churches of Jesus Christ, who would shine as lights in the world amidst the darkness of surrounding corruption, must exhibit to the eyes of each other and all around that "good confessions," which they are commanded to profess before many witnesses. Upon this interesting subject the history of near eighteen centuries should admonish us. To live as a society with a confession of faith has been often attempted, but we have yet to be informed of the first instance of its succeeding. We understand that the congregational churches of Massachusetts have made the dangerous experiment, and like those who have embarked before them in the same presumptuous enterprise, they have fallen a prey to dissention and heresy, to a degree equally instructive and mournful.

Some suppose that a new order of things is about to open in the church, bringing as great a change as ever marked the progress of the Redeemer's kingdom in any preceding age. In this new and undefined prospect they seem to themselves to see the approaching prostration of most of those fences, and the dissolution of most of those ties, which have heretofore been regarded as indispensable for the maintenance of unity and harmony in the family of Christ. We consider it time enough to provide for the new order of things when it shall arrive. Were all religious societies to give in to that scheme which proposes to assemble and to amalgamate them into one church while they retain their various conflicting and opposite views of the Bible, the era would be new, unprecedented and unparalleled. But who, or what, could dwell in this non-descript community? It is possible that genuine Arianism, which believes in two Gods, a great and a lesser one; and in two Creators, one supreme and the other subordinate, might dwell there. That modern Unitarianism, the votaries of which affect to call themselves "rational Christians," who deny our Lord's divinity and the distinct personal existence of the Holy Ghost, the doctrines of original sin, and the atonement; who discard the belief of the miraculous conception, and the worship of Christ in which they outstrip the Tuscan Apostle, Faustus Socinus himself. These might dwell there and Socinianism of the lowest dye, which ridicules the very idea of the existence and agency of the devil, of the spirituality and separate existence of the soul, of an intermediate state between death, and the general resurrection, and of the eternity of future punishments; all this might dwell there. And even the disciples of Robert Sandeman, who believe that the whole benefit of the work finished by Christ in His death, is conveyed to man only by the apostolic report concerning it, that everyone who understands this report to be true or is persuaded that the event actually happened, as testified by the apostles, is justified and finds relief to his guilty conscience. That he is relieved by finding their report to be true; that the event itself, which is reported, becomes his relief so soon as it stands true in his own mind that all the divine power which operates on the minds of men, either to give the first relief to their consciences or to influence them in every part of their obedience to the gospel, is persuasive power or the forcible conviction of truth. Of course they have no use for the Holy Spirit in this business. All these might possibly dwell there, those who have made shipwreck of the faith; those tossed to and fro and carried about with every wind of doctrine; those who consider erroneous views of the plan of salvation quite innocent or unimportant, who have sunk into a state of stunning indifference to the gospel and suppose all contending for its essential and distinguishing doctrines, useless and perhaps criminal. All these may be found there. But to a conscientious Christian, who has received the truth as it is in Jesus, who scorns to compromise away his principles, would aspire to a name and a place in this church without a creed: this Babel confederacy.

Beloved brethren. Be ye steadfast, unmovable, always abounding in the work of the Lord; be strong in the Lord and in the power of His might by a continual reliance on Him for protection, support and assistance; put on the whole armor of God which in the fullness of Christ and in the graces of the Spirit is provided for every believer, that ye may be able to stand against the wiles of the devil. By prayerful, vigilant, ardent and persevering efforts labor to strengthen and draw closer the bonds of union; strive to hold on your way, turning neither to the right hand, nor to the left, esteeming it your highest honor and happiness, to be employed as humble instruments in building up that kingdom which is from generation to generation. Pray for the coming and enlargement of God's kingdom, for when it shall be fully come, the whole earth shall be filled with its glory; wars shall cease unto the ends of the earth, the kingdom and dominion, and the greatness of the kingdom under the whole Heavens shall be given to the people of the saints, of the Most High. Then shall the bride, the Lamb's wife, look forth as the morning, clear as the sun, fair as the moon, and terrible as an army with banners. She shall come out of the wilderness like pillars of smoke, leaning upon her Beloved and shall dwell in peace. Till then, she must try the spirits while sailing through seas of conflict and tribulation. Brethren, let us be admonished and encouraged by the voice of the Spirit unto the churches. These things saith the first and the last which was dead and is alive; I know thy works, tribulation and poverty (but thou art rich) and I know the blasphemy of them which say they are Jews and are not but are the synagogue of Satan. Fear none of those things which thou shalt suffer. Be thou faithful unto death and I will give thee a crown of life. Amen.

Chapter Six

"High Doctrine
and Broad Doctrine"

Charles H. Spurgeon

"All that the Father giveth me shall come to me; and him that cometh to me I will in no wise cast out" (John 6:37).

These two sentences have been looked upon as representing two sides of Christian doctrine. They enable us to see it from two standpoints—the Godward and the manward. The first sentence contains what some call high doctrine. If by "high" they mean "glorious towards God," I fully agree with them; for it is a grand, God-honoring truth which our Lord Jesus declares in these words: "All that the Father giveth me shall come to me." Some have styled this side of truth Calvinistic; but while it is true that Calvin taught it, so also did Augustine and Paul and our Lord Himself, whose words these are. However, I will not quarrel with those who see in this sentence a statement of the great truth of predestinating grace.

The second sentence sets forth blessed, encouraging, evangelical doctrine, and is in effect a promise and an invitation: "Him that cometh to me I will in no wise cast out." This is a statement without limitation of any kind. It has been thought to leave the free grace of God open to the free will of man, so that whosoever pleases may come and may be sure that he will not be refused. We have no permission to pare down either sentence, nor is there the slightest need to do so. The first sentence appears to me to say that God has chosen a people, and has given these people to Christ, and these people must and shall come to Christ, and so shall be saved. The second truth declares that every man who comes to Christ shall be saved, since he shall not be cast out, and that implies that he shall be received and accepted. These are two great truths; let us carry them both with us, and they will balance each other.

I was once asked to reconcile these two statements, and I answered, "No, I never reconcile friends." These two passages never fell out: they are perfectly agreed. It is folly to imagine a difference, and then set about removing it. It is like making a man of straw, and then going out to fight with it. The grand declaration of the purpose of God that He will save His own is quite consistent with the widest declaration that whosoever will come to Christ shall be saved. The pity is that it ever should be thought difficult to hold both truths; or that, supposing there is a difficulty, we should have thought it our duty to remove it. Believe me, my dear hearers, the business of removing religious difficulties is the least remunerative labor under heaven. The truest way is to accept the difficulty wherever you find it in God's Word and to exercise your faith upon it. It is unreasonable to suppose that faith is to be exempted from trials: all the other graces are exercised, and why should not faith be put to the test? I often feel a joy within my spirit in having to believe what I cannot understand; and sometimes when I have to say to myself, "How can it be?" I find a joy in replying that it is so written, and therefore it must be so. Instead of all reasoning stands the utterance of God. Our Father speaks, and doubts are silenced: His spirit writes, and we believe. I feel great pleasure in gliding down the river of revelation, upon a voyage of discovery, and hour by hour obtaining fresh knowledge of divine truth; but where I come to an end of progress, and see my way blocked up by a sublimely awful difficulty, I find equal pleasure in casting anchor under the lee of the obstacle, and waiting till the pilot tells me what next to do. When we cannot go through a truth, we may be led over it, or round it; and what matters? Our highest benefit comes not of answering riddles, but of obeying commands by the power of love. Suppose we can see no further into the subject— what then? Shall we trouble about that? Must there not be an end of human knowledge somewhere? May we not be perfectly satisfied for God to appoint the boundary of understanding? Let us not therefore run our heads against difficulties of our own invention, and certainly not against those which God has seen fit to leave for us.

Take, then, these two truths, and know that they are equally precious portions of one harmonious whole. Let us not quibble over them, or indulge a foolish favoritism for one and a prejudice against the other; but let us receive both with a candid, large-hearted love of truth, such as children of God should exhibit. We are not called upon to explain but to accept. Let us believe if we cannot reconcile. Here are two jewels, let us wear them both. As surely as this Book is true, God has a people whom He has chosen, and whom Christ has redeemed from among men; and these must and shall by sovereign grace be brought in due time to repentance and faith, for not one of them shall ever perish. But yet is it equally true, that whosoever among the sons of men shall come and put his trust in Christ shall receive eternal life. "Whosoever will, let him take the water of life freely."

"None are excluded hence but those
Who do themselves exclude.
Welcome the learned and polite,
The ignorant and rude."

The two truths of my text are by no means inconsistent the one with the other: they are perfectly agreed. Happy is the man who can believe them both, whether he sees their agreement or does not see it.

I was cruising one day in the western Highlands. It had been a splendid day, and the glorious scenery had made our journey like an excursion to Fairy Land; but it came to an end, for darkness and night asserted their primeval sovereignty. Right ahead was a vast headland of the isle of Arran. How it frowned against the evening sky! The mighty rock seemed to overhang the sea. Just at its base was a little bay, and into this we steamed, and there we lay at anchorage all night, safe from every wind that might happen to be seeking out its prey. In that calm loch we seemed to lie in the mountain's lap while its broad shoulders screened us from the wind. Now, the first part of my text, "All that the Father giveth me shall come to me," rises like a huge headland high into the heavens. Who shall scale its height? Upon some it seems to frown darkly. But here at the bottom lies the placid, glassy lake of infinite love and mercy: "Him that cometh to me I will in no wise cast out." Steam into it, and be safe under the shadow of the great rock. You will be the better for the mountain—truth as your barque snugly reposes within the glittering waters at its foot; while you may thank God that the text is not all mountain to repel you, you will be grateful that there is enough of it to secure you.

First, I shall bid you view that goodly mountain, and then we shall sail into that pleasant loch.

The Eternal Purpose

Consider, then, with reverential joy the eternal purpose. Our Lord Jesus Christ, when He found that the mass of the people rejected Him, turned round upon them, and said, "Ye believe not, because ye are not of my sheep." He knew in His own heart, however, that if they refused Him all would not do so: a number would assuredly believe on Him. Therefore He boldly said, "All that the Father giveth me shall come to me." He threw this grand fact in the teeth of His fierce revilers. It was His own comfort and their rebuke. Now, I do not want to throw it at anybody tonight; on the contrary, I desire to use it as a beckoning finger to any troubled heart that longs to come to Jesus and be saved.

I saw the other day, round a gentleman's park, a very strong and lofty palisade, and to complete the exclusive apparatus a superabundant number of tenter-hooks were nailed upon the top of the fence, and a liberal quantity half-way up. I somewhat jocosely observed upon the kindness of the proprietor, in placing so many nails for the boys to climb up by, and so many more for them to hold on by when once they were up. "Why," said my companion, "those tenter-hooks would tear fingers and clothes to pieces; they are no help to climbers." "No," I replied, "no more help to climbers than the remarks which your minister made upon the sovereignty of God could be considered to be a help to seekers of the Lord Jesus." The good man set forth the truth in the most awkward and pernicious manner possible; not making thereof steps for earnest climbers, but tenter-hooks to keep them out: but I do see so many tremblers needing encouragement, and so many doubters needing instruction, that I delight to turn every word, and promise, and doctrine of the Lord into sweet invitations to all around me to come and welcome to the great heart of the crucified. I am not afraid that too many will come; my fears are all in the opposite direction. Oh, that I could hope that all my present hearers would come to Jesus at once!

First notice, carefully, that if all that the Father giveth to Christ shall come to Him, then some people shall most surely come to Christ; and why should not you be among them? This seems to me to be a sweet suggestion for the help of despondency when she is at her worst: some must come to Christ, why should not I come? When the devil says to you, "You cannot come to Christ," and you yourself feel as if you could not come; when sin hampers you, when doubt drags you down, when you cannot do what you want to do—still it is decreed and determined that some people must come, then why not you? By divine decree they shall come. Why should not you be among them? Does not that help you? If God blesses it, you will not longer sit on the borders of despair. Suppose there is a plague in the city, but there are some people predestinated to be healed. I should be glad to know of that fact. I should be almost glad of it if I was sure that I was not one of the favored ones, for I rejoice in the good of others. But I should be still more glad to press to the physician with this assurance upon my mind—some must be healed: why should not I? There is a famine in the land. I hear that it is revealed by a sure prophet that a certain number never shall die of famine. Then why should not I outlive the dreadful days and be among them? Why not? I hear one say, "Suppose I am not one of God's elect." To him I answer, "Suppose you are." Better still, suppose that you leave off supposing altogether, and just go to Jesus Christ and see. To go to Him is your wisdom; your immediate business, as laid down in His Word, therefore, delay not. Instead of shutting myself out, as some do, because it is written, "All that the Father giveth me shall come to me," I shut myself in, and say, "Then I will be among them." Why should I not? Oh, Lord, if Thou hast ordained that some shall come, then I see that to them no difficulties can be insuperable, and I will therefore come to Thee myself, and in Thy name enter in where every coming one is welcome.

In the next place I find that those that come to Christ, according to this text, come because of the Father and the Son. Read it. "All that the Father giveth me shall come to me." That is, they come to Jesus. Why is it that they are made to come? Because the Father has given them to Christ. Why is it that they shall come? Is it because there is some good thing in them? No, there is nothing said upon that point either one way or the other. Is it because they have strong wills and firm determinations, and therefore come? The Scripture is equally silent upon that point, except that it says elsewhere that the New Birth is not of the will of man. The reason that is given why they shall come to Jesus is because something was done for them by the Father and by the Son. Why, then, should not I come? Suppose I am weak: suppose I am sinful: suppose I am seven times more sinful than anybody else; yet since this "shall come" depends not on the character of those to whom the promise is made, but upon a certain something done for them by the Father and the Son, why should not I be among those for whom the Father and the Son have done this certain thing, and why should not I therefore be made to come to Jesus? There never was a soul that I really wanted to come to Jesus but what it could come and did come. There never was a pining, longing sinner that was long kept away from Christ. When he wanted Christ, Christ wanted him a hundred times as much. If thou hast the least desire or the faintest longing after the Lord Jesus Christ, then the cords of love are about thee, and His mighty hands are drawing home those cords. Yield to the sweet pressure and thou shalt come, not because of what thou art, or what thou ever hast been, but because of what the Father is doing, and because of what the Son is doing. It is written, "No man can come to me, except the Father which hath sent me draw him": but when He is drawing thou canst come. The Father is drawing you, since you are longing to come, and are anxious to find a Savior. Now, do not turn this truth about so as to set it edgeways, and make a "chevaux de frise" of it to keep yourself from getting to Christ. The doctrine of the divine purpose is not a thornhedge to keep you off from the tree of life. On the contrary, you are bound to regard it as an open door. "Some must come. Why not I? Those that come do so because of something done for them of the Father and of the Son; and why should not that have been done for me? Why should not I also draw near to God?"

Notice, thirdly, that these people are all of them saved because they come to Christ. Observe the words: "All that the Father giveth me shall come to me." They are not saved otherwise than by coming to Christ. Here are certain people that are different from others, for the Father has given them to Christ. Yes, but it does not matter how different they are from others. They have to be saved in the same way as other people. There is no way of salvation specially prepared for these peculiar people; they must follow the King's highway. The one common way of salvation is by coming to Christ, and all that the Father has given to Christ must come in by this gate. This is the one door that God has opened: there is no other; there never shall be any other. Come, pluck up heart, my dear friend, thou that art bowing thy head like a bulrush, the best saint in heaven found his way thither by a simple trust in Jesus Christ. Why canst not thou get there in the same way? Many sinners of the deepest dye have been saved through Jesus Christ, and why should not you be saved in the same way? Ask Peter, and James, and John, and Paul, and all the rest of them, whether they entered into heaven by a private bridge thrown across for them alone; and they will tell you that they were saved by the one Redeemer. As no Scripture is of private interpretation, so be sure that there is no private and secret Savior for a few favored persons. "Other foundation can no man lay than that which is laid, which is Jesus Christ. God's elect can only be saved by coming to Christ." Jesus says, "All that the Father giveth me shall come to me;" for they cannot be saved else. Coming to Christ is the one essential thing. "Oh," says one, "I sometimes wish that I knew whether I was one of God's elect." Why should you wish to know anything out of its turn, when you can learn every truth that you need by studying other truths which lead up to it? You come to Christ, and you shall know that you were given to Christ; for none come to Him but those who are His, and by their coming to Him they give the best evidence of their election. You know what the brother in Cornwall said to Malachi, who was rather a stout Calvinist. He said, "Now, Malachi, I owe you two pounds. Before I discharge the debt I want you to tell me whether I am predestinated to pay you." Malachi opened wide his hand, and said, "Put the two pounds there, and I will tell you directly." Like most sensible folk, he preferred to prophesy after the event; and there are many advantages in keeping to that method. It is evidently the natural order to things for uninspired folk. Whether the Father gave me to Christ or not, I cannot discover till I know whether I have come to Christ. When I know that I have truly come to Christ with all my heart, then I am certain that I was given to Christ, and I find no difficulty in so believing; yea, my heart is glad to think that I am saved in the same way as others are saved.

Yet, once again, from this text it is most clear that, if I come to Christ, the Father gave me to Christ. If I, whoever I may be, do but simply trust Jesus—for that is the coming here meant—then

I am one whom the Father gave to His Son. If, just as I am, I cast myself upon His blood and righteousness and become His disciple, sworn to follow Him, hoping by His help to tread in His footsteps: then I may know that, long before the day star knew its place, or planets ran their round, the Eternal Father had looked upon me with eyes of everlasting love, and that He still accepts me, and will never cast me away. Is it not so? "All that the Father giveth me shall come to me"; and if I have come, then the Father hath given me to Christ; the great question is answered, the eternal mystery is unveiled, and my spirit may rejoice in God my Savior, and in all the precious things of that everlasting covenant which is ordered in all things and sure.

So much about that huge, overhanging mass of rock. Of that I am going to say no more; only under its lee I have anchored long ago, and at that anchorage I mean still to remain. Since I have come to Jesus I know that I belong to Him by the Great Father's gift, and I am right well assured that the purpose of God shall be fulfilled in me, and that He will assuredly bring me, with all the rest of His elect, to His kingdom and glory, where we shall see His face forever. This may be called old-fashioned doctrine; I care not what it is called, it is my life, and I dare rest my soul's weight upon it for time and for eternity.

The Everlasting Gospel

Now we enter into smooth water. The mystery is opened, let us partake of the joy of it. We have, in the second place, to speak to you for a little time on the everlasting gospel. "Him that cometh to me I will in no wise cast out." You may forget my first head if you like, especially if you are troubled by it, but I earnestly beseech you to recollect the second.

"Him that cometh to me I will in no wise cast out." This is one of the most generous gospel texts that I do remember to have met with between the covers of this book. Generous first, as to the character to whom the promise is made. "Him that cometh to me": that is the character. The man may have been guilty of an atrocious sin, too black for mention; but if he comes to Christ he shall not be cast out. To that atrocious sin he may have added many others, till the condemning list is full and long; but if he comes to Christ he shall not be cast out. He may have hardened his neck against the remonstrances of prudence, and the entreaties of mercy; he may have sinned deeply and wilfully; but if he comes to Christ he shall not be cast out. He may have made himself as black as night—as black as hell; yet, if he shall come to Christ, the Lord will not cast him out. I cannot tell what kind of persons may have come into this hall tonight; but if burglars, murderers, and dynamite-men were here, I would still bid them come to Christ, for He will not cast them out. I suppose that the most of you are tolerably decent as to moral character; and to you I say, if you come to Christ He will not cast you out. Children of godly parents, hearers of the word, he will not cast you out. You who lack only one thing, but that the one thing needful, He will not cast you out. Backsliders! Are there some such here, who have almost forgotten the way to God's sanctuary, for whom the Sabbath-bell proclaims no Sabbath now? Come you to Jesus, and He will not cast you out. Oh, you Londoners, you have grown weary of God's house, and of God's day—millions of you; but if with all your religion you are here tonight, the truth holds good of you also, if you trust in Jesus, He will not cast you out.

If, amidst this company, there should be some whose characters we had better not describe, and who already shrink into themselves at the very idea of being picked out, and mentioned by name; yet if such persons come to Jesus, He will gladly receive them. Be your character what it may, you who are wrapped in mystery, you shall not be cast out. I wish that I could put this to those who are troubled about a life of grievous sin; for to the life-long transgressor the text is still true. My Lord proclaims an act of oblivion concerning all the past. It shall be as though it had never been. Through Jesus Christ, if you will but believe in Him, the whole past shall be rolled up and put away, as though it had never known an existence, and you yourself shall be born again. When Naaman came up from washing in the Jordan we read that "his flesh came again like unto the flesh of a little child, and he was clean"; and so it shall be with you. The old man took the fair-haired child upon his knee, and threaded his fingers through its locks, and said, "Young child, God keep you from the sin into which I have plunged. My old life is full of evil. It is now almost over, and I am past hope. Would God I were a child again!" Lo, the angel of mercy whispers to anyone in that condition, "You may be a child again!" The man a hundred years of age may yet be made a child; and he that is a grey-beard in infamy may yet become a babe in innocence through the cleansing power of the water and the blood which flowed from the riven side of Jesus. Go ye, and write it athwart the brow of night; write it in new stars if you can. "Him that cometh to me I will in no wise cast out." Then hang it up over the midday heavens, and let the sun cast all his beams upon it, till it seems writ in the splendor of God: "Him that cometh to me I will in no wise cast out." The character who will be received is excluded. No limit is set to the extent of sin: any "him" in all the world—any blaspheming, devilish "him" that comes to Christ shall be welcomed. I use strong words that I may open wide the gate of mercy. Any "him" that comes to Christ, though he come from slum or taproom, betting-ring or gambling-hell, prison or brothel, Jesus will in no wise cast out.

Further, this text is a very generous one because it gives no limit to the coming. The only limit to the way of coming is that they do come to Christ. I have known some come to Christ running to him—a willing, speedy, earnest pace. You read of that in the Gospels. They were so glad to hear of a Savior that they flew to Him at once. Many young children and young people do this, and they are blessed in the deed. Come along with you, ye lively and tender spirits; He will not cast you out if you leap and rush to Him. If you run all on a sudden to Him tonight—if you make a dash for Christ—He will not cast you out.

Alas! A great many, when they come to Christ, advance very limpingly. They are burdened with a huge load of sin and fettered with doubts and fears, and so they make slow progress. They do not look to Jesus and live, all at once. They keep looking here and looking there, instead of looking to Him. They are a long while in coming, for they are afraid and ignorant and dull.

Never mind, brother. The snail got into the Ark; and if you come to Christ He will not cast you out though your pace be sadly sluggish. Some look to Christ as soon as they hear of Him, with clear, bright eyes like those of Rachel. Oh, such a look! They seem to drink in Christ and His salvation all at once with those bright eyes. But I have met with many whose look is like that of Leah, who had tender eyes: they look through the mists of their doubt, and the showers of their tears, and they do not half see Christ as they should. Ay, but that half-clouded look will save them. Any looking will save you if it is looking to Christ; and any coming, if it is coming to Christ, will save you. Coming to sacraments may condemn you; coming to priests will ruin you; but coming to Christ will save you. If your simple faith takes hold of Christ's salvation, there is life in that grip. If your thoughts think of Him, if your heart embraces Him, if your soul trusts Him, however weakly and imperfectly you do it, He will not cast you out. Oh, this is glorious truth to my mind; is it not so to yours? So long as we do but come to Him, our Savior will not cast us away: I feel glad to be preaching this gospel in Exeter Hall; are you not glad to hear it? If you are not you are a sorry set.

Thirdly, there is no limit here as to time. "Him that cometh to me I will in no wise cast out" is a glorious, free utterance, compassing every age. There may be some little children here; indeed, I am glad to see boys and girls mingling with the congregation. Listen to me, my children! I am always glad to see you, and we preachers make a great mistake if we do not preach to you. Oh, dear John and Jane, Mary and Thomas, I wish you would come to Christ while you are yet young, and put your trust in Him, and become young Christians. There is no reason why you should not. You are old enough to die, and you are old enough to sin, and you are old enough to believe in the Lord Jesus Christ. Why should you not do so at once? When I was just about fifteen years of age I was helped by God's Spirit to cast myself upon Christ; and did I ever repent that I came to Jesus so soon? No, I wish that I could have come fifteen years before, and that I had known Christ as soon as ever I learned to know my mother. Some of you have heard about Jesus from your infancy; His name was part of the music with which your mother sang you to sleep. Oh, that you may know Jesus by faith as well as by hearing! Do not think that you have to wait till you are grown up before you may come to Jesus. We have baptized quite a number of boys and girls of ten, eleven, and twelve. I spoke the other day with a little boy nine years of age; and I tell you that he knew more about Christ than ever so many grey-headed men do; and he loved Jesus most heartily. As the sweet child talked to me about what Christ had done for him, he brought tears into my eyes, to see how happily and brightly he could speak of what he had felt in his own soul of the Savior's power to bless. You young children are like rosebuds; and you know everybody likes a rose-bud better than a full-blown rose. My Lord Jesus will gladly receive you as rosebuds. Offer yourselves to Him, for He will not cast you away. I am sure He never will.

If any here are in the opposite extremity of life, I would remind them that "Him that cometh to me I will in no wise cast out" applies to the aged as well as to the young. I heard it said by a minister—a very earnest man—that if persons were not con-verted before they were five and forty, he hardly believed that they would ever be converted afterwards; and he gave it as a note of his observation that he had not seen any persons converted after five and forty. I wished that I had been in his pulpit. I should not have questioned his statements, but I would have overlaid them with others of another character. Surely this brother had been living in some minute hamlet or other; or else he had not preached the gospel in its fullness to every creature. Perhaps he did not believe in the conversion of the aged, and consequently no aged persons were converted by his means. I have seen as many people converted of one age as another: that is to say, in proportion to the number of them, for there are not so many people in the world over fifty as there are under fifty; and consequently a large proportion of those persons who make up our congregations are young. We have in our regular gatherings a fair number of all ages, and as to the additions to the church, I have noticed that there is about the same proportion of very young children as of very old men and women. We have baptized, upon profession of faith, men and women over eighty years of age, about whose conversion we had as firm a conviction as we had about the conversions of the little ones; neither more nor less. Who shall dare to say that there is an age after which God's grace does not work? I challenge anyone to bring a text which looks that way; furthermore, I challenge the truth of any observations which arrive at such a result. My own preaching has been such that young and old in equal proportions have attended it, and in equal proportions they have been saved. However old you may be, my Master bids me say to you, "Him that cometh to me I will in no wise cast out." Come along, come along, dear old friend, though you cannot come without your stick. Come along, though your eyes are failing: come in your spectacles. Though you cannot do much for my Master, He can do everything for you. Though you have only a little time to live on earth, you will have all eternity in heaven through which you can praise Him. I am sure you will be one of the most eager at that work. I think you will be like an old woman of my acquaintance. When I spoke to her about her conversion at an advanced age, she said, "Sir, if the Lord Jesus Christ ever does save such a poor old sinner as I am, He shall never hear the last of it." That is just why I want Him to save you; for then He never will hear the last of it. You will praise Him forever and forever for what He has done for you. Will you not?

Oh, my dear hearers, come to Jesus! Come in the morning when the dew is on your branch, for He will not cast you out. Come in the heat of noon, when the drought of care parches you, and He will not cast you out. Come when the shadows have grown long, and the darkness of the night is gathering about you, for He will not cast you out. The door is not shut; for the gate of mercy closes not so long as the gate of life is open. Oh, fly to Christ, and find mercy now!

Once again, dear friends, I want you to notice in my text the blessed certainty of this salvation. "Him that cometh to me I will in no wise cast out." Two or three negatives in the Greek language make a negation stronger, though they have no such effect in the English tongue. It is a very strong negative here. "Him that cometh to me I will not NOT cast out"; or, "I will never never cast out." As much as to say, On no account, or for no reason, or on no pretense, or from no motive whatever, will I ever in time or in eternity cast out the soul that comes to Me. That is how it stands—a declaration of absolute certainty from which there can be no escaping. What a blessed thing it is to get your foot on certainties! Certain preachers, who are much cried up nowadays, are very uncertain preachers, for they do not themselves know what they will be propounding tomorrow. They make their creed as they go along, and a very poor one it is when they make it. I believe in something sure and certain; namely, in infallible Scripture, and that which the Lord has written therein, never to be altered while the world stands. My test is certain as the truth of Christ Jesus; and if we had ever seen that beautiful face of His we could not distrust Him. Can your imagination picture for a minute the ever-blessed face of the Son of God? Could you look into that face, and suspect Him of a lie? And when He says, "Verily, verily, I say unto you, he that believeth in me hath everlasting life," the saying must be true. If you believe in Him, you have everlasting life. When He says, "Him that cometh to me I will never never cast out," the declaration must be true. He never, never, can cast you out, whoever you may be, however long you may live, or whatever else may happen, if you do but come to Him. There are plenty of reasons, apparently, why He should cast you out, but He has knocked them all on the head by saying, "I will in no wise cast out": that is, "In no way, and under no pretext, will I ever cast out a soul that comes to Me." Now, if Christ does not cast us out, then He receives us; and if He receives us, we are received into the heart of God; we are received into eternal life; and by and by we shall be received into everlasting blessedness. Oh, the joy of my text, in that it is so certain!

The Personality of My Text

So I shall close here, dear friends, with just a word or two of further encouragement by noticing the personality of my text;

for in this a part of the liberality consists. Do you observe that the first part of the text began with, "All that the Father giveth me shall come to me." Ay, but when Christ began to deal with sinners with broken hearts, He dropped the "all" and every form of general statement, and He came to the personal pronoun singular: "Him that cometh to me I will in no wise cast out." Now, herein He meant to say to everyone in this Hall, "If thou doest come to Me, I will not cast thee out." It is not, "If thou and another come"; for, if so, it would be put in the plural: "If you come." But it is, "Him that cometh." You alone; your servant alone; your child alone; but specially yourself alone: if you come to the Lord Jesus He will not cast you out. You cannot doubt this. Come, then, my dear hearers, believe your Savior. I am not talking tonight to persons who doubt the veracity of the Son of God, I am not talking to persons who think Christ a liar. You know that He would receive you if you would come. Then, why do you not come? But you mean to come, do you, by and by? Then why not now? What is it that holds you back? How dare you delay? Will you be alive next week? How can you be sure of a day, or an hour? When money is to be given away, I do not find that persons generally delay to receive it, and say, "I would rather have it next year." No, they say, "A bird in the hand is worth two in the bush." Oh, to have a Christ in the hand, and to get Him now! And why not now? Is it because you really do not understand what it is to receive Him, or to believe in Him? It is indeed the simplest thing in the world, and that is the only reason why it is so difficult; it is so exceedingly simple, that men cannot believe that it can be as we put it. Indeed, it is so. Faith is simply to trust Christ; and trusting Christ brings with it the new life, and salvation from sin. I sometimes put it in Watt's way: "A guilty, weak, and helpless worm, On Christ's kind arms I fall."

But after I had once been preaching, a young man said to me, "Sir, I cannot fall." "Oh dear," I said, "then I do not know how to talk; for I meant not a thing you could do, the cessation of all your efforts, just falling or if you will see it better, just tumbling down, because you cannot stand upright; and that is it." Because I cannot save myself, I fall into Christ's arms. Ceasing to hold to anything of my own, I just drop upon Him. "Still," you say, "there must be something more than that." There is nothing more than that. If thou believe that Jesus is the Christ, thou art born of God. "He that believeth and is baptized shall be saved; but he that believeth not shall be damned." "He that with his heart believeth, and with his mouth maketh confession of him, shall be saved." "Oh, but I must—I must—I must do something mysterious, or feel something which at present is far beyond me." Thus you give God the lie, and put away from you the life eternal.

Have you never read the story of the good ship that had been a long time at sea, and the captain had lost his reckoning; he drifted up the mouth of the great river Amazon, and, after he had been sailing for a long time up the river without knowing that he was in a river at all, they ran short of water. When another vessel was seen, they signalled her, and when they got near enough for speaking they cried, "Water! We are dying for water!" They were greatly surprised when the answer came back, "Dip it up! Dip it up! You are in a river. It is all around you." They had nothing to do but to fling the bucket overboard, and have as much water as ever they liked. And here are poor souls crying out, "Lord, what must I do to be saved?" when the great work is done, and all that remains to them is to receive the free gift of eternal life. What must you do? You have done enough for one lifetime, for you have undone yourself by your doing. That is not the question. It is, "Lord, what hast Thou done?" And the answer is, "It is finished. I have done it all. Only come and trust Me." Sinner, you are in a river of grace and mercy. Over with the bucket, man, and drink to the full; for you will never exhaust the stream of grace.

A river is free to every dog that runs along the bank: every cow that stands by the river may drink to the full. So is the mercy of God free to every sinner, be he who he may, that does but come to Jesus. That river runs near to you tonight. Stoop down, you thirsty one, and drink and live. But you say, "I must feel different from what I do now." But you need not: come with your bad feelings. "Oh, I have not yet a broken heart," says one. Come to

Christ and He will break your heart. "But I do not feel my need as I ought." Come to Christ and He will help you to feel your need. "Oh, but I am nobody!" You are the very person that Christ delights in, for to you He will be everybody.

Do you see that beautiful tree in the orchard loaded with fruit? It is a pear tree. From top to bottom it is covered with fruit. I think I never saw such a sight: every branch is bowing down. Some boughs are ready to break with the luscious burden. As I listen to the creaking boughs, I can hear the tree speak. What does it say? It says, "Baskets, baskets, baskets! Bring baskets!" Now, then, who has a basket? "I have got one," cries yonder friend, "but it is of no use, for there is nothing in it." Bring it here man: that is the very kind of basket the tree wants. A person over there says, "Oh, I have a basket—a splendid basket. It is just the thing. It is full from top to bottom." You may keep your basket to yourself. It is of no use to my loaded tree. Where is there an empty basket? Who has an empty basket? Come along with you: come and pick from the tree as long as you like. Bring all your baskets. Bring thousands and thousands of baskets, all empty, and fill them all! Do you notice as we fill the baskets that the fruit begins to multiply? There is more when we have filled the baskets than there was at first, for this inexhaustible tree produces more and more fruit, as far as we pluck from it. What is wanted by the Lord Jesus is an empty soul to receive out of the fullness which God has treasured up in him.

God bless every one of you, for His name's sake. Amen.

Chapter Seven

"The Duties of Pastors to Their Churches" (1857)

John W. Brown

"Take heed therefore unto yourselves and to all the flock over which the Holy Ghost hath made you overseers, to feed the church of God which he hath purchased with his own blood" (Acts 20:28).

In order to ensure faithfulness and efficiency on the part of pastors and churches, it is essential that they should understand their relative duties. "The duties of churches to their pastors" have been faithfully presented on a former occasion. The duties of churches to their pastors, as specified in that discourse, are as follows:

1. Churches owe it as a duty to their pastors to provide for their temporal support.

2. The churches owe it to their pastors carefully to shield their reputation from injury.

3. The pastor ought to be supported and cheered by the cordial sympathies of his people.

4. It is the duty of the church to make her pastor and his ministry subjects of earnest and habitual prayer.

It is our object to specify some of the duties of pastors to their churches. A church, scripturally defined, is an assembly of baptized believers, associated for the purpose of maintaining the worship of God, promoting His cause, and observing the ordinances of the gospel. The church has a high responsibility and heavenly mission to accomplish. That she may be better prepared for the fulfillment of this high mission on earth, and for the enjoyment of the heavenly rest, God has constituted the gospel ministry for the edification, encouragement, and comfort of His people. Hence says the apostle, "And he gave some apostles and some prophets, and some evangelists and some pastors and teachers, for the perfecting of the saints, for the work of the ministry, for the edifying of the body of Christ."

Ministers are not only to take heed to themselves, that is, to be sure that their own hearts are right before God, but they are commanded to watch over the spiritual interests of their people. The intimate and endearing relation subsisting between a pastor and his people is most beautifully represented under the similitude of a shepherd and his flock. A pastor literally means a shepherd, but figuratively a minister of the gospel. While Christ is the great and good shepherd of His people, having pledged His infallible word for their protection here, and final preservation in heaven, ministers are His under-shepherds, and should be full of the spirit of their Divine Master, who cherished the strongest compassion and most tender sympathies towards His disciples. The man who undertakes to preach the gospel to others, and to oversee the household of faith, must possess a large measure of that love which prompted our blessed Redeemer to give His life for His people—to shed His blood that they might be redeemed from all their sins and purified unto Himself as a peculiar people, zealous of good works.

The Obligation of the Pastor to Preach the Gospel to His Flock

The first and most important duty that we shall specify is the obligation of the pastor to preach the gospel to his flock. This is the primary and highest duty of a faithful pastor. It must be performed in the spirit of a good minister of Jesus Christ. The gospel, with its precepts and promises, is the bread of life to the soul of the believer. It is the most potent instrumentality that he can employ to infuse into the hearts of his people the spirit of Christ, and urge them to a prompt and efficient discharge of Christian duties. It is from this source that the people of God derive spiritual nutriment. It improves and develops their graces. The gospel, like the refreshing and reviving showers of heaven, enlivens and invigorates them, prepares them for extensive usefulness on earth, and matures them for the enjoyment of the inheritance of the saints in glory. The pastor who endeavors to edify, please, and encourage his people by philosophical lectures, metaphysical disquisitions, and rhetorical flourishes, will soon find them sinking into barrenness and inactivity. In his pulpit labors he cannot substitute anything for the faithful presentation and clear illustration of God's Word. In proportion as the promises, motives, and claims of the gospel are pressed upon the minds of Christians, will their zeal, usefulness, and happiness be enhanced.

What does the apostle mean by feeding the church of God? He certainly means that it is the duty of the pastor, as a good shepherd, to conduct his flock into the fertile fields of God's grace, in the gospel of His Son. It is in the rich pastures of grace, and by the fountains of His love, that their souls are refreshed and strengthened, comforted and animated in their earthly pilgrimage. Appropriate, nutritious food is not more essential to the support and growth of the body than the truths and doctrines of the gospel are to the spiritual sustenance and growth of believers.

The gospel must be preached doctrinally and practically. The great doctrines of the gospel are designed to enlighten and strengthen the minds of believers, and lead them to practical godliness. We find that the apostles in their instructions to the churches adopted this method. They presented the great fundamental truths of the gospel, and urged them, in view of these truths, to the practice of holiness and the performance of duty. The apostle, in his epistle to the Romans, inimitable for its eloquence and argument, enforces the doctrinal and practical parts of the gospel.

The judicious and vigilant pastor will not only adapt his discourses to the condition and capacity of his flock, but will adopt that method of preaching best calculated to render them efficient in the service of Christ, and to supply their spiritual wants.

He will feel that the great end of all his ministrations is to expound and enforce the word of his Divine Master. In his regular ministrations to his people, he should judiciously combine the expository and topical methods of preaching. Expository preaching possesses less of human thought and arrangement, and is the best to edify a church, and render them familiar with the true sense of the Scriptures. The pastor must preach the great truths of the gospel proportionally. Every truth should be so presented to the minds of his people, that they may discover its due importance in the gospel system. Each doctrine, promise, and precept is essential to the development of the Christian character. If one be preached to the exclusion of others, the church will be ignorant of her whole duty, inconsistent in her practice, and fearfully defective in her doctrinal views. Every doctrine, truth, and command should be so presented as to render the gospel one grand harmonious system.

The gospel should be preached with zeal, energy, and faithfulness. In order that the pastor may thus address his charge, it is indispensable that his soul be full of the love of Christ. His people must witness in every word, action, and gesture, the spirit of his Divine Master. Words proceeding from a man whose mind and heart are thoroughly imbued with the spirit of Christ, will have the desired effect. He will often find his people, who are necessarily connected with the pursuits and cares of the world, and who frequently forget the great end of their conversion to God, immersed more or less in secular business.

If he would inspire them with energy in the work of the Lord, and awaken in them a sense of their responsibilities to God, he must speak with a voice that alarms the indifferent with words that burn, and with a countenance that glows with the fire of heaven. Much of the coldness and lukewarmness that prevails in the churches is ascribable to a want of zeal in ministers. His people expect him to commune with God by study, meditation, and prayer, and to come forth from this spiritual atmosphere in the spirit and power of the gospel. From such faithful preaching his people will catch the spirit of true consideration to God, and ever be ready to support him by their presence, prayers, and means. Therefore, O man of God, pastor of God's chosen flock, if thou wouldst be a good minister of Jesus Christ, making full proof of thy ministry, preach the Word. Preach it in season and out of season, in simplicity and power, in the hovels of the poor and the palaces of wealth, in the pulpit and out of the pulpit, to the bereaved and disconsolate, to the afflicted and dying.

"I charge thee before God and the Lord Jesus, who shall judge the quick and the dead at his appearing and kingdom, preach the Word—nothing but the Word."

We mention in this connection, because of its importance, that the pastor should thoroughly indoctrinate his people, and labor firmly and perseveringly to fortify their minds against the encroachment and ultimate triumph of error. When the apostle delivered this solemn charge to the elders of Ephesus, he foresaw that grievous wolves or false teachers would make their appearance, and endeavor to divert the minds of the disciples from the doctrines and simplicity of the gospel. The good minister will endeavor to satisfy himself that his flock are thoroughly established in the faith. Rooted and grounded in the truth, and confirmed in the doctrines and practice of the gospel, they will successfully withstand the floods of error that sometimes sweep over the world, corrupting the hearts and perverting the minds of Christians. Thousands are arrayed this day on the side of error for the want of fidelity and stability in their spiritual guides. What God said to His prophet He says to every pastor,

"So thou, O son of man, I have set the watchman unto the house of Israel; therefore thou shalt hear the word at my mouth, and warn them from me." Woe unto that pastor who has failed to fortify the minds of God's people against the inroads and assaults of errorists.

We would also specify here that it is the duty of the pastor to teach his flock thoroughly and faithfully what they are required to do as disciples of Christ. A disciple is one who has been and is to be taught. The pastor sustains to believers the important relation of spiritual teacher. His people look to him for instruction, and have a right to expect it. Defective instruction produces inefficient and inactive churches. The pastor is to train his church for usefulness here, and for glory, honor, and immortality. Let the churches be thoroughly indoctrinated and instructed, and there will be a harmony of views and feelings, and a consistency of practice, that will array them in one unbroken phalanx against the host of darkness. We now see and feel the evil effects of the neglect of this duty. Had the duty of ministerial support and the obligation to make sacrifices for the spread of the gospel been duly impressed upon the minds of the church in this country years ago, pastors would be much better sustained at the present day, and our missionary operations more effectively prosecuted.

That He May Be an Argumentative, Eloquent Preacher, and an Efficient Teacher, It Is the Duty of the Pastor to Labor for His Intellectual Improvement

He who would consecrate himself to the good of the church must be a man of intellectual industry. This is a duty that the pastor owes to himself, to the church, and to his God. If he would meet the fearful responsibilities of his high position, he cannot neglect it. The church is expected to give him a competency, and having done her duty, she expects him to give his time and consecrate his talents and energies to the great work before him. The apostle admonishes Timothy to give himself to reading, study, and meditation. The same apostle speaks in another place of "approving ourselves as the ministers of God by knowledge"(2 Cor. 6:4–6). He who would rise to intellectual greatness and attain to extensive usefulness, must do it by dint of application. The pastor who would secure the constant esteem, affection, and confidence of his people, must prove to them in his discourses that he is a man of thought and research. A popular writer has justly said,

> The churches demand a higher instruction and an ampler reasoning from the pulpit than can be gleaned from the narratives of the nursery. They may be pleased for a time with the pleasant voice and pathetic tale; but, like the prodigal, they will soon turn away from the husks, and long for a more nutritive aliment, though presented in a homelier dish. The bare belief that a preacher has no excellence but that of elocution, and no grace but that of attitude, will soon degrade his authority; while the bare belief that he is a consummate theologian will invest his teachings with commanding importance.

The man of thought and investigation will outlive in the estimation of his people, and, ultimately, outshine the coruscations of genius. He must study the Scriptures thoroughly, critically, and systematically. He should furnish himself with the best theological and critical works to help him to understand the Word of God. He ought to be acquainted as far as possible with the history of biblical criticism and interpretation. He ought to possess sufficient knowledge of history, philosophy, astronomy, and geology, to enable him to refute the arguments, and answer the objections of infidels. If infidelity penetrate the earth in search of arguments to unsettle the faith of Christians, let him, like the indefatigable and immortal Miller, make the rocks speak in attestation of the truth of the Scriptures. If infidelity soar to the heavens to accomplish wicked purposes, let him make the stars and planets pour their combined light upon the pages of revelation, that its truth may shine forth with insufferable brightness. Thus laboring and toiling in defense of the truth, and for the good of the church, God's blessing will crown his efforts with success.

The Pastor Should Give Himself Wholly to the Gospel and the Services of the Church Unless Circumstances Render It Impossible for Him So to Do

There are circumstances sometimes beyond his control that render it expedient that he should pursue some honorable and useful avocation in connection with his pastoral duties. If it is impossible for him to procure a competency from the church, he must seek a livelihood either by manual or mental labor. "For ye remember, brethren, our labor and travail, for laboring night and day, because we would not be chargeable unto any of you, we preached unto you the gospel of God" (1 Thess. 2:9). He did not toil, however, for personal aggrandizement and for the accumulation of wealth, but, from the necessity of the case that he might not be chargeable to anyone, or oppressive and burdensome to the brethren.

Pastoral and ministerial duties are not to be considered as of secondary, but of primary importance. Hear the apostle's instruction to Timothy: "Meditate upon these things, give thyself wholly to them, that thy profiting may appear in all things" (1 Tim. 4:15). The pastor must not unnecessarily entangle himself with the cares of the world. "No man that warreth entangleth himself with the affairs of this life, that he may please him who hath chosen him to be a soldier" (2 Tim. 2:4). A worldly-minded pastor cannot reprove the sin of worldliness in others. Precept and example must go together. His usefulness will decline in proportion as he becomes involved in secular business. He must live above the ostentation, vanity, and pride of the world. "But thou, O man of God, flee these things, and follow after righteousness; godliness, faith, love, patience, meekness."

The Pastor Must Be an Example of Piety and Practical Godliness to the Church

He must raise the standard of piety high, and himself live up to it. Faithful preaching united with a life of holiness will exert a powerful influence upon the church and the world. He cannot successfully exhort others to walk with God unless he maintain this walk himself. The good pastor will ever say, "Brethren, be followers together with me, and mark them which walk so as ye have us for an example" (Phil. 3:17). He should be an example in deportment and conversation. "Let no man despise thy youth, but be thou an example of believers in word, in conversation, in charity, in spirit, in faith, in purity" (1 Tim. 4:12). Piety is the very life of all his ministerial and pastoral labors. The pastor must take the leadership in every good work. He should inaugurate and advocate such plans and measures as shall best promote the welfare of his people and the cause of Christ. The influence of a good and exemplary pastor shall outlive himself. It shall be said of him as of Abel, "Being dead, he yet speaketh." The influence of Baxter and Bunyan still lives to bless the church and the world.

It Is the Duty of the Pastor to Visit His Flock as Often as It Is Necessary and Consistent with His Other Duties

Although churches sometimes make unreasonable demands in the number of visits, yet it must be admitted, that it is the duty of the pastor to hold frequent intercourse with his people in this way. By this means he gains the confidence and esteem of his church, and he will find his pastoral visits of great service to him in his public ministrations. Here we should draw the distinction between mere social visiting and pastoral visiting. The object of a social interview may be recreation—to promote cheerfulness in pastor and people. The object of a pastoral visit is to promote the spiritual welfare of God's people. It should be rendered instrumental in awakening in them new zeal and interest in the cause of Christ, and in deepening their piety. He should impress upon the minds of his flock that the object of his pastoral labor is to make them better and happier Christians. Here the pastor learns the spiritual wants and condition of his people, and he will naturally adapt the matter and character of his discourses to their necessities. Hearing the experiences of others will make him an experimental preacher, one great want of the present day. He should visit the feeble and afflicted, the young and unstable, that he may encourage and comfort the former, and guide and confirm the latter.

It Is the Duty of the Pastor to Exercise His Judgment and Influence to Guard the Church Against the Admission of Unworthy Members

Mark the distinction. We only affirm that he should exercise his discrimination to prevent the reception of unconverted members. He has no authority either to admit or exclude—this is the prerogative of the church. He has a better opportunity to judge of the qualifications of candidates for membership, and the church is generally governed by his recommendation; hence the necessity of caution on his part. It is to be feared that churches and pastors are becoming too lax in their manner of receiving members. Receive none into the fellowship of the church except those who know what it is to repent and believe in the Lord Jesus Christ, and have found Him precious to their souls by believing in His name. The pastor who encourages either tacitly or openly the admission of unconverted members, inflicts a positive injury upon the church.

It Is the Duty of the Pastor to Refuse to Assist in the Ordination of Any Man Who Is in Any Way Incapable of Exercising the High and Responsible Functions of a Minister of Jesus Christ

Paul says to Timothy, "Thou, therefore, my son, be strong in the grace that is in Christ Jesus. And the things that thou hast heard of me among many witnesses, the same commit thou to faithful men, who shall be able to teach others also." No man that is incapable of filling the ministerial and pastoral office should ever go forth bearing the credentials of a Presbytery.

The Pastor Should Pray for the Temporal and Spiritual Welfare of His People

"For this cause we also since the day we heard of it, do not cease to pray for you, and to desire that ye might be filled with the knowledge of his will in all wisdom and spiritual understanding" (Col. 1:9).

The Pastor Should Not Dissolve His Connection with His Church for Trivial Causes; but Seek to Render His Pastoral Office Permanent

There are sometimes good reasons why he should make a change. Among these may be enumerated the incompetency of his salary, and the prospect of enlarged usefulness. Where those causes do not exist, he is unjustifiable in breaking away from his people who love him. Pastors are becoming too migratory and unsettled. Numerous evils arise from the want of permanency in the pastoral relation that we cannot now mention.

A Pastor Should Be Impartial in His Attentions to His Flock, Making No Distinctions between the Rich and the Poor, and Uniform in His Conduct

"I charge thee before God, and the Lord Jesus Christ, and the elect angels, that thou observe these things without preferring one before another, doing nothing by partiality" (1 Tim. 5:21). He should exercise great prudence in his attentions to his people, so as not to create the impression that he prefers one to another. His conduct should be uniform. He should not be friendly and social today and tomorrow indifferent. He must recognize them as members of his flock at all times and under all circumstances; at home and abroad, on the Sabbath and the week day, in the shop and the fields, let him make them feel that he is the same God-fearing, faithful, kind, and affectionate pastor.

In conclusion, we observe that the pastor should cherish an ardent affection for his people, and entertain for them a spirit of kindness and gentleness, and ever live in hope of that perfect and indissoluble union that he will form with them in heaven. The apostle says, "As ye know how we exhorted and comforted, and charged every one of you as a father doth his children, that ye would walk worthy of God who hath called you unto his kingdom and glory" (1 Thess. 2:11–12). The faithful pastor, in serving the church, is serving his Lord and Master. Every act of love and kindness done to His people He regards as done to Himself. If the communion and fellowship of a pastor and his flock be so endearing and joyous on earth, how much will this joy and happiness be heightened in heaven. "The elders which are among you I exhort, who am also an elder, and a witness of the sufferings of Christ, and also a partaker of the glory that shall be revealed. Feed the flock of God which are among you, taking the oversight thereof, not by constraint, but willingly; not for filthy lucre, but of a ready mind; neither as being lords over God's heritage, but being examples to the flock. And when the chief shepherd shall appear, ye shall receive a crown of glory that fadeth not away." The faithful pastor shall receive an unfading crown. All shall enjoy the presence and smiles of the chief Shepherd. Heaven shall sweeten all our enjoyments, heighten all our pleasures, and consummate our mutual love and happiness. "Therefore, my beloved brethren," pastors, and people, "be ye steadfast, immoveable, always abounding in the work of the Lord, forasmuch as ye know that your labor is not in vain in the Lord."

Chapter Eight

"Dangers of Denominational Prosperity" (May 26, 1843)

Jacob R. Scott

(Delivered before the Portsmouth Association convened at Mill Swamp, Isle of Wight Co., May 26, 1843)

"Let him that thinketh he standeth take heed lest he fall" (1 Cor. 10:12).

I could wish, my brethren, that someone older in the Christian ministry, and older in his connection with this association, were to address you at this time; but as you have been pleased to devolve the duty on me, I obey; and this with some degree of cheerfulness, as the present occasion affords me an opportunity of giving expression to a few thoughts suggested by the recent progress of our denomination—thoughts which have of late rested with considerable weight on my mind, and which seem to me worthy of being deeply infixed in the minds of all who desire the speedy reign of truth and holiness in the world. I doubt not, the same, or similar reflections have occurred to many of you. I should be sorry indeed if they should prove trite and uninteresting; but I am confident that the necessity of urging them upon our churches is not past, and never has been greater than at this very time. You have already anticipated that my remarks are to be cautionary in their nature; and here again when I consider that caution and counsel are the province of age and experience, I am almost deterred from proceeding with my design. But as I have lived long enough at least to learn that apologies oftener spring from vanity than diffidence, I shall not detain you by the offering of any, but pass at once to my observations.

The apostle Paul spoke of his own care and exertion to mortify the lusts of the flesh, so that he might at last secure the incorruptible crown of a faithful servant of Christ. From this he goes on in the tenth chapter of Corinthians to admonish his Corinthian brethren to do the same, and not to suffer themselves to be lulled into security, as was the case with too many, by the consideration of the great spiritual gifts they had received from God. These gifts were far from putting them beyond the reach of danger, whilst they did create an additional obligation to watchfulness, diligence, and zeal. This he shows to be shadowed forth in the history of the Israelites in their journey from Egypt to Canaan, who, notwithstanding they had been distinguished by the miraculous protection of God, and the communication of various blessings, still incurred the displeasure of Jehovah by their misconduct, and were overthrown in the wilderness. The external favors conferred upon those Hebrews prefigured the rich spiritual gifts of the Christian dispensation. See to it then, the Apostle would say, that you do not abuse the blessings you enjoy, as they did, and thus cause their fate to prefigure your destiny. They, by their presumption and iniquities, tempted God, until He came out against them in wrath; beware lest the correspondence between their case and yours, be not merely a correspondence in point of blessings received, but also in respect to the forfeiture of blessings, and the incurring of a disastrous overthrow. "Now all these things happened unto them for examples: and they are written for our admonition upon whom the ends of the world are come. Wherefore, let him that thinketh he standeth take heed lest he fall."

There is hardly any doctrine more clearly revealed in the Word of God than that of the saints' final perseverance. But clearly as it is revealed that the true believer will be kept by the power of God through faith unto salvation, we are told, he that shall endure unto the end, the same shall be saved—implying that it is the result of our course which must determine whether we are indeed true believers, and that even the real child of God will persevere only in the exercise of strict watchfulness and effort.

And so the sacred oracles leave us in no doubt that as long as the world stands, God will have a church on the earth; and yet, in some sense He has left it to the church herself to preserve and perpetuate her existence. Her prosperity also, at any given period will be proportionate to the zeal and fidelity of her members. I would not by any means, here lose sight of the necessity of sovereign, divine grace in the preservation and upbuilding of Zion; but I say God has clearly instituted and made known the connection alluded to. We may have the truth, the whole truth, and nothing but the truth, on our side, and yet we are taught that the success of our cause is coupled with the measure of our watchfulness, activity, and prayer. The arm of the Lord must indeed awake, and put on its strength, but His people must not be deaf to the call, "awake, awake, put on thy strength, O Zion!"

There are two respects in which the adherents of any system may be mistaken, and wherein they should take heed. They may think that they are firmly planted in the truth, when they are really in error; and they may be confident of triumph, when they are destined to disaster, if not total defeat. Where the truth is actually entertained there is no question, but that is the side which must ultimately prevail; and yet, it does not follow before the final consummator, that its success in any given struggle will be proportionate to its superiority in point of truth. Does not universal history teach us that truth, though immortal, may yet long lie crushed to earth, while error is rife and rampant in the world?—that the ground which she gains, if she would maintain it, she must watch with eagle eye, and defend with a vigorous arm?—and that if she would make new conquests, she must march boldly forth, and win them on fields, where every inch will be desperately disputed? Thus has it been in every past age. Truth and error, like two sturdy gladiators, have held each other in close grapple, and now one has seemed uppermost, and now the other. When it may please God that the mortal blow shall be inflicted upon error, and the ultimate triumph of truth shall arrive, the Omniscient only knows; but it is certain, as yet, no one can say, I am right, because my opinions are triumphant; or my opinions must triumph, because I am right. Let him that thinketh he standeth, then, either in respect to the truth or the triumph of his particular sentiments, take heed, lest he fall.

As Baptists, we trust, and we are confident in the persuasion, that we have the truth, as nearly as human imperfection can approximate to it, on our side. We cannot doubt, but our views, founded as they are, on the simple Word of God, irrespective of the traditions of men, are destined ultimately to complete triumph. And from the rapid progress they have made, and are still making, we fondly believe that the day when they shall universally prevail, is not distant. That day cannot be distant, if Baptists are only true to the sacred trust committed to them. But here we have just ground for apprehension; and a little reflection will convince you, brethren, that our most serious fears must actually be based on our apparent prosperity. We are bound, indeed, to thank God and take courage, for what our ears have heard, and our eyes have seen. In this land, we have already come to outnumber any other denomination, and the leaven of our views is diffusing itself more and more widely in every direction. We have a right to rejoice; we do, and we will rejoice; but let us be careful that we do not give ourselves up too exclusively to exultation; let us not blind ourselves to the fact, that with this advance has come an accession of dangers, which should keep us incessantly on our guard. I ask your prayerful attention, whilst I shall endeavor to point out some of these dangers—the perils of our prosperity—perils, which if not guarded against and counteracted, may give a retrograde movement to the cause of truth, and involve the world once more in the darkness of error and superstition. Heaven forbid it! Heaven forbid that we prove faithless to the high and holy trust committed to us!

Point 1: Purity

The first danger I specify, as springing from our prosperity and threatening to mar it, has respect to our purity—our soundness both in doctrine, and in practice. Bodies as they grow large are very apt to grow corrupt. It is as true in the moral as in the natural world, that rapid growth is not always a symptom of health. It becomes our churches then, as their numbers increase, to see to it that there be no relaxation of sound doctrine, and that a healthy tone of piety be maintained. However the bulk of a church may have been augmented, there has been no advance in real prosperity if, take the church through, the average attachment to the great truths of God's Word and the tone of practical religion have been lowered. And is there not danger of this? Where there have been large additions, is it improbable that among them are many whose views of divine truth are very partial and defective; and many, who, having no definite views at all, are in danger of imbibing notions exceedingly erroneous, or of being tossed about by every wind of doctrine? And so, does not experience teach us, that where many present themselves for membership, at a time, we are apt to be less particular, as to the evidence of a real change in the candidates, than where only one, or but a few present themselves? And is it not peculiarly difficult, in the flush of such an occasion, to judge accurately what weight is to be allowed to the statements presented?

At all times there is danger of deceived persons being admitted to the church; but is not the danger especially great, at a time, when the kingdom of heaven suffereth violence? It is a critical time with a church when membership in it is popular. But, allow that all who have been received are genuine converts, and sound in their doctrinal views, so far as they have any, this is the point to which I would come; is there not danger, where there are so many more to be instructed, and watched over than formerly—and who will not admit the necessity of such watch-care, and instruction?—that less attention will be bestowed on the members individually? That where many are to be looked after, the business will be done in a more hasty and general manner, than where there are but few? Is it unlikely, that neglects, inconsistencies, and abuses, which before would have been promptly rebuked, will be suffered to pass unnoticed? You know how it is in tillage. A farmer may be increasing his acres and still be growing poorer. We should not forget that a small estate, constantly improving, is better than a large one running to waste. This deterioration in the church may not be very perceptible at once, but let some emergency arise, in which it is necessary for her to vindicate her purity—to speak out, and act out boldly against heresy or sin—and then it will be seen whether the church has improved, on the whole, by comparing the present degree of her union and promptitude with the past. Look in at the prayer meeting also. Have the attendance and interest there kept pace with the increase of the church? Is as large a proportion of the whole number to be found there now as when the church was smaller? Do you witness the cheerfulness of that little band, who in days gone by enjoyed such sweet seasons together? Or does gloom preside, and do you hear little else than lamentations, that out of so many so few only feel love enough to the Savior and love enough to one another, to draw them out to meeting? And how is it in respect to the interest of the church in the various objects of Christian liberality and exertion? Has the church enlarged her contributions and operations, in proportion to the enlargement of her ability?

If an unfavorable answer is given to these questions, is not the conclusion inevitable, that the church is not so sound as when it was smaller? Understand me, brethren, I say nothing against the large and rapid accessions to our churches; would to God they were larger and more rapid; I do not say that the evils referred to necessarily follow, but only that there is danger of their following, because, where there are so many more to be instructed and trained, there is a liability that individual cases will not be looked after so carefully. Now what makes this a point of great importance is these two things: (1) The objects of church association, it must be obvious to all, can be carried out only in proportion to the soundness and piety of the body; and (2) It is only in that proportion that a church can expect to enjoy the smiles of her great Head; and what, brethren, what is a church without God's blessing? I pass to notice another danger.

Point 2: Liability to Disunion

It is the increased liability to disunion. All must be aware that this liability is much greater in a large body than in a small one. The more materials there are for parties, the more schisms there are likely to be. Philosophy itself cannot furnish a stronger illustration of cohesive attraction than is found in that union, which binds together a little, despised, persecuted handful, cemented together by a common faith. But let their number be increased; let them come to assume an aspect of respectability and importance in the eyes of the world; destroy the powerful bond of sympathy in suffering for conscience' sake; introduce a greater diversity of interests and outward circumstances; instead of all knowing each other intimately, let numbers be unacquainted with each other, and generally the acquaintance be slight, compared with what it was before; let them come to feel that rupture, after all, will not be death to them—I say, let the condition of that little band be thus changed, and will not discord find much easier admittance than before? No one can doubt it. Besides, the greater the number of members, the greater will probably be the diversity of views and feelings to be reconciled; consequently the more numerous the occasions which can be wrested by disaffected persons to the purposes of faction. And still further: the larger and more influential the body, the stronger are the allurements to pride, ambition, and cupidity in it; and what more fruitful parents of disunion than these?

And so we might go on to enumerate many other ways in which the increase of a church widens the entrance for disunion. But time forbids. This curse need not enter, and it should not be suffered to enter; everything should go on harmoniously in the church of God; all I say is, there is danger on this score, and the more numerous the body, the greater the danger. Hence, with the augmentation of our ranks, the necessity of increased vigilance to prevent the evil, and promote mutual conciliation and love.

Point 3: Threatened Humility

The next danger I notice is that which threatens our humility. The Lord will not bless a proud denomination, or a proud church, let their creed be ever so orthodox. When David, at the instigation of Satan, numbered Israel, Jehovah was indignant, and sent Gad, the seer, to him with this fearful message: "Choose thee one of these three things, that I may do it unto thee. Choose thee either three years' famine; or three months to be destroyed before thy foes, while that the sword of thine enemies overtaketh thee; or else, three days the sword of the Lord, even the pestilence in the land, and the angel of the Lord destroying throughout all the coasts of Israel." Thus when David, in the pride of his heart, went to numbering the people, the Lord determined to diminish the people, and there fell of Israel 70,000 men.

Let us learn a lesson from the history of Hezekiah also. The king of Babylon having heard of his recovery from sickness, sent messengers to him, with a present and letters of congratulation. Hezekiah, flattered at the attention of the heathen monarch, and doubtless, wishing to show that the distinction was not unworthily bestowed, takes the ambassadors to the house of his precious things, and there makes an ostentatious display of his wealth. The light in which God regarded this vain act may be learned from the message He sent by Isaiah: "Behold the days come, that all that is in thine house, and that which thy fathers have laid up in store unto this day, shall be carried into Babylon," the very country from which these ambassadors have come, "nothing shall be left, saith the Lord." And when we, my brethren, show symptoms of elation, in consequence of the great prosperity with which the Lord has crowned us, when we, as a denomination, or as separate churches, begin to boast of the great numbers in our ranks, the wealth, the talents, the respectability, the influence, that have been added to our communion, when we begin to lose that spirit of simple, lowly, unsophisticated piety, which characterized us in the days of our fewness and contempt, it will be high time for us to begin to tremble also. We may expect the withering frown of Jehovah, and the tide of our prosperity will be turned backward. We may rejoice indeed, that the Lord has blessed us; and let us be glad; but let us exult only because in our success, we see the advancement of truth, which is the cause of God, and essential to the enfranchisement, the glory, and the felicity of our race. It cannot be doubted, brethren, that with the enlargement of our denomination, there has come a tendency to this vain-glorying. I say it with regret, I fear the indications of this tendency have already made their appearance. What means the boastful parade so often made in our publication, or our superiority in numbers over other denominations? And especially of any inroads we may chance to have made on their ranks? Let us beware of this spirit. Let us see to it that we be not puffed up with arrogance. The devil cannot be better gratified than to witness this. Let us take heed lest we make shipwreck here, and it be left for us merely to furnish a beacon to some remoter generation, who, thus warned of the rock on which they are most likely to split, shall safely bear the holy trust now in our hands, into the port to which we had had the honor of bearing it but for our folly.

Point 4: A Diminution of Energy

Another danger to which our prosperity renders us peculiarly liable, is a diminution of energy in propagating the truth. Let us not forget that our obligation to exert ourselves for the glory of God is as great now as ever it was, and we are found to exert ourselves as vigorously as ever. What has been accomplished will afford us no apology for suspending, or in any degree relaxing our efforts. Had our churches been tenfold more active and faithful than they have been, no excuse could possibly be offered for the slightest flagging in our solicitude and labors for Zion's good. Too much still remains to be done, too much lost time, and too many wasted opportunities remain to be redeemed, too many enemies are waiting for our halting, to allow the least apology for folding our arms yet. No, when we consider how remiss in fact we have been, when we contrast all the labor that has been bestowed with the tremendous demand for exertion, and with what might actually have been done with proper fidelity, do we not really seem to have been asleep? So far then from thinking of rest, let us feel that we are called upon to arouse ourselves and redouble our diligence and energy; let us tremble at a single symptom of indisposition to continue, nay, to increase to the utmost, our attacks upon the power of the prince of darkness.

But, I repeat it, our past success brings with it a peculiar liability to such indisposition. We are apt to be satisfied too soon, before our Master is, or to fancy because so much has been accomplished, what remains can be done at our leisure; or, since because there are so many more in the service, each one may do less. It is the natural tendency of prosperity to enervate; and this tendency, if not counteracted, will eat out our vitals. When the world frowns upon the church, and Satan threatens to devour; when Christians are few and despised, there is every thing to stimulate to activity. It is then a struggle for life, and no one feels excused from fighting as hard as he can. But when large numbers have enlisted, and we imagine that we are too many, and too strong, to be scorned down, or beat down, we are prone to rest contented at this point. Many relax their exertions, while not a few cease their aggressions upon the enemy altogether. Like Job, we say, "I shall die in my nest." Like the Laodiceans, we say, "I am rich, and increased with goods, and have need of nothing." Like Babylon, we say, "I shall be a lady forever." We feel safe, we feel respectable, we feel at ease, and so do not bestir ourselves, forgetting that our own personal safety, and comfort, and respectability, are not the ends set before us, but the total defeat of Satan, the extermination of sin, the complete subdual of the earth to Immanuel's reign. Thus, brethren, are we in danger of being satisfied with what the Lord has already done for us, of feeling that we are strong enough, and sinking down into ignoble indolence, of restraining prayer, and neglecting all the means He has made it our duty to employ for the advancement of His glory. I pass just to hint at another danger intimately connected with this.

Point 5: Regarding Activity

I refer to the danger of activity not being so general through-out the churches as when they were smaller, of every church and every individual not coming up so much, as a body, to the help of the Lord. The churches being so much more numerous, the smaller ones will be apt to be overlooked in the calls which are made for the support of our various denominational enterprises; and not being particularly called upon, come themselves to forget the duty to do their proportion towards supporting those enterprises. And so, take any given church, I think this fact cannot have escaped your notice, brethren: that as the members and resources of a church increase, instead of each member doing what he can, as in the days when it was necessary for every one to work, or see the church die, a portion of the members come to be thrown out from bearing their share in supporting the different operations. The mites and the one talents thus fail to come into the Lord's treasury. Where the church can get along respectably without them, they are not considered worth the trouble of collection. The fact is, there ought to be no trouble about it; a church should have its regular treasuries for good objects, and every member should know where the treasuries are, and have that spirit, which will lead him to bring in, system-atically and punctually, his contributions himself. But the evil I refer to is not a mere matter of dollars and cents. It is the loss of a sense of individual responsibility, of obligation on the part of every member, not merely to pay money, but to pray and labor in every way for the prosperity of Zion. From the very nature of things, it cannot be avoided that some members should become more prominent in the affairs of the church than others; but this is no reason why any one should feel that he has less personal interest in the church than any other. Alas! In too many of our churches there may be noticed a class, who hardly seem to regard themselves as part and parcel with the church, but rather, as in some sort mere useless appendages to the body. This ought not to be so. All should feel that they are members one of another; that each one has a part to perform in the upbuilding of the spiritual edifice; and that direct action, personal exertion in some way for the glory of God, is essential to the safety and prosperity of every soul. The danger on this score attendant on the progress of our denomination must be apparent to all. Let us see to it that the appropriate preventives be promptly and effectually applied.

Point 6: Secularized by Prosperity

Another danger of no inconsiderable magnitude, and to which I designed calling your particular attention, but which I can barely notice, is that of our denomination becoming secularized by its prosperity. From being a small body, we have become so numerous, that, united for secular and political purposes, we would wield no small amount of influence and power. How strong the temptation to this is liable to become, you need not be told. But Heaven defend us against it! The moment we attempt to erect ourselves in to a great establishment, and proclaim ourselves banded together on any other grounds, and for any other ends, than those which are purely spiritual, that moment will be disastrous indeed to us. So soon as we, in our denominational capacity, take a stand of this kind, are to be bartered with for objects of mere worldly advantage—bought and sold in the market of demagogues and speculators, we may inscribe Ichabod upon our banners, for the glory will have departed.

Point 7: Influence
of Denominational Prosperity on Others

Another point of danger on which it were perhaps worth while to dwell, but which I will only suggest, is the influence of denominational prosperity on the toleration of others. I confess, brethren, when I read the pages of history, I feel proud of the stand that Baptists have always taken on the subject of religious freedom. I say it not in the spirit of boasting, truth will bear out the assertion, that the great, invaluable principle of toleration in spiritual matters, if not discovered by a Baptist, has, at least, been more clearly developed, more powerfully enforced, and more unwaveringly acted on by no denomination than ours. No denomination has shown less disposition to abuse its advantages, more freely and cheerfully conceded to others the right of judging for themselves what is truth, and of carrying out the convictions of their judgment. God has blessed us in thus respecting the rights of others. We have reason to fear His frown, should we ever consent to abuse our advantages by the invasion of those rights. God forbid that we should ever set ourselves up as spiritual dictators in the world, and attempt to tyrannize over the consciences of men. Let us go on, as we ever have gone, trusting to no sword for our victories, but the sword of the Spirit, which is the Word of God. Let us especially abhor and despise that petty despotism, which we sometimes see wielded over a community by a dominant sect, so abhor and despise it, as never to tolerate the slightest approach to it in our own case. There cannot possibly be any thing lost, by the exhibition of that noble disinterestedness and generosity, which will lead us always cheerfully to concede to others as unshackled an exercise of the understanding and conscience, as we claim, or wish for ourselves.

Point 8: Incurring Heaven's Displeasure

I will detain you brethren, to notice but one danger more; and that is, the danger of incurring the displeasure of Heaven by ingratitude. The Lord hath done great things for us, and He expects us to make corresponding returns. He expects that we will be thankful, and manifest our thankfulness by our increased devotedness to His service. He expects that, as He has enlarged our ability, we will enlarge our operations. As there are more laborers in the vineyard, He expects that more work will be done. And He expects an increase of service, not merely in proportion to our increase of means, but that we will exert ourselves to supply the deficiencies of the past, that we will make Him special thank-offerings, and that being taught by experience how certain our outlays are of being crowned with a rich return, we will never hesitate to make our investments correspond with our absolute ability.

I feel, my brethren, that this is a point of unspeakable importance. I fear we are not alive as we ought to be to its importance. I fear so, because I cannot learn that there is any more self-denial in our churches; I hear no more frequently than before of young men longing to proclaim the gospel to perishing sinners; I cannot hear that our churches are much more willing to do justice to their ministers, and let them prosecute their work undistracted by worldly cares; I cannot see that our benevolent institutions are any better sustained now than they have been for years past. Our missionary boards have been put to their wit's end more the last year than ever before. I know it has been a year of almost unprecedented embarrassment in the commercial world; but I do not see in this depression an adequate reason for the falling off which has taken place in the support of our holy enterprises. I fear that our retrenchment is too apt to begin at the sanctuary instead of our own houses. I fear that this multitude of new converts are not properly instructed in the principles of true Christian consecration, and in the claims of benighted millions. I fear that this vast mass of material is not growing up as it ought to "into him in all things, which is the head, even Christ."

If this be true, my brethren, how shamefully, or rather, shamelessly unthankful does it prove us! Have we not reason to fear that the gratification we feel at the increase of our denomination is of a very unholy and selfish kind? Have we not reason to apprehend that God will change His method of dealing with us, that He will turn our prosperity into desolation, that He will drive us from His vineyard, and commit the culture of it to those who will make Him more worthy returns? O my brethren, the distinguished favor of God devolves a weighty responsibility upon us. Would that we felt it more. Let us implore the grace of God to make us feel it. Let us dwell much upon the goodness of the Lord to us, as a denomination, as separate churches, and as individuals. Let us praise Him for His goodness, and be it our earnest endeavor henceforth to serve Him with greater fidelity.

But it is time for me to close. I have endeavored, brethren, plainly and faithfully to portray the dangers, in which I conceive our present position involves us. Your attention has been directed to the perils which threaten us on a variety of particulars. I trust that the views presented have convinced you of the importance of our taking heed in relation to our future course. Many other considerations might be offered, but I hope these will suffice to put us on our guard, to make us instant and earnest in our supplications, and cause us to advance with renewed and vastly augmented zeal in the service of our adorable Redeemer. It is a high trust that has been committed to us. We concede, and that cheerfully, to other evangelical denominations that not a little truth may enter into their systems, and that they are doing not a little to promote the happiness of mankind, for time and for eternity; but so long as they cling to a single error, or corruption of "another Gospel," a degenerate Christianity, it is not for them to lead forth the world, completely unshackled, from its house of bondage. This I sincerely believe to be the vocation of the Baptist denomination. I am not a bigot, and no one who knows me will accuse me of an excel of zeal for the peculiarities which distinguish us from every other body of Christians; but I believe firmly, that religion will never stand forth, emancipated, and in her native majesty, dispensing her richest blessings, until all who love the Lord Jesus shall have united in the belief and practice of His simple teachings, just as He left them with His church, and of nothing else. Believing, brethren, that God has called us to this high work, and seeing, in the success with which He has already crowned us, the earnest of victory complete, but fearing that that victory may be retarded by the abuse of past success, I have been moved to raise a voice of warning on this occasion. May the great Head of the church own and bless the feeble endeavor! Church of the living God "peace be within thy walls, and prosperity within thy palaces! For my brethren and companions' sakes, I will now say, peace be within thee!"

Chapter Nine

Reminiscences
of the Old-Time Baptists

S. G. HILLYER

In these reminiscences, I shall devote some time to the consideration of Georgia Baptist churches as they appeared during the early decades of the present century [the early 1800s].

They were built upon the apostles and prophets, Jesus Christ Himself being the chief corner-stone. Hence they contended earnestly for the faith once delivered to the saints and firmly held the New Testament to be their only authoritative creed and their only binding rule of practice. Accordingly, they would not admit any one to baptism and to church membership till he was able to give for himself credible evidence of regeneration in the experience of sincere repentance towards God and in the exercise of genuine faith in Jesus Christ. The logical result of these views compelled them to repudiate the baptism of infants, and also to adhere to immersion as the New Testament form, and, therefore, the only valid form of administering the ordinance.

195

The old-time Baptist meeting-house was a simple structure. As has been stated, our Baptist people generally, seventy or eighty years ago, lived in the country, and there they built their meeting-houses. They were built sometimes of logs, but the average meeting-house was a framed building varying in size to suit the supposed wants of the neighborhood. It was often without ceiling on the inside and sometimes its windows were left without glazed sashes. And in many cases no provision was made for warming the house. Now it is simply wonderful how preachers or people could keep up their meetings under such conditions in cold weather. Think of a preacher riding in his buggy ten miles on Sunday morning to meet a candidate for baptism (received the day before at conference), and after baptism having to dress himself in the woods and then leap in his buggy and drive four miles to the meeting-house and conduct the morning service as usual, and then, after the benediction, to step into his buggy again and drive twelve miles, without seeing fire, till he reached his own home, while all day the mercury was near the freezing point. Of this case I had personal knowledge. Was it a hard case? No doubt the administrator and the spectators felt the cold severely. And the subject, who was a humble colored woman, no doubt felt it more than all. But I venture to say that neither the pastor nor the subject regarded the physical inconvenience (I need not call it suffering) as worthy to be compared with the transcendent privilege that each enjoyed.

Nevertheless, it is readily admitted that the stove or furnace, with a baptistery flanked by two comfortable dressing rooms, is a wonderful advance upon the simple arrangements of the old-time meeting-house, while the joy of obedience has suffered, from the change, no diminution whatever.

The Conferences

Regarded in its visible aspects, a church conference was about as unattractive a gathering as could be found. Its place of meeting was, in all probability, that old-time meeting-house with its uncouth and rough equipments. Its members were men and women who had left their farms, their shops, and their household cares that they might fill their places in the meeting of the church. They usually met on Saturday which preceded the Sunday that was set apart for the public worship of the church, and for the preaching of the gospel to the congregation which might assemble with them on that day.

The conference on Saturday was usually preceded by a sermon, accompanied with prayer and hymns of praise. Then generally after a short recess, the church met in conference. It was emphatically an independent body. It acknowledged, outside of itself, no power on earth that had a right to control its action. Clothed with such complete self-government, the question may well be asked: What was the business or work that engaged their attention? This question, if answered in all its fullness, would fill several pages; but it may be answered comprehensively in a few words, thus: The business of a church conference is to promote the kingdom of God among men at home and abroad. Did the early churches of Georgia so understand their duty? Only to a very limited degree. They were on the right line of duty, but only at the beginning of it.

That beginning was first to watch over one another in love, to maintain a wholesome discipline among themselves, and to provide a preached gospel as often as they could for themselves and for the community around them. These things they understood. I have stated them almost in the words of their church covenants. And when they were trying to perform these duties, they were really aiming, perhaps, without being aware of it, to promote the kingdom of God in themselves and among their neighbors.

Now, taking these principles with us, let us search the minutes of our old-time churches. I am sure it will appear from those minutes that those old churches did, with great fidelity, watch over the morals and the religion of their members, and they did it in love. The evidence of this is found in the fact that their minutes are often studded with cases of discipline. This fact I know may show that the offenders were many, but it also proves that the majority of the church, in each case, was faithful and true to put away evil from among them. And yet they did it in love, for how glad were they to receive back to their fellowship a penitent offender as soon as he approached them with a proper confession.

In the light of what has been said I think we may conclude that the chief work of those old conferences was to maintain a high standard of morals and of piety among their members.

Their Discipline

It was a rule with many churches fifty and eighty years ago to have the roll called at each conference, and absentees were marked, and at the next conference those who were absent at the previous meeting were expected to explain their absence. This was not an "iron rule." It did not apply to the female members at all, and the male members were not called on for their excuses by name unless they had been absent three times in succession. In that case, when one had failed to attend the meetings, the clerk was required to report him if he did not report himself, and then he was called on to explain his absences. Nor was the church severe as to the character of the excuse required. He was allowed to plead any reasonable inconvenience.

Though the enforcement of the rule was very lenient, yet its effect was decidedly wholesome. It kept before the minds of all the precept of the Apostle, "Forsake not the assembling of yourselves together"; and it was easy for them to see that the precept included attendance, not only on the conferences, but upon all the appointments of the church—its prayer-meetings and its Sunday services. The existence of such a rule is a constant appeal to the consciences of church members to fulfill the covenant they have made with their brethren.

I doubt not that there are many Baptist churches in Georgia today which have this rule, and I am just so certain that when it is efficiently observed it will lead on to other good works and to greater prosperity.

I have said that the rule should be enforced leniently, but there comes a time when forbearance ceases to be a kindness. When one neglects his church meetings persistently and continuously, he becomes justly a subject of dealing. The pastor and other brethren should labor with him. Peradventure, they may save their brother. But if he should prove incorrigible, then he should be excluded.

Another phase of discipline found in the early churches was manifested in their dealings with the grosser vices. I need not, however, enlarge upon this topic, for I think it is well understood that the churches in those days would not tolerate any gross immoralities. It did not matter who was the offender. So far as their discipline was concerned there was no respect of persons. The offender might be their pastor, or the richest man in the church; but if he was proved guilty of immorality, his high position could not protect him.

There was still another exercise of discipline among the old-time Baptist churches in Georgia that deserves a passing notice. It was not an uncommon thing for them, in conference, to settle disputes between brethren. In such cases the church did not act precipitately. They would wait till the aggrieved party had sought redress in the way prescribed by our Savior in the eighteenth chapter of Matthew. Then if he had failed to obtain what he believed to be his rights, it was his privilege to bring the case before the church. True, such cases were sometimes mere quarrels growing out of bad tempers and unkind words.

I witnessed, nearly sixty years ago, just such a case. It was a quarrel between two prominent sisters. The feeling on both sides became intense, till at length the husband of the aggrieved lady brought the case before the church. He preferred no charges against the offending sister, but only asked for letters of dismission for himself and wife. For a moment there was silence in the house. Then the offending sister rose to her feet and said substantially: "Brother Moderator, I can't consent for two such people as Brother and Sister ———— to leave this church on my account. I believe them to be Christian people." What else she might have said along the line of tenderness and conciliation, I do not know, for just then the pastor interrupted her and said: "Sister, are you willing now to come forward and offer them your hand of Christian fellowship?" Instantly the good lady started down the aisle that she might reach the other parties, who were on the opposite side of the house. They saw her coming, and promptly moved forward to meet her and to grasp cordially her offered hand, and there the three stood weeping together, while many in the audience were also bathed in tears. When they returned to their seats the brother gladly withdrew his request for letters. Thus passed away this threatening cloud, while the beams of the Sun of righteousness adorned its retreating form with the beautiful bow of peace and reconciliation.

Sometimes the disputes among brethren involved the payment of debts and the fulfillment of contracts. How many of the present generation are aware that the conference of a Baptist church would sometimes become, practically, a court of justice? And yet a case of that kind occurred in 1828 in one of the counties of Middle Georgia.

There were, indeed, some churches who would not allow their members to go to law with one another before the State courts. They held this position under Paul's teachings in his first letter to the Corinthians, with which we are all familiar.

There was one other matter that in former years furnished occasion for discipline to our Baptist churches. I allude to the complicated subject of social indulgences and amusements. There is no doubt about it, the New Testament warns the people of God against the love of the world. And it is also true that one mode of gratifying this love is found in the pleasures and indulgences of social life.

Our honest forefathers, impressed with these facts, made an earnest effort to protect church members from the contaminations of the world. To this end they placed some worldly amusements under the ban of stern disapprobation, and made them subjects of discipline. In making these discriminations they made, we must admit, some grave mistakes. But I think it will be found that their mistakes were in allowing some things which they ought to have forbidden rather than in those things which they condemned. For instance, they condemned social dancing and card playing, because they judged these amusements to be hurtful to spiritual growth and dangerously alluring to other and grosser vices. In this judgment they were certainly right. But they allowed social drinking without a word of censure. In this they were inconsistent. But it should be observed that they were not knowingly inconsistent. I can distinctly remember when a moderate "dram" (so called) was deemed as harmless as the same amount of milk. Not only so, it was considered, in hundreds of cases, to be actually helpful and sustaining to the physical system. Hence the most prudent farmers of the country would often furnish it to their hands, especially when their work happened to be more than usually heavy. Religious people did the same thing. Even preachers, after a long sermon, would often relieve their fatigue with a dram.

In the light of these facts it is not surprising that our fathers, seventy years ago, should overlook the evils of moderate drinking. But remember that they did not tolerate drunkenness. Their church minutes show many cases of discipline, which evince their watchfulness over the morals of their brethren.

There are other social evils that our fathers failed to condemn in any very strong terms. These are theaters, operas, and circuses. In their days they were very rare in Georgia. Their true character and hurtful influence were not understood. I do not know that the old minutes contain any cases at all growing out of these amusements. But the evils of dancing and card playing were well known. They saw in them "a love of the world" that was intense—so intense as to crush all the elements of true piety in those who habitually indulged in them. Hence it is not strange that our fathers gave them no quarter.

Their opposition, in some cases, was so strong that they transferred to the fiddle the abhorrence which they felt for the dance. I knew a good pastor—a man eminent for his piety and learning—who was very fond of the fiddle. He owned one and often played it. He was serving a church in the country, of which he was not a member, and somehow his brethren heard of his fiddle. They couldn't stand it. At conference one of the brethren told the pastor what they had heard and asked if he really played the fiddle. He frankly confessed that he did, and in a very affectionate way tried to convince them that he did it innocently. But the brethren were not satisfied. After a full debate he at last said to them, "Well, brethren, I see my playing the fiddle hurts your feelings. This I am not willing to do. I will therefore agree that I will not play another tune on the fiddle as long as I am your pastor." This was enough. The brethren accepted his promise as all that they had a right to ask. The moral of this story is plain. When you know that an indulgence which you think innocent hurts the feelings of your brethren, it is generous and lovely to deny yourself rather than wound them.

Their Reception of Members

The New Testament idea of a church is that it should be an assembly of converted and baptized members who have Christian fellowship with each other. This beautiful ideal Baptists have always and everywhere desired to realize, and to this end have adopted such methods of receiving new members as they hoped would most successfully secure its realization. The New Testament prescribes no particular method of testing the sincerity of one who professes to have exercised "repentance toward God and faith toward our Lord Jesus Christ." But it would be a grave mistake to suppose that the Apostles and the primitive churches took no pains to guard against the admission of unfit members. True, in that early period, it may not have been needful to adopt such stringent methods to protect the purity of the churches as have become necessary in these modern times. The "offense of the cross" was so intense and wide spread that very few, save those who were truly "born of God," were willing to endure its shame. Hence, those who became willing to confess Christ in baptism by that very consent gave a signal proof of their sincerity. And with this proof the apostolic churches may have been and, no doubt, in many cases were constant.

But times have changed. The "offense of the cross" has well-nigh ceased. It is no longer a disgrace and a shame to become a Christian. Becoming a Christian now no longer exposes one to the loss of his citizenship or his social position, and much less does it expose him to the fagot and the stake. Nay, it has come to pass that the way into the church is easy, and often inviting, for it sometimes leads to respectability. Indeed, in some sections of the so-called church there lies a way that leads to honor and to great emolument.

Under such conditions as are above set forth a people who insist upon a converted church membership must faithfully watch against intruders. If it be needful to watch over one another in love that we may maintain a "wholesome discipline," much more is it needful that we should begin that watchfulness at the very door of the church.

Accordingly it has been the custom with our Baptist churches in America and throughout the world to require every candidate for church membership to give a relation of his Christian experience in order that the brethren may know whether it affords a credible and reasonable evidence of a genuine conversion. This relation always, save in a few exceptional cases, precedes baptism, for the simple reason that a genuine conversion is as essential to the validity of a baptism as it is for admission into the church.

The rule, as above explained, was rigidly observed by Georgia Baptists from their very beginning in the state. Where a church met in conference, it was usual to spend a little while in devotional exercises, except when a sermon with its usual services of prayer and praise had preceded the church meeting. The next thing in order was to "open the door of the church." This was done by the pastor. With kind and gentle words he invited any one present who might feel a desire to unite himself with the people of God to come forward to the front seat during the singing of a hymn selected by the pastor. Here was an interesting crisis. The pastor might have in his mind's eye some dear youth who he believed ought to come forward, but whose timidity might restrain him. To suit such a case, he would select a hymn like this:

"In all my Lord's appointed ways,

My journey I'll pursue;

Hinder me not, ye much-loved saints,

for I must go with you."

As the voices sing these sweet words of holy purpose and high resolve, that timid believer catches the inspiration and, just as the song ceases, walks to the front and takes the seat assigned him. He comes to ask for a place among the people of God. He tells them how he had felt himself to be a sinner, and how he had vainly tried to attain unto righteousness by reforming his life, till he should build up for himself a character exempt from all sin. And then he tells them of his deep distress when he found his own righteousness only a "filthy rag," and how he then cried unto the Lord for mercy, till at length he was able to believe in Jesus as his Savior, and being thus justified by faith found peace with God through our Lord Jesus Christ, and was able to rejoice in hope of His glory.

The account just given of the experience which a candidate for admission to a Baptist church was expected to give is only an outline, with all details omitted, but I think it covers every essential point.

When the candidate had finished his story, it was then in order for some brother to move that he should be admitted both to baptism and to the church. (Admission to both, though not always expressed, was always implied.) If the motion prevailed, then followed a song and the giving to the new brother the right hand of Christian fellowship.

Now, I know very well that the facts above set forth are perfectly familiar to many thousands of the present generation, for the mode of receiving members which I have described still lingers in many sections of our state. Forty years ago it was perhaps universal. But before leaving the subject, I wish to notice what seems to me to be some of the advantages of the old-time method of receiving members into the church.

First of all the relation of one's experience before the church is in many cases a cross. It is perhaps the first cross that a young convert finds in his path. To be able to take it up and joyfully to bear it affords him the opportunity to win the first victory in his religious life, and thus to strengthen himself for still greater struggles that are sure to follow. Jesus said: "If any man will be my disciple, let him deny himself and take up his cross and follow me." Self-denial and cross-bearing often involve each other and both are demanded when we propose to follow Christ.

Another advantage of this mode of receiving members is the fact that it promotes the fellowship of the churches. This is no small matter. It is well known that a common experience is one of the strongest ties that unite the people of God together. It endures through ages. The Christian of today, as he reads the experimental Psalms of David finds his own heart echoing the thoughts of those ancient songs. If these things are true, then a knowledge of one another's experience must promote our mutual fellowship.

A third advantage deserves to be noticed. The young convert, when he tells to the whole church the story of his conversion, begins to be a witness for Christ—he is another example of the saving power of the gospel. And many a time a thoughtless listener in the house may hear a word from a young convert that may send him home to repent and weep. Indeed, the very scene may produce a good effect. There was once a young lady with no thought of piety, as far as I know, who accompanied her pious mother to her church. It was conference day. When the door of the church was opened only one came forward, and he was a middle-aged Negro. The young lady said to herself: "Surely the church is not going to receive such a creature as that, he cannot tell an experience." Perhaps she scarcely deigned to listen to his words, preferring probably to indulge in her own thoughts. But presently, very much to her surprise, the members rose to their feet and, with a sweet song of welcome, began to give the humble candidate the right hand of fellowship. He had told an experience that was responded to by every pious heart in that house.

The lady saw that humble slave receiving from those who were high above him in social life a boon which she, at that time, dared not ask. The incident made a lasting impression upon her mind, and it was not very long before she told her experience in that same country church and received from those same brethren and sisters the right hand of fellowship. And her after life well illustrated the genuineness of her conversion.

That lady was my own beloved mother. She told me the above story when I was well advanced towards young manhood, which shows that the incident had deeply impressed her.

May this method of receiving members be perpetual among our Georgia Baptists.

Their Baptisms

Baptists hold that the first duty of a new convert is publicly to confess his repentance towards God and his faith in Christ by being baptized according to the Savior's commandment, and then to become a member of the church. When, therefore, he relates to the church his experience and they vote to receive him, that vote does not take effect to make him a member till after he has been baptized. As soon, therefore, as the church votes to receive him, the next thing to do is to arrange for his baptism, in order that he may be qualified to become a member of a church of baptized believers. All these points our Baptist fathers well understood, and practiced accordingly.

It was their custom to meet with the candidates for baptism at a convenient hour, under the blue sky, and beside some suitable body of water. Large congregations were generally on hand to witness the baptisms. There was something that made those baptisms exceedingly attractive. Else why should so many come together to witness them? Mere curiosity might have influenced some of the young and giddy, but it cannot explain the continued attendance of the matured and old men and women who were wont to assemble on such occasions. Curiosity is easily satisfied, and when satisfied ceases to act as a motive. No mere curiosity will not explain the phenomenon. May not the true explanation be found in the fact that a baptism, rightly performed, is a thing of divine origin? God is in it. It is the effective influence of His unseen presence that gives to it its attractiveness and its power.

Take these ideas away from the ordinance and how silly would a baptism appear! Think of that man who, nearly 2,000 years ago, came out of the wilderness, with his uncouth apparel and his unkempt locks. Was he not a fit subject of derision and ridicule? But, mark, he is not ridiculed. He utters strange words. He proclaims a startling fact—that "the kingdom of heaven is at hand" and, as a preparation for it, exhorts the people to repent and be baptized. We learn from his own lips that it was God who commanded him to baptize. Great multitudes attended his ministry, and many were baptized by him in the Jordan, confessing their sins. It was his privilege also to baptize our Savior and to proclaim Him to the people as the "Lamb of God which taketh away the sin of the world."

Such was the origin of baptism. And just such scenes as were enacted on the banks of the Jordan have been repeated through all the centuries down to the present time. The rivers of Georgia for more than a hundred years have often been signalized by Christian baptism, attended with thronging congregations. When Jesus gave the Great Commission to His disciples, He promised to be with them to the end of time. According to this promise, Christ is with His servant in baptism, and it is His unseen but effective presence that draws the people to the baptismal waters.

But this is not all. Baptism has a more important significance. Jesus Himself used it to represent His awful sufferings in the work of redemption. He said to James and John, "Are ye able to be baptized with the baptism that I am baptized with?" Here He speaks metaphorically. What does He mean? He must have meant that there was some great ordeal before Him whose fearful nature He expressed by calling it a baptism. He did the same thing on another occasion. He said to His disciples: "I have a baptism, to be baptized with, and how am I straitened till it be accomplished?" In both these cases He had reference to that great sorrow which ended in His burial and His resurrection, of which His baptism was a prophetic symbol. It foreshadowed His own death and resurrection.

But the significance of baptism reaches yet farther. After the day of Pentecost, while it still represented, retrospectively, the Savior's burial and His resurrection, and is now the memorial symbol of both, Paul turns it to the believer, and makes it represent to him his burial with Christ unto sin and his resurrection with Christ to a new and a better life, and finally his resurrection with Christ from the grave to the glories of the new heavens and the new earth.

The foregoing thoughts are not original. How could they be, while every baptism of a true believer has been, through the centuries, an object-lesson designed especially to teach them? Yet still they deserve to be often repeated, for they made baptism, when rightly administered, a witness for Christ and our holy religion, wherever it may be exhibited. I knew a learned infidel once who frankly confessed that there were two facts in support of Christianity which he could not set aside. These were the memorial supper and baptism.

The administration of the ordinance of baptism was as simple among our Baptist fathers as it well could be. When the church and candidates were assembled at the water's side, the pastor would open the services by calling for a suitable hymn. It was sung with feeling and pathos. Then followed a short address, sometimes to the candidates, explaining to them the need of consecrating themselves to the service of Christ, or, perhaps, expounding the significance of baptism. Sometimes he would exhort the church to watch over the young lambs that were coming into their fold. Or he might make a loving appeal to the unconverted, persuading them to come to Jesus. Then one by one, and sometimes two by two, he would gently lead them in their watery grave and bury them with Christ in baptism.

The effect of such baptisms we shall never know till we get to heaven. I will tell you, however, a few things that I have seen and heard. I have seen a mother overcome with holy joy because her daughter was one of several others who were about to put on Christ in baptism. The emotion overflowed and she praised God aloud for His goodness to her beloved child.

Again, I have seen a man, who was a sinner, weep before a large congregation when he led his wife whom he loved to the water's edge and gave her to the minister to be baptized. Then, at another time, there was a young man at a baptism. He had, while the people were gathering, not a serious thought about him. The services were conducted as usual, with no extra occurrences. But that young man confessed to a friend that the service from its very beginning to its close had affected him with unexpected and deep solemnity. What became of him afterwards I do not know, but the incident is significant. Here I must stop. It is enough for me to say that the memory of my baptism affords me some of the sweetest reminiscences of my life. And no doubt the same was true with the thousands of Baptist preachers who lived and died in Georgia during the last eighty years.

I tell you, brethren, there has been an unseen power in our baptisms. And is it to be wondered at? Did not Jesus say to His disciples: "Lo, I am with you always, even unto the end of the world"? And it is worthy of notice that He gave this promise in connection with the formula of baptism.

Now, what I have said in the foregoing paragraphs is not new to Georgia Baptists of today. Thank God, we still have the baptism of our fathers. But do we appreciate it as we ought? Are our pastors sufficiently careful so to minister it as not to abate its solemnity, nor to hinder its effect?

If the lives and conduct of Baptists were truly as scriptural as is their baptism, they would be an irresistible power in promoting the kingdom of Christ. May the Lord make our lives as pure as our creed—the Word of God.

Our Baptist fathers believed in a call to the ministry with full assurance of faith. It was a settled item of their creed that no man should take this office unto himself unless he was "called of God as Aaron was" (Heb. 5:4). As long ago as I can remember, these words were sure to be quoted when any attempt was made to explain the way into the Christian ministry. Those good brethren did not perceive that the writer to the Hebrews, when he used those words, was not speaking of the Christian ministry at all, but only of the Jewish priesthood. Failing to notice this fact, they applied the words to ministers of the gospel and made, therefore, a divine call an essential condition for admission to the ministry and, accordingly, it became an established rule among them to admit no one to ordination who could not give satisfactory evidence of having received such a call.

This rule has been perpetuated in our churches to the present day. It is true there are other qualifications besides a divine call that are deemed essential for ordination, but a divine call has been as much insisted upon as any other and especially by our Baptist fathers in Georgia. Were they right?

They who ignore the direct agency of the Holy Spirit in the religious life of a Christian will, of course, regret the rule and will contend that the fathers were wrong in adopting it. But those who believe in such agency of the Holy Spirit need not find any difficulty in answering the above question emphatically in the affirmative. Admit that our fathers supported the rule by one text, which, as had been already shown, was not relevant, it does not follow that they were wrong; because the doctrine of the Holy Spirit, as given in the New Testament, would justify us, "a priori," in expecting that He would exercise His agency in calling and qualifying men for so important a service as the preaching of the "glorious gospel of the blessed God." How can we suppose, for a moment, that the Holy Spirit should exercise His agency in "helping the infirmities" of the humblest saint and in "teaching him how to pray as he ought," and in "making intercessions for him with groanings that can not be uttered," and yet be indifferent to the selection of those who are to go forth to contend for the truth against all the powers of darkness? Such a thought is simply preposterous. This "a priori" argument might well be deemed sufficient, even if it stood alone. But it is triumphantly sustained by Paul's testimony.

His testimony is found in Rom. 12:3–8; 1 Cor. 12:4–11; Eph. 4:8–11. I can not conveniently quote these passages. If the reader, however, will turn to them and carefully read and compare them, he will discover that all special gifts bestowed upon church members that were to be exercised in public for the benefit of others and for the advancement of the gospel among men were bestowed by "one and the same Spirit, dividing to each one severally even as he will." These gifts include the preaching of the gospel. And forasmuch as it, as well as all the others, was bestowed by the sovereign will of the Spirit, it follows that its bestowment constituted to all intents and purposes a divine call to the ministry of the Word. It happens, therefore, that the fathers were right in demanding from every one who sought admission with their sanction and good will to that most sacred office a reasonable evidence of having received a divine call to the work.

In view of the foregoing facts we may well be proud of our spiritual ancestors. When we remember how little learning they had and to what extent they were dependent upon the Bible only for all that they knew, we are compelled to admire not only their loyalty to what they believed to be the truth, but also their wonderful correctness in the interpretation of the Scriptures. True, they found some passages which they could not comprehend. Others they may have treated allegorically when they were only literal narratives, and some they may have misapplied; but as to matters of faith and practice they were, indeed, seldom mistaken. They certainly were not mistaken when they believed in a divine call to the ministry. But what are the tests of such a call?

This question implies that it is possible to be deceived in this matter. Both the church and the applicant may be deceived, and thus one may be admitted to the ministry whom God has not called to that work. This melancholy fact invests the above question with grave importance. I wish I could answer it as fully as it deserves, but I can offer only a few suggestions.

In the first place, I think it may be assumed that the Holy Spirit does not call any man who is not truly regenerated to be an evangelist, i.e., a preacher of the gospel—or a pastor or bishop in the church. If this be true, then all the evidences of a true regeneration become a part of the evidences that one may be called to the ministry. But the evidences of regeneration are common to all true Christians. And we know that no one should be admitted to baptism and the church without these evidences; then much more, no one should be admitted to the ministry without them. The case may be concisely stated thus: The Holy Spirit does not call all true Christians to the ministry, but every one whom He does call must be a true Christian. And, therefore, his being indeed a child of God is an essential evidence that he is at least within the reach of the Spirit's call.

Another test of a divine call may be found in one's conformity to the character of a bishop as described by Paul (1 Tim. 3:2–7). The passage is too long to quote. It must suffice to say that the character drawn by Paul was intended to fit all the conditions of human life. But those conditions vary in different individuals. Paul speaks of the bishop whom he describes as a married man and as having a family. Now Paul could not have meant that a bishop, elder or pastor (these terms are only different titles of the same office) must of necessity be a married man, for that would have excluded himself and other apostles. He meant only this: that a married man to be a bishop should have but one wife and should rule his household in a proper manner. In a word, a bishop or pastor of today must have the character of the one which Paul described just as far as his conditions and opportunities will allow. And having such a character is an evidence that the Spirit may have called him.

There is yet another test which deserves to be noticed. It is found in the candidate's own experience. And this is the test which is the most important of all; for without it, unless he is a willful hypocrite, he would never consent to be ordained even if his brethren should advise it.

But suppose he is not a hypocrite, but a true Christian—willing to serve the Master in any way that may open before him.

Now, when we see such a man as this, after advice with his pastor and other pious friends, consenting to be set apart to the work of the ministry, we may know that he has what he thinks is a good reason for doing so. And that reason is found in the exercises of his own mind and heart. These exercises, carried on in the realm of his own consciousness make up an experience which is regarded as his "call to the ministry," which means that the experiences are the evidence of the call. It is, therefore, just as proper for the church to require a candidate for the ministry to give an account of his call to that work, as it is to require a candidate for baptism to give an account of his conversion.

What Constitutes a Call to the Ministry?

The importance of this question deserves a brief notice. During the first century of Baptist history in Georgia the attractions to the pulpit were very few. It promised no emolument or worldly glory. On the contrary, an entrance into the work of preaching the gospel demanded, from the very start, self-denial, sacrifice and hard labor, often attended with severe privations. Nor were these trials limited to the preacher only. Had this been so, he might have borne them with greater resignation. But the good wife shared fully the privations of her husband, while she had burdens of her own that were largely increased when he was away filling his regular appointments, or making a missionary tour to the regions beyond.

Another obstacle to one's entering the ministry in those days has been often alluded to in these reminiscences. It was the want of educational advantages. How could a plain man, without an education, undertake to expound to others that gospel which is declared to be the wisdom of God? Looking at the case from a human standpoint, it is truly wonderful that in those days any one should have consented to become a preacher. But the mystery is solved as soon as we admit that he was called of God by the agency of the Holy Spirit.

Let us then consider what are the constituent elements of such a call. They may be divided into two classes. Some are found in the soul itself. These are invisible and known only to him who has felt their influence. For this reason they may be named the subjective elements of a divine call. Others are found outside of us. These we can see and hear and touch. Hence they may be named the objective elements of a call. The subjective elements are perhaps the most important. They are impressions, feelings, inclinations, love and desires, having their place in the soul itself and culminating at length in one steady earnest purpose to go forth, with God's help, to proclaim the "glad tidings" of salvation to dying men and women, whether at home or abroad.

I have given only a general statement of the case. Let me amplify a little. The experience above mentioned may include on one side a joyful sense of all the glory involved in the saint's salvation and on the other side a profound sense of the awful doom of the sinner. The soul impressed by the touch of the Spirit with these vivid pictures would naturally become affected with intense feelings of thanksgiving for the saved, and of sympathy, pity, and love for the lost. These again, under the same Spirit, would lead on to earnest desires and active efforts to lift the lost from the sinner's doom up to the glories of the saints. All these affections, having their place in the soul of one who is seeking to know what the Lord would have him to do, may be well regarded as the voices of the Spirit calling him to the ministry of the Word. So much for the subjective elements of such a call.

The objective elements are no less real. They are made up of a series of providences so adjusted and directed by the unseen Spirit as to lead the subject of them straight into the pulpit. These providences are sometimes apparently trivial events—so trivial, indeed, that but for the results flowing from them they would not be remembered for a week. I know two cases that illustrate this point. One is the case of Dr. Albert Spalding. When quite a young man, while a student at Mercer University, it happened one day that a friend said to him in substance: "Brother Spalding, I heard Doctor Dagg this morning say of you, 'Brother Spalding ought to devote himself to the ministry.'" That was all; the young man smiled and went his way. But only recently I heard that dear brother confess that those brief words, coming from such a source, so impressed his mind that he began to inquire what the Lord would have him to do. We all know the result. For about forty years he has been a faithful laborer in the harvest fields of the Master.

The case of Dr. W. L. Kilpatrick affords another example. He too was a student at Mercer. On a certain day he happened to be in conversation with one of the professors, who it seems had been thinking that his young friend ought to be a preacher. The professor embraced the opportunity to talk to him upon the subject. In kind and gentle words he tried to set before him the claims of the ministry upon his heart and life, and earnestly advised him to seek, with humble prayer, how he might most successfully serve the Lord. Many years afterwards I heard Brother Kilpatrick allude to that conversation as the very beginning of his call to the ministry. It was then he took the first step in that noble life which has placed his name high on the roll of honor among Georgia Baptists.

The world may laugh at such incidents as these, and ascribe the importance we give them to an idle superstition. But we know that nothing is so small as to be beneath our Father's notice, and no means are too trivial to become efficient in the hands of His Holy Spirit. So it was in the cases mentioned. The words spoken were few and simple, but somehow they deeply impressed the hearers of those young brethren, somehow they were never forgotten, and somehow those brethren when far advanced in life, referred to those words as giving them their first impulse towards the ministry.

What does all this mean? Does it not mean that through those objective words the Holy Spirit was calling those young men to their appointed work?

Now these two cases may be generalized thus: When a good brother discovers, in any way, that his pious friends or his pastor, or all together, are somehow thinking of him as a suitable man for the ministry, he should certainly consider the matter prayerfully and earnestly. It may be that the approbation of his brethren is the medium through which the Spirit is whispering His gentle call to the path of duty. Indeed this conclusion becomes certain when we remember that the very qualifications which have enabled the young man to win the approbation of his brethren are the gifts of the Spirit. And in the same way, the honest inquirer may safely interpret any and all of those outward providences that shed light upon his pathway.

Then, when these objective evidences are carried inward, and added to the subjective affections already explained, they form together a proof of a divine call to the ministry that need not be doubted.

It has been shown that the old-time Baptists believed firmly in the reality of a divine call to the ministry. But many of them had some queer notions in regard to it. Not such, however, as to affect its reality. In this they believed. And hence every applicant for admission into the ministry was subjected to a critical examination as to his call.

Ordination—Deacons

The Baptist churches of America, as far as I know, have always inducted men into the ministerial office by the authority of the church with the aid of a council of elders, sometimes called a presbytery. Being themselves ministers in good standing, it was thought that they were better able to judge of the fitness of a candidate for the ministry than the members of the church would be if left to themselves; and their official position was supposed to qualify them to carry through the whole ceremony of setting apart the candidate for the work to which he was appointed.

Here two questions occur. Who shall choose or elect these officials? How shall they be set apart to their work? Baptists answer the first question by claiming that the New Testament clothes the church itself with full authority to elect its own officers. And in answer to the second, they claim that those chosen should be set apart to their official work in the way indicated by the example and teachings of the apostles, which, in the case of deacons, was by prayer and the imposition of hands, and in the case of ministers, by fasting and prayer and imposition of hands. These modes of setting apart church members to some official position are what we call ordinations. Our Baptist fathers practiced these ordinations with great care and with deep solemnity.

In the case of a deacon, they would call in one or two neighboring ministers to unite with the pastor in performing the service. The brother-elect was placed before elders. They proceeded to examine into his qualifications for the office. He was expected to relate his first religious experience that the elders might judge of the genuineness of his piety, and then he was examined on the doctrines of the gospel. When the elders were satisfied with his fitness for the office, then, with the concurrence and under the authority of the church previously given, the elders kneeled around the kneeling brother and one of them led in prayer, while all laid their hands upon his head. With that prayer, the whole church, usually on their knees, fervently united. When the prayer was ended, it was not uncommon for one of the council to address the newly appointed deacon, that he might explain to him the duties of his office and emphasize their great importance. And it was also in order for another elder to follow the first speaker with an address suited to the church, designed to explain their obligation to cooperate willingly and promptly with their deacons in all the services required of them.

Making allowance for slight variations, such was the ordination of a deacon in the old-time churches of Georgia Baptists.

I can remember when no Baptist in Georgia would venture to question its scriptural authority. And I well remember when and by whom I first heard it questioned. But I prefer not to mention names. It is enough to say that the argument against the practice was based upon two assumptions. One was this, that the "seven brethren" chosen by the church at Jerusalem, who were full of the Holy Spirit, and whom the apostles set apart to a special service, were not deacons at all, and therefore the setting of them apart by prayer and the imposition of hands can furnish no precedent for setting apart officers of a different kind in the same way.

Now, it is clear that this argument is based upon the assumption that the seven brethren set apart by ordination to a new and special service in the church at Jerusalem were not deacons. For the truth of this assumption there is no valid evidence. It is true, Luke does not call them deacons, but this omission is easily explained. The polity of the church was in its inchoate state. Jesus did not enact in advance a complete system of polity. He left it, in part, to be developed gradually as circumstances might require, under the guidance of His inspired apostles. And it is interesting to notice that the very first addition made by them to the polity of the church was the creation of a new order of church officials. They were appointed at first without a name, being designated only as "the seven." The design of their appointment, however, is clearly stated. It was that they should take charge of the resources of the church and so disburse them as to give to all what was just and equal, in order that the apostles might be freed from such work and be able to devote themselves exclusively to the "ministry of the Word." And this clearly means that they were also designed to help the apostles, who at that time were the acting elders of the church at Jerusalem.

Now, it came to pass in after years that churches were planted far and wide over many parts of the Roman Empire. And we learn, from the writings of the apostles, that there was in those churches an order of servants called deacons. The word "deacon" is a generic term, it is true, of wide application, according to its etymology. Its Greek origin in the New Testament is often applied to apostles and preachers, and when so applied it is rendered in our translation "minister," or by the more general term, "servant." Nevertheless, there was an order of servants in the churches distinct from all others, who were called, specifically, deacons.

Now it is, I think, universally conceded that to this class of officers was assigned the care of all the temporal interests of the churches, so that the pastors (or bishops or elders) might give undivided attention to the spiritual welfare of their people. This being granted, it follows that the duties assigned to the deacons were identical, in kind, with those assigned to the "seven" at Jerusalem. Therefore, we may conclude that the seven, though not so called, were really the very order to servants which was afterwards specifically named deacons. They were deacons, and hence the mode of their ordination does furnish us a clear example, under apostolic authority, which it is wise and safe to follow. Nay, are we not bound to follow it?

Those who reject the ordination of the "seven" as an example for us to follow, make another bold assumption. They say that the apostles who laid hands on the seven did so that they might confer upon them the Holy Spirit or some special spiritual gift.

Upon this assumption it is argued that as the power of imparting the Holy Spirit by the laying on of hands passed away with the apostles, it is now utterly useless to continue it.

But how do those who reason thus know that the apostles laid their hands upon the seven to impart to them some spiritual gift? This is a mere assumption, and altogether improbable. For the seven were already "full of the Holy Spirit," which means, at least, that they were men of deep and fervent piety, and hardly needed extra gifts from the hands of the apostles. They, indeed, had the power of conferring spiritual gifts upon whom they would, but it is reasonable to suppose that they would impart only to those who lacked. Let us then look for another reason.

Notice here that the apostles knew that they were about to establish a new order of servants; one which the church at Jerusalem already needed, and which all other churches, as they came into life and activity, would be sure to need. Was it not, therefore, discreet and proper to make the introduction of these new servants into their office impressive and solemn? If so, what better method could have been adopted than the one which we find reported? The record is very brief, but let us notice the several items which it gives us.

- The men were elected by the whole church as an independent body.

- The men chosen were expected to be "men of good report, full of the Spirit and of wisdom."

- They were placed before the apostles.

- "And when they had prayed, they laid hands on them," not to confer a spiritual gift, but in connection with the prayer to confer upon them only official position.

This the ceremony did do; and we do not know that it did anything else. I think, therefore, the argument based upon the second assumption is fairly answered.

Now, our Baptist fathers, as a rule, were not learned men or critics. And yet they took substantially the same view of this interesting subject that I have presented. This will appear more fully when I come to speak of the ordination of ministers. Let us still seek the old paths.

Ordination—Ministers

The two services were very similar, both in their conditions and in their forms. In each case the candidate was expected to be a man of deep piety and in each case he was set apart to his official position by prayer and the imposition of hands. But in the case of ministers something more was required. They were expected to be not only pious men, but also men who could give credible evidence of a divine call to the ministry. And they were set apart to their work not only by prayer and the imposition of hands, but these were preceded by fasting. At least, the members of the council, or presbytery, and the candidate were expected to come to the service fasting. This was considered of as much importance that if one of the appointed council happened to forget himself and to eat his breakfast on the day set apart for the service, he felt himself disqualified for assisting in the ordination. He would take a seat with the church members as only a spectator. If in this we should admit that he was overscrupulous, still the fact shows with what profound reverence those early Georgia saints approached an ordination service.

When the elders whom the church had invited to attend were assembled at the proper time and place, and were duly organized, then the candidate, with the consent and under the sanction of his church, came before the council.

I should have mentioned, however, that the candidate, before the ordination service began, was usually expected to preach on that morning in order to let the invited elders hear him, that they might have personal knowledge of his gifts as a public speaker. After this the candidate took his seat before the elders, who proceeded with the service. The chairman of the council conducted the examination.

He first requested the candidate to relate his experience, then to give a statement of his doctrinal views. The next step was to test his personal character and his life. To this end the chairman could either recite verbatim, or read from the Scriptures, the qualifications, given in 1 Tim. 3:1–7, which should adorn the life and character of one who desires to be made a bishop (elder or pastor). Here they touched his social and religious standing, both in the church and in the outside world. Of course they did not expect that candidate to speak for himself in regard to these qualifications. They knew that the church had enjoyed the best opportunity to know the brother's standing, and therefore, they could take it for granted that the church would not have given him their endorsement and called him to ordination if they had not believed that he possessed the requisite qualifications. Nevertheless, the Apostle's specifications were publicly read, and it was assumed, if no objection was made, that the candidate fairly met their requirements.

The next step in the examination was to have the candidate give some account of his call to the ministry; for our Baptist fathers believed with all their hearts in the reality of such a call. And their experiences on the subject were sometimes wonderful to tell. Some of them seemed to feel that it might show a little self-conceit if they should hearken at once to certain impressions which might indicate the drawings of the Spirit. They, therefore, from modesty and self-distrust, would resist the wooings of the Spirit for months and sometimes for years.

Such hesitation and delay not infrequently afforded occasion for the intervention of startling and sad providences. A man deeply impressed with his duty to labor for the salvation of souls, yet resisting his impressions, might be suddenly visited by some unexpected calamity. It might be the death of some beloved member of his household. Being already burdened with his inward experiences, is it strange that such a one should regard his bereavement as a judgment of God designed to make him yield to the monitions of the Spirit? And is it strange that, in the face of such incidents, a brother before a council should relate them as among the reasons why he believed that the Lord had called him?

However, it is pleasant and, no doubt, correct to believe that a great many of the old-time preachers did not wait to be scourged, as it were, into the ministry. They wisely gave heed to the impressions that weighed upon their hearts in respect to the question of duty before them. These impressions may have varied greatly in different persons. But I think there are three that are manifestly found in all true ministers. One is a sincere desire to promote the glory of God in the advancement of His kingdom. Another is a deep, abiding concern for the ungodly, accompanied with a strong desire, if possible, to lead them to Jesus. And the third is an earnest desire to build up the children of God in their faith and to promote, as far as possible, their growth in grace and in the knowledge of Christ.

These impressions may differ very much in degree, and they may be described in various terms, but each has its basis in the inspired Word. The first rests upon the injunction, "Whatsoever ye do, do all for the glory of God." the second rests upon the Savior's words, "Go, therefore, and make disciples among all nations." And the third rests upon His words to Peter, "Feed my lambs . . . feed my sheep." And taken together, they voice the sentiment of the Apostle when he says, "The love of Christ constrains us" that we should live, not for ourselves, but for him who died for us and rose again.

When these impressions become paramount in a believer's heart, there is a preacher in embryo. It will not be long before he will appear before the council, and it will not be difficult for him to relate his call to the ministry.

But it is time to return to the ordination.

The preliminary examination being closed, then the presbytery, or council, proceeded to the ordination proper. This was accomplished, as in the case of the deacons, with the consecrating prayer and the laying on of hands. Then followed one or more addresses, first to the candidate, designed to impress upon him the obligations which he had assumed and the great work upon which he had entered; and second, to the church, designed to remind them of their obligations to give to the brother, whom they had caused to be set apart to the work of preaching the gospel, all the moral support, sympathy and encouragement that might be in their power to give.

When the addresses were ended, the exercises were finally closed with an appropriate hymn, accompanied with the right hand of fellowship given to the newly made preacher as a token of the sympathy and love which the presiding elders and the church felt for him. Thus they sent him forth upon the great and solemn work assigned him.

I think that I have fairly set forth in the foregoing paragraphs what was the usual ordination service in our old-time churches of Georgia Baptists. And I am glad to hope and believe that our churches of the present generation follow very closely the example of our fathers in their ordination services.

But did our fathers have scriptural authority for their methods? They certainly did in every essential particular. We find it in the thirteenth chapter of Acts. We there learn that in the church at Antioch were prophets and teachers: viz., Barnabas, Simeon, Lucius, Manaen, and Saul. In all, five persons are named. We learn also that two of them—Barnabas and Saul—had not yet been set apart by any formal or visible action to the work to which God had called them. Subsequent events plainly show that that work was the preaching of the gospel—the work of the ministry, as it is called in our day. Again, we learn that while they were engaged in some sort of service, "the Holy Spirit said, Separate me Barnabas and Paul for the work whereunto I have called them." How was this separation accomplished? The record gives the answer: "Then, when they had fasted and prayed and laid their hands on them, they sent them away." Simeon, Lucius, and Manaen were, no doubt, the officiating ministers. The narrative is very short, but as far as it goes, it certainly affords a clear example in all essential particulars of what we call an ordination of a minister.

I close with a single admonition. Let us most carefully avoid all departures from the New Testament. The only example of the ordination of a minister found in the New Testament mentions fasting as a part of the service. And our fathers observed it. Let not our churches now fail to follow their example in adhering closely to the inspired Word.

In approaching this topic let us bear in mind that Georgia Baptists have generally lived in the country. During the early decades of the century there were hardly a half-dozen towns in the state that had in them a Baptist church. And even now the great majority of our people are in the country, and there are their churches. Under such conditions it is not surprising that their social privileges, especially in the early days, were greatly hindered.

Their Visits and Special Occasions

Nevertheless they did make visits occasionally to one another. The visits were not "pop calls." The visitor, or visitors, would make arrangement to be absent from home at least for a day, and sometimes for several days. It was perfectly in order for the lady visitors to take their work baskets with them, that they might not have to sit with idle hands during the passing hours. And it was equally in order for the kind hostess, after she had greeted her visitors and put away their shawls and bonnets and seated them in her best room, to withdraw awhile to the pantry to arrange with the cook for a dinner that should be worthy of her guests. Having thus provided for the claims of hospitality, she would return to her company, and, sitting down by her own work basket and resuming her task where she had left it, she would open with her friends the fountains of social enjoyment, aided by her husband and perhaps by her older children.

Besides these occasional visits, there were a few other opportunities of social intercourse. There were the quilting parties, which some of our older readers may remember. To these may be added the barbecues, which are still well known as means of bringing into social contact chiefly the male population of the country. Then there were the everlasting marriage festivals that have survived the ravages of time and are likely to continue to the end of the present era.

I have made special mention of these phases of social life, because church members, of all denominations, felt themselves at liberty to enjoy them. But after all, they afforded only an occasional opportunity of coming together, for the reason that in any given neighborhood years might pass without any one of them. However, as often as there was opportunity, it was deemed admissible for religious people freely to share them, for they brought together the best elements of each neighborhood and cultivated among the people pleasant and lasting friendships.

But the social life of our fathers and mothers of the olden time had in it an element that deserves to be most strongly emphasized. This was their religious conversation.

I do not mean to claim this element of social life for Baptists only, but it is a matter of joyful thanksgiving to God that they possessed it (and in a high degree) in common with all truly religious people of other denominations. They might meet on social visits, as already mentioned, or at the quilting, or at a dinner, or at a wedding—no matter where—they would not be together long without speaking of Jesus and His love, or of some item in the Christian experience. In a word, religion, when Christians were together, and time and opportunity allowed, was sure to be, in all its phases, the leading staple of conversation.

Some good effects of this custom were to strengthen their own spirituality and to promote their own growth in grace. Another effect was to impress their children with the importance of religion. When they saw how much their parents delighted to talk about religion, they could not fail to see that their parents regarded it as the chief concern of this present life. So great a place did religious conversation hold in the social life of early Georgia Baptists.

Their Social Worship

Another element of that life was found in their social worship.

What is social worship? It is the worship of two or three pious souls who have met for the purpose in the name of Jesus. The number may be few or many. The place may be anywhere under the blue sky that Christians may choose to meet that they may worship the Father in spirit and in truth. It is not too much to say that in social worship the social life of the saints reaches the very highest development that it can ever reach this side of heaven. For it is social worship that weaves the golden threads of Christian fellowship that bind together, in one body, the consecrated brotherhood of the saints. Such is the power of social worship.

When a father and a mother have around them a family of children whom they would train up in the nurture and admonition of the Lord, they can not safely dispense with family prayer. And this is the first form of social worship. What a privilege it is for anxious parents! It makes their house a Bethel, nay, it makes the little chamber, when they gather around the old Bible that lies upon the stand ever ready to pour forth from its inspired pages the light of the great "Shekinah," the antitype of that "most Holy Place," with its golden altar and mysterious "mercy seat," which lay behind the curtain within the ancient tabernacle (see Heb. 10:1–23). Can we ever overestimate the value of family prayer? The father who conducts it is the priest of his household.

He brings to the domestic altar, not the blood of dumb animals, but the blood of Christ, "which speaketh better things than the blood of Abel." Yes, in many a poor man's cottage, in many a widow's home, there goes up to heaven, through faith in the crucified One, a purer worship than even Solomon was ever able to render.

Now, I do not claim that family prayer was universally observed in every household of our Baptist fathers, but I do say that as far as my memory can reach it was not the exception but the rule in truly pious families.

Again we have another form of social worship. It is found in the prayer meeting. This is only the expansion of family worship. It is a meeting together of one or more from several families for prayer and praise and thanksgiving, and for hearing some scriptural lesson read and expounded. Under favorable conditions it is the natural outgrowth of family worship, with a larger circle of social influence and of religious power. How did the old-time churches regard the prayer meeting? They dearly loved it.

I am sure that this is true, although they did not often have the privilege of attending a prayer meeting. Their churches were, with few exceptions, located in the country, which was so sparsely settled that church members were too widely scattered to meet at night, with any sort of regularity, either at private houses or at the meeting house. They were, therefore, limited for the most part to occasional opportunities. These occurred sometimes during district and associational gatherings. At such times delegates and visitors would be distributed in groups among the neighboring families for the night in sufficient numbers to make up a prayer meeting. I know from personal experience how delightful such prayer meetings could be made. The services at the meeting house during the day and in the neighboring cottages at night afforded much enjoyment to pious people.

Their Public Worship

This was held, with a few exceptions, but once a month. Only in the cities and in some of the more important towns were the

Baptists able to have public worship more frequently. And many of them had to be satisfied with two Sundays.

At such meetings the pastor, if present, would of course preach, unless a visiting minister was on hand. In that case the pastor would generally invite the visiting brother to preach for him, and it was not unusual for both to preach, sometimes with and sometimes without an intermission. When the visitor came unexpectedly and no second service was anticipated, then the two sermons would both be preached, one right after the other, without any recess; but if two services were anticipated, and the good sisters had brought refreshments, then there would be two services—one in the morning, followed by a recess, during which it was in order to enjoy the refreshments provided by the sisters. It is true, they had no booths woven of green boughs, for they did not need them. They had for their shelter the rich foliage of the majestic oaks and other lofty trees that shaded the ground around the meeting house, and yet, a Bible reader, in looking upon such a scene, would be reminded of "the feast of tabernacles" which the ancient Hebrews loved so well. It was a scene of social enjoyment, modified to a large extent by the prevalence of the religious sentiment, and the effect was to cultivate the most friendly relations among all the people of the neighborhood, and to develop among church members a deeper sense of Christian fellowship.

On such occasions, the preaching was based, in a large measure, upon the Christian experience. This was a subject which the preachers understood. They could present it in all its many-sided aspects, and they knew the Scriptures that served to illustrate it from Genesis to Revelation. Hence it became in their hands a mighty means of "strengthening their brethren" and of building them up in the faith and hope of the gospel.

Nor was this all. While such preaching was more especially designed to instruct and to comfort believers, yet it was by no means intended only for them. It often passed beyond the saints and carried enlightenment and comfort to many a mourning soul and troubled penitent. Indeed, these sermons of the experience often sent arrows of swift conviction to pierce the hearts of the ungodly. When the preacher had strengthened and comforted his people with the sweet realities of a genuine experience, he could then, with great power and pathos, appeal to the unconverted before him with that fearful warning "the sinner must be born again"—a warning which the Christian's experience both strongly emphasizes and clearly confirms. The sinner must be born again. And the preachers of the olden time made the people feel it.

In noticing the customs of our Baptist fathers when met for worship, it is certainly in order to say something about their singing.

Religious music is as old as Moses and Miriam. It was illustrated by David, and became at an early day an important part of the services that were offered to the great Jehovah. And Jesus gave it His sanction, for we learn that when He was with His disciples for the last time, they sang a hymn before they went forth to meet the dreadful scenes that were so soon to follow. Then, years afterwards, we read that Paul and Silas, in the prison at Philippi, cheered the midnight hours with sacred song.

With such antecedents, it is not strange that music should accompany the worship of the saints through all the succeeding centuries. In the face of such facts, we need not doubt that it was a part of the divine purpose to make singing one medium through which the pious worshiper might lift his thanksgivings and his longings up to the very throne of God. That it was designed to be such a medium is clearly taught by Paul. Speaking to the Ephesian church he says: "Be filled with the Spirit, speaking to yourselves in psalms and hymns and spiritual songs, singing and making melody in your heart unto the Lord."

According to these words, sacred song should be the outward expression of the inward affections of the soul towards God.

The world has its songs; thus we hear the lover praising in song the charms of his mistress. Then we hear the votary of nature describing in song her diversified beauties as they shine on earth from all its varied scenery, or glow in the skies with all the glory of the stars. Again, we hear the patriot celebrating in song the good and the great, the heroes and the statesmen—in a word, all distinguished benefactors, who have lived to honor and to bless the land of their nativity. In all these cases it is manifest that the function of song is to express the feelings of the soul.

In the cases above mentioned, it is obvious that in each case the music should be rightly adapted to the object which it is designed to celebrate. Who would think of celebrating the towering heights of Mont Blanc, with all its awful wonders of crag and cliff and avalanche, in the same strain with which a lover would serenade his sweetheart?

But there is an object higher than Mont Blanc, more awful than the avalanche, and yet, more lovely than the flowery earth, or the garnished skies, and far more worthy of gratitude and of thanksgiving than any human friend or benefactor can ever be. That object is God. And it is in His worship that song should find its highest and noblest exercise. And surely it ought to be in measures worthy of the exalted being whose praises it is designed to celebrate.

Now where shall we find such music? Not in the organ, or cornet, or flute, or violin. These are, or should be, only accompaniments. When they stand alone, their volume of sound can rise no higher than the vaulted ceiling of the auditorium. Such music can be found only in the "scriptural songs" wherewith the worshiper makes sweet "melodies in his heart" unto God.

I think this was the kind of music which was often heard in the old-time churches. They wanted music that would voice their religious affections of every kind, and their hymns were adapted to supply this want. They might be sometimes affected with penitential sorrow, perplexed with painful doubts, or they might be in full assurance of faith rejoicing in the love of God and in the hope of heaven, or they might be melted with tender compassion for the ungodly who are without hope. Well, there were hymns suited to express all these emotions, and when our fathers and mothers sang them, their holy desires were wafted up to heaven. There may have been but little culture, there may have been some harsh sounds and perhaps some discords, but the Lord, in spite of such imperfections, could discern the melodies that came up from the heart, and these He graciously accepted. Oh, that we could have again some of the old-time hymns! Well do I remember them, and greatly do I miss them.

Their Doctrinal Views

Throughout these reminiscences, it has been assumed, and often mentioned in terms, that our Baptist fathers were sound in their faith. But before leaving the old-time churches it may be well to treat their doctrinal views a little more fully than has yet been done.

The Baptists of Georgia, from the very beginning of their development in this state, acknowledge no authority in matters of "faith and of practice," except the Scriptures. It is true, each church had what was called its abstract of principles, or its confession of faith. But this abstract, or confession, was adopted by each church, as an independent body, for itself, and it was held to be valid only so far as its subscribers believed it to be in harmony with the Bible. In controversies with their opponents, Baptists never appeal to the confessions found in their church records, but directly and exclusively to the inspired Word. And so did our fathers of the long ago. They were loyal to the Scriptures as they understood them.

I do not mean to claim that those early Baptists had no diversities of opinion among them. This could hardly be expected. When we consider how people differ from one another in environment, in intelligence, in habits of thought, and in the structure of their sensibilities, is it any wonder that they should differ somewhat when they undertake to discuss the grave questions of religious truth? Is it not rather wonderful that they should agree at all? And yet our fathers did agree to such an extent that they were one people in Christian fellowship.

I do not propose here to formulate their creed, for their creed was the Bible, and to attempt to outline its teachings would far exceed my limits. I propose rather to state the things they believed in a way of my own, and yet all the essential elements of their faith.

They believed in the God of the Bible. I put the item in this form because it distinguishes them, at once, from every other class of theists known upon the face of the earth. This distinction has become important in these modern times. There are people who openly declare the God of the Bible to be unworthy of their love or worship. Then there are others who, less bold, will not go quite so far in their blasphemy. They even profess to accept the Bible as in some degree a revelation from God. But those passages that express the burning wrath of God against the wicked, that foretell the coming judgment and the perdition of ungodly men, are erased by a reckless criticism as altogether unworthy of their conceptions of what the character of God ought to be. Which means, that if the rejected passages should prove to be genuine, then these wise critics would claim that they could no longer reverence or love the God of the Bible. The God which they pretend to worship is a God which they have constructed for themselves under the dominating influence, not of right reason (as they proudly claim), but of their carnal sensibilities. And the thing which they have thus thought out is as truly an idol as if it had been cut by the hand of the sculptor from a block of marble.

Against all such perversions our Baptist fathers accepted the God of the Bible. And they claimed no other. Nay, they would have no other. Hence, it followed, as a matter of course, that their theology was the theology of the Bible. True, they could see the glory of God as it shines in the phenomena of nature; but they saw that glory more effulgent as it shines through the revelation which God has given of Himself in His own inspired Word. In all this our fathers were thoroughly agreed.

They believed all that the Bible teaches us about God. This, indeed, is a logical inference from what has gone before, but it may be useful to notice briefly what the fathers believed that the Bible does teach about God.

- They believed that God has revealed Himself to us as the Father, the Son, and the Holy Spirit, constituting a compound Unity, which, in modern times, we have learned to call the "Holy Trinity."

- They believed that this triune God is the creator of the heavens and of the earth, and of all that is in them.

- They believed that He is a being absolutely perfect in all the attributes of His exalted nature, and is in fact the absolute sovereign of the universe which He has created, and its rightful Lawgiver and Ruler.
- They also believed that God created man in His own image, or likeness, and endowed him with such faculties of mind and heart as qualified him to be an intelligent and voluntary agent, and a fit subject of moral government.

In regard to all these points also, our Baptist fathers were in perfect agreement. But this is not all.

They believed that God had devised before the foundation of the world a plan for the salvation of mankind. Account for it as we may, it is a fact that the human race has suffered through all the centuries of its existence as if it had been from the beginning accursed of God. But behind the curse, there lay in the bosom of God a purpose of mercy. It was the great scheme of human redemption. Its first intimation to man was heard amidst the curses which drove him away from the Garden of Eden. It was then announced that "the seed of the woman should bruise the serpent's head." These words spanned the dark cloud of divine wrath that overhung our first parents at the Garden of Eden with a bow of promise far more precious than the sevenfold arch that gilded the clouds of the retiring deluge. This was a promise of exemption from only a future deluge of water, but the words at the Garden betokened a deliverance of men from the awful flood of moral guilt and ruin into which the great adversary had plunged them.

The scheme of redemption thus foretold brings to our view the three exalted persons of the Godhead. "The Father so loved the world that he gave his only begotten Son, that whosoever believeth on him might not perish, but have eternal life." Then we learn that the Son, when speaking of His approaching death, said: "I lay down my life for the sheep; no man taketh it from me. I have power to lay it down, and I have power to take it again." Here it is clear He made Himself a free will offering to His Father as a ransom for His people. Then the Holy Spirit is often mentioned as the divine agent who gives efficiency to the Word of God upon the heart of the sinner that he may be quickened into spiritual life and become a child of God. Thus it is manifest that the triune God, in the great work of redemption, is One. Hence it is evident, and it is a great comfort to know it, that the Holy Three are working together in perfect fellowship for the salvation of lost sinners.

What has been said so far brings to our view another great truth. It is that the plan of salvation is founded upon the expiatory sufferings of our Lord and Savior Jesus Christ who was the Son of God. He took upon Himself our nature, sin only excepted, and made Himself an offering for sin, that "God might be just and the justifier of him who believeth in Jesus." The Scriptures abound with proof that Jesus "died for our offenses, and was raised again for our justification." So He became "the Lamb of God who taketh away the sin of the world."

I have already said that our Baptist fathers believed in the plan of salvation. And I feel sure that they also believed in the important truths which we have found to be included in its conditions and which have been briefly set forth in the foregoing paragraphs.

Our Baptist fathers believed in the fall of man from his first estate of innocence and purity into a state of moral guilt and pollution, and they believed that the effect of this fall of our first parents, from innocence to a state of guilt, was transmitted to their posterity to such an extent that every human being comes into the world with a proclivity to moral evil so intense that he inevitably falls into transgression and sin. This proclivity to moral evil is what we call human depravity.

Our fathers believed in this depravity. They sometimes called it "total depravity," and for doing so they were often severely criticized, and even ridiculed, by their opponents. Well, it is needless, at this late day, to discuss the propriety or impropriety of qualifying depravity with the word "total." It is better, far better, to notice what the Scriptures say about it. We learn from them that the human heart is "desperately wicked," that "the carnal mind is enmity against God: for it is not subject to the law of God, neither indeed can be," and that men, by nature, are "dead in trespasses and in sins." Such are the terms in which man's moral condition is described in the Bible. It is certainly a condition of depravity so deep that the sinner, if left to himself, is, and must be, inevitably lost. And this is the depravity in which our early Baptists believed.

The doctrine of human depravity renders it logically necessary that the sinner, if he is ever saved, must be "born again." Simple as this proposition is, there are thousands, even of cultivated minds, who ignore the new birth. Nicodemus was one of this class. When, in John 3:3, Jesus said to him, "Except a man be born again, he can not see the kingdom of God," he did not know what the Savior meant. But our Baptist fathers had sense enough to see the necessity of the new birth. They knew that the sinner, being at enmity with God, not subject to His law but dead in trespasses and in sins must forever perish, unless he could be brought, somehow, into a new condition of life. By their confidence in the teachings of the Scriptures they were able to discover that the "new birth" which Jesus taught to Nicodemus metaphorically represents this coming into a new condition of life, and this they had realized in their own Christian experiences.

Their first condition of life, into which they had come by a literal and natural birth, was a condition of deep moral depravity. They did not love God, nor did they desire a knowledge of His ways. They were willing to be worldly-minded, hard-hearted and impenitent, and were, perhaps, indulging in many practical sins. And such was the degree of depravity that, if left to themselves, they would have chosen to live and die in that sad condition.

But it came to pass that they were brought within the reach of the preached gospel, and by its instrumentality, under the direct agency of the Holy Spirit, they were brought through the successive steps of the Christian experience into a new condition of life. Now this coming into a new condition of life is just what the Savior meant when He said: "Except a man be born again he can not see the kingdom of God."

Notice the word "again." It is represented in the Greek by the word "anothen." It has three meanings: again, anew, from above. It is interesting to notice that each one of these meanings will translate the word "anothen" so as to yield a good sense. If we say a man is born again, it means that he had been born before and is now born a second time. Well, that is true of the Christian, for he was first born into his natural life and afterwards into his spiritual life. If we say that a man is born anew, it means that he has left his old life and come into one that is new and fresh. This also is verified in the experience of the Christian. For of him it is written: "Old things have passed away, and all things have become new." And, in the third place, if we say a man is born from above, the phrase is used figuratively to denote that he is born of God. And this, too, is confirmed by other Scriptures; for we learn that believers are born, "not of blood, nor of the will of the flesh, nor of the will of man, but of God." And again, it is said: "Of his own will begat he us, by the word of truth." Therefore to be born from above, as already stated, is to be born of God.

The nature of the new birth is still more fully expressed, and yet on the same line of thought, in the fifth verse of the same chapter: "Verily, verily, I say unto thee, except a man be born of water and of the Spirit, he can not enter into the kingdom of God." When the metaphorical terms of this text are correctly interpreted the meaning of the Savior's words may be expressed in plain language thus: Verily, verily, I say unto thee, except a man be brought into life (which is to be born) through the instrumentality of divine truth (often represented in the Scriptures by water) and by the direct agency of the Holy Spirit, he can not enter into the place where God reigns.

This paraphrase is in harmony with Dr. J. L. Dagg's interpretation of the text, and fully sustains the correctness of his definition of the new birth. I have not his definition before me, but it is to this effect, that the new birth denotes a great moral change of a sinner's affections towards God, analogous to a coming into a new life, of which God is the author, and whose manifestations are found in the sinner's desire to glorify God and to obey His commandments. This change is sometimes called a conversion, sometimes a change of heart, and sometimes it is spoken of as a new creation.

Our Baptist fathers believed with all their hearts in the necessity of this great moral change in the heart and life of the sinner before he could be prepared for heaven. And to describe its process through all the stages of the Christian experience engaged a large proportion of their conversation and their preaching.

I have dwelt thus long on the new birth because of its transcendent importance. It is one of the distinctive doctrines of Christianity that separates it, by an immeasurable distance, from every other religion on this globe. And yet, strange as it may seem, two-thirds of all Christendom have for many centuries so merged it in water baptism that they have nothing left of the grand idea save a fruitless ceremony of their own invention. The baptismal font, and that for unconscious babes, is made to do the work of regeneration.

Only a few religious denominations of the present day stand for the doctrine of the new birth as it was taught by Jesus and His inspired apostles. But out Baptist fathers stood for it with unwavering fidelity. They found it in the words of Christ and they found His words illustrated in their own happy experiences.

Now, beloved brethren of the present day, let me close this paper with a word to you. You have succeeded to the responsibilities of your fathers. That you are spiritually and denominationally so prosperous is because they were so faithful. True, they were not perfect, they made some mistakes and held some queer notions but, for all that, they did contend earnestly for the faith once for all delivered to the saints, and especially did they teach with all their hearts that "the sinner must be born again, or sink in endless woe." Let your choruses sound aloud this awful refrain till every soul shall hear it.

Election was also a cardinal point in the faith of our fathers, and their preachers gave it conspicuous place in their sermons. They believed that God knew from the beginning who would be saved. And then they believed that no sinner, if left to himself, would ever repent towards God and believe in Christ, inasmuch as he is by nature "at enmity with God, not subject to his law, neither indeed can be." Putting these ideas together, our fathers were able to see that whoever is saved must be renewed in the spirit of his mind, that is, he must be quickened into spiritual life, by the direct agency of the Holy Spirit. In other words, no man can be saved without that great moral change called the new birth, of which God is the author. And in every new birth God must take the initiative step. He must, of His own will, beget the sinner by His word of truth (see James 1:18). Each case is of his own will, which means of his own choice. When did God make choice of this or that sinner as a subject of His saving power? Surely His choice, or election, must be as old as His foreknowledge. Therefore the election must have been before the foundation of the world.

The doctrine of the final perseverance of the saints is a logical sequence of the doctrine of election, so closely connected with it that to accept one is to accept the other. Those good people of whom I am writing believed in it, of course. They called it the "final perseverance of the saints." And to this day our Baptist folks are accustomed to use the same phrase. But it is not accurate, and, moreover, it puts a weapon into the hands of our opponents. They sometimes point to some backslider among us and tauntingly ask: "What has become of his perseverance?" The question is hard to answer.

The truth is, the phrase does not express exactly what it is used to express. The thing which our fathers believed in, and which is so closely connected with election, was the doctrine of the final preservation of the saints. This mode of expressing the certainty of the saint's salvation clearly suggests the divine power by which it is accomplished. For we read that the saint is "kept by the power of God through faith, unto salvation, ready to be revealed in the last time." This is by far a much safer reliance than can be found in the perseverance of the individual.

Our fathers gained great comfort from these doctrines. Think for a moment what the doctrine of election means. It means the certain salvation of a multitude whom no man can number. Remember, without election no one of Adam's apostate race would have been saved, for the whole race was dead in trespasses and in sins, and under sentence of condemnation. But God was moved with compassion for the lost race. Out of that compassion arose the great scheme of redemption by which he could offer free salvation to all who would accept it. But none would accept it. Here occurred the gravest problem in the counsels of the Godhead that can be found, perhaps, in all the annals of eternity. It was the election that solved this mighty problem. God, in the exercise of His infinite sovereignty, chose whom He would have to be saved. These are the people whom He foreknew, "whom he did predestinate to be conformed to the image of his son." And these are the people whom, in the course of time, He has been effectually calling and sanctifying and glorifying (Rom. 8:29–30).

But for this electing grace, not one sinner would have been saved; for such is the depravity of human nature that if left to himself the sinner would not accept the gospel and Christ would have died in vain. But God, in foretelling the mission of His Son, has already declared, by the lips of His prophet Isaiah, that the great Messiah should "see of the travail of his soul and be satisfied," which means that He should not die in vain.

To this divine purpose the Savior Himself alludes. He says to the unbelieving multitude around Him, "All that the Father giveth me shall come unto me, and him that cometh unto me I will in no wise cast out" (John 6:37). These words mean that Jesus knew that He had a people secured to Him, by the gift of the Father, whose salvation was assured. Therefore, Jesus knew that He should not die in vain—that His blood should redeem such a multitude of the lost as to satisfy the travail of His soul.

Such were the doctrines that our fathers loved. They found in them streams of living water flowing from the "smitten Rock" that cheered and comforted them. They were able to see that the powers of darkness might mass their forces round the globe, but they could never separate the elect of God from His eternal love (see Rom. 8:38–39).

In treating of the doctrinal views of the old-time churches, I have thus far confined myself to those elements of faith for which they were generally distinguished. Thus far I have presented them as beacon lights of orthodoxy to which the churches of today would do well to give good heed. And just here I would gladly stop. But it may be useful to notice briefly what may be called the other side.

While our early Baptists believed, with great harmony, in all the "doctrines of grace," as they were often called, yet this common faith did not bring forth in all exactly the same fruit. The effect of that faith on some minds was to make them willing to live, not for themselves, but for Him who died for them and rose again. Some reasoned, perhaps, in this way: I was a lost sinner, so completely in bondage to a depraved nature that if I had been left to myself I should have certainly perished, but God, for the great love wherewith He loved me, quickened my soul into spiritual life that I might believe and be saved. The idea that that love was from the beginning only intensified its force. All who reasoned thus were ready to engage in every good work that promised glory to God or good to man. When, therefore, the great missionary enterprise burst upon them, they were prepared to meet it. They knew that Christ has a people by the gift of the Father who shall come to Him and be saved, but they knew also that the gospel is the ordained instrumentality whereby the elect are to be gathered unto Christ. And, therefore, they were called "Missionary Baptists."

But all did not reason thus. Their argument was about this: God's purposes are fixed and immutable. Therefore the salvation of His elect is certain and man has nothing to do with it. Here was a most hurtful perversion of the doctrines of grace. Those who held to it were call anti-missionaries. But their opposition did not stop at missions. They denounced Sunday schools, temperance societies, and all efforts that aimed to give a better education to our ministry.

The history of this sad division among our fathers is too well known to need recital here. We rejoice to know that it has wellnigh passed away. Our church polity allows to every church absolute independence. Therefore, as our churches grew more enlightened, one by one, or in groups, they became missionaries and without a shock transferred themselves from the one body to the other. This process is still going on, and the Georgia Baptists are rapidly becoming again one people.

Chapter Ten

Baptists and Religious Liberty (May 16, 1920)

GEORGE W. TRUETT

Foreword

This address was arranged for weeks before the Southern Baptist Convention met in Washington. Washington City Baptists are directly responsible for it. The speaker, Dr. George W. Truett, pastor First Baptist Church, Dallas, Texas, was chosen by a representative group of Baptists to deliver the address. It was delivered to a vast audience of from ten to fifteen thousand people from the east steps of the national capital, three o'clock Sunday afternoon, May 16, 1920. It was not a convention session, though the convention was largely represented in the audience by its members.

Since Paul spoke before Nero, no Baptist speaker ever pleaded the cause of truth in surroundings so dignified, impressive, and inspiring. The shadow of the capitol of the greatest and freest nation on earth, largely made so by the infiltration of Baptist ideas through the masses, fell on the vast assembly, composed of Cabinet members, Senators and members of the Lower House, Foreign Ambassadors, intellectuals in all callings, with peoples of every religious order and of all classes.

The subject was fit for the place, the occasion, and the assembly. The speaker had prepared his message. In a voice clear and far-reaching he carried his audience through the very heart of his theme. History was invoked, but far more, history was explained by the inner guiding principles of a people who stand today, as they have always stood, for full and equal religious liberty for all people.

There was no trimming, no froth, no halting, and not one arrogant or offensive tone or word. It was a bold, fair, thoroughgoing setting out of the history and life principles of the people called Baptists. And then logically and becomingly the speaker brought his Baptist brethren to look forward and take up the burdens of liberty and fulfill its high moral obligations, declaring that defaulters in the moral realm court death.

Truett's address advances the battle line for the denomination. It is a noble piece of work, worthy the wide circulation it is sure to receive. Intelligent Baptists should pass it on.

A serious word was said in that august presence concerning national obligations as they arise out of a civilization animated and guided by Christian sentiments and principles. As a nation we cannot walk the ways of selfishness without walking downhill.

I commend this address as the most significant and momentous of our day.

J. B. Gambrell, President, SBC

Southern Baptists count it a high privilege to hold their Annual Convention this year in the national capitol, and they count it one of life's highest privileges to be citizens of our one great, united country. . . .

It behooves us often to look backward as well as forward. We should be stronger and braver if we thought oftener of the epic days and deeds of our beloved and immortal dead. The occasional backward look would give us poise and patience and courage and fearlessness and faith. The ancient Hebrew teachers and leaders had a genius for looking backward to the days and deeds of their mighty dead. They never wearied of chanting the praises of Abraham and Isaac and Jacob, of Moses and Joshua and Samuel; and thus did they bring to bear upon the living the inspiring memories of the noble actors and deeds of bygone days. Often such a cry as this rang in their ears: "Look unto the rock whence ye were hewn, and to the hole of the pit whence ye were digged. Look unto Abraham, your father, and unto Sarah that bare you; for when he was but one I called him, and I blessed him, and made him many" (Isa. 51:1).

Religious Liberty: A Supreme Contribution

We shall do well, both as citizens and as Christians, if we will hark back to the chief actors and lessons in the early and epoch-making struggles of this great Western democracy, for the full establishment of civil and religious liberty—back to the days of Washington and Jefferson and Madison, and back to the days of our Baptist fathers, who have paid such a great price, through the long generations, that liberty, both religious and civil, might have free course and be glorified everywhere.

Years ago, at a notable dinner in London, that world-famed statesman, John Bright, asked an American statesman, himself a Baptist, the noble Dr. J. L. M. Curry, "What distinct contribution has your America made to the science of government?" To that question Dr. Curry replied: "The doctrine of religious liberty." After a moment's reflection, Mr. Bright made the worthy reply: "It was a tremendous contribution."

Indeed, the supreme contribution of the new world to the old is the contribution of religious liberty. This is the chiefest contribution that America has thus far made to civilization. And historic justice compels me to say that it was pre-eminently a Baptist contribution. The impartial historian, whether in the past, present or future, will ever agree with our American historian, Mr. Bancroft, when he says: "Freedom of conscience, unlimited freedom of mind, was from the first the trophy of the

Baptists." And such historian will concur with the noble John Locke who said: "The Baptists were the first propounders of absolute liberty, just and true liberty, equal and impartial liberty." Ringing testimonies like these might be multiplied indefinitely.

Not Toleration, but Right

Baptists have one consistent record concerning liberty throughout all their long and eventful history. They have never been a party to oppression of conscience. They have forever been the unwavering champions of liberty, both religious and civil. Their contention now is, and has been, and please God, must ever be, that it is the natural and fundamental and indefeasible right of every human being to worship God or not, according to the dictates of his conscience, and, as long as he does not infringe upon the rights of others, he is to be held accountable alone to God for all religious beliefs and practices. Our contention is not for mere toleration, but for absolute liberty. There is a wide difference between toleration and liberty. Toleration implies that somebody falsely claims the right to tolerate. Toleration is a concession, while liberty is a right. Toleration is a matter of expediency, while liberty is a matter of principle. Toleration is a gift from man, while liberty is a gift from God. It is the consistent and insistent contention of our Baptist people, always and everywhere, that religion must be forever voluntary and uncoerced, and that it is not the prerogative of any power, whether civil or ecclesiastical, to compel men to conform to any religious creed or form of worship, or to pay taxes for the support of a religious organization to which they do not belong and in whose creed they do not believe. God wants free worshipers and no other kind.

A Fundamental Principle

What is the explanation of this consistent and notably praiseworthy record of our plain Baptist people in the realm of religious liberty? The answer is at hand. It is not because Baptists are inherently better than their neighbors—we would make no such arrogant claim. Happy are our Baptist people to live side by side with their neighbors of other Christian communions, and to have glorious Christian fellowship with such neighbors, and to honor such servants of God for their inspiring lives and their noble deeds. From our deepest hearts we pray: "Grace be with all them that love our Lord Jesus Christ in sincerity." The spiritual union of all true believers in Christ is now and ever will be a blessed reality, and such union is deeper and higher and more enduring than any and all forms and rituals and organizations. Whoever believes in Christ as his personal Savior is our brother in the common salvation, whether he be a member of one communion or of another, or of no communion at all.

How is it, then, that Baptists, more than any other people in the world, have forever been the protagonists of religious liberty, and its compatriot, civil liberty? They did not stumble upon this principle. Their uniform, unyielding and sacrificial advocacy of such principle was not and is not an accident. It is, in a word, because of our essential and fundamental principles. Ideas rule the world. A denomination is molded by its ruling principles, just as a nation is thus molded and just as individual life is thus molded. Our fundamental essential principles have made our Baptist people, of all ages and countries, to be the unyielding protagonist of religious liberty, not only for themselves, but as well for everybody else.

The Fundamental Baptist Principles

The Absolute Lordship of Christ

Such fact at once provokes the inquiry: What are these fundamental Baptist principles which compel Baptists in Europe, in America, in some far-off seagirt island, to be forever contending for unrestricted religious liberty?

First of all, and explaining all the rest, is the doctrine of the absolute Lordship of Jesus Christ. That doctrine is for Baptists the dominant fact in all their Christian experience, the nerve center of all their Christian life, the bedrock of all their church polity, the sheet anchor of all their hopes, the climax and crown of all their rejoicings. They say with Paul: "For to this end Christ both died and rose again, that he might be Lord both of the dead and the living."

From that germinal conception of the absolute Lordship of Christ, all our Baptist principles emerge. Just as yonder oak came from the acorn, so our many-branched Baptist life came from the cardinal principle of the absolute Lordship of Christ. The Christianity of our Baptist people, from Alpha to Omega, lives and moves and has its whole being in the realm of the doctrine of the Lordship of Christ. "One is your Master, even Christ, and all ye are brethren." Christ is the one head of the church. All authority has been committed unto Him, in heaven and on earth, and He must be given the absolute pre-eminence in all things. One clear note is ever to be sounded concerning Him, even this, "Whatsoever He saith unto you, do it."

The Bible: Our Rule of Faith and Practice

How shall we find our Christ's will for us? He has revealed it in His Holy Word. The Bible and the Bible alone is the rule of faith and practice for Baptists. To them the one standard by which all creeds and conduct and character must be tried is the Word of God. They ask only one question concerning all religious faith and practice, and that question is, "What saith the Word of God?" Not traditions, nor customs, nor councils, nor confessions, nor ecclesiastical formularies, however venerable and pretentious, guide Baptists, but simply and solely the will of Christ as they find it revealed in the New Testament. The immortal B. H. Carroll has thus stated it for us: "The New Testament is the law of Christianity. All the New Testament is the law of Christianity. The New Testament is all the law of Christianity. The New Testament always will be all the law of Christianity."

Infant Baptism Unthinkable

It follows, inevitably, that Baptists are unalterably opposed to every form of sponsorial religion. If I have fellow Christians in this presence today who are the protagonists of infant baptism, they will allow me frankly to say, and certainly I would say it in the most fraternal, Christian spirit, that to Baptists infant baptism is unthinkable from every viewpoint. First of all, Baptists do not find the slightest sanction for infant baptism in the Word of God. That fact, to Baptists, makes infant baptism a most serious question for the consideration of the whole Christian world. Nor is that all. As Baptists see it, infant baptism tends to ritualize Christianity and reduce it to lifeless forms. It tends also and inevitably, as Baptists see it, to the secularizing of the church and to the blurring and blotting out of the line of demarcation between the church and the unsaved world.

Surely, in the fact of these frank statements, our non-Baptist neighbors may apprehend something of the difficulties compelling Baptists when they are asked to enter into official alliances with those who hold such fundamentally different views from those just indicated. We call God to witness that our Baptist people have an unutterable longing for Christian union, and believe Christian union will come, but we are compelled to insist that if this union is to be real and effective, it must be based upon a better understanding of the Word of God and a more complete loyalty to the will of Christ as revealed in His Word.

The Ordinances Are Symbols

Again, to Baptists, the New Testament teaches that salvation through Christ must precede membership in His church, and must precede the observance of the two ordinances in His church, namely, baptism and the Lord's Supper. These ordinances are for the saved and only for the saved. These two ordinances are not sacramental, but symbolic. They are teaching ordinances, portraying in symbol truths of immeasurable and everlasting moment to humanity. To trifle with these symbols, to pervert their forms and at the same time to pervert the truths they are designed to symbolize, is indeed a most serious matter. Without ceasing and without wavering, Baptists are, in conscience, compelled to contend that these two teaching ordinances shall be maintained in the churches just as they were placed there in the wisdom and authority of Christ.

The Church: a Pure Democracy

To Baptists, the New Testament also clearly teaches that Christ's church is not only a spiritual body but it is also a pure democracy, all its members being equal, a local congregation, and cannot subject itself to any outside control. Such terms, therefore, as "The American Church," or "The bishop of this city or state," sound strangely incongruous to Baptist ears. In the very nature of the case, also, there must be no union between church and state, because their nature and functions are utterly different. Jesus stated the principle in the two sayings, "My kingdom is not of this world," and "Render unto Caesar the things that are Caesar's, and unto God the things that are God's." Never, anywhere, in any clime, has a true Baptist been willing, for one minute, for the union of church and state, never for a moment.

A Free Church in a Free State

That utterance of Jesus, "Render unto Caesar the things that are Caesar's, and unto God the things that are God's," is one of the most revolutionary and history-making utterances that ever fell from those lips divine. That utterance, once for all, marked the divorcement of church and state. It marked a new era for the creeds and deeds of men. It was the sunrise gun of a new day, the echoes of which are to go on and on and on until in every land, whether great or small, the doctrine shall have absolute supremacy everywhere of a free church in a free state.

In behalf of our Baptist people I am compelled to say that forgetfulness of the principles that I have just enumerated, in our judgment, explains many of the religious ills that now afflict the world. All went well with the early churches in their earlier days. They were incomparably triumphant days for the Christian faith. Those early disciples of Jesus, without prestige and worldly power, yet aflame with the love of God and the passion of Christ, went out and shook the pagan Roman Empire from center to circumference, even in one brief generation. Christ's religion needs no prop of any kind from any worldly source, and to the degree that it is thus supported is a millstone hanged about its neck.

An Incomparable Apostasy

Presently there came an incomparable apostasy in the realm of religion, which shrouded the world in spiritual night through long hundreds of years. Constantine, the Emperor, saw something in the religion of Christ's people which awakened his interest, and now we see him uniting religion to the state and marching up the marble steps of the Emperor's palace, with the church robed in purple. Thus and there was begun the most baneful misalliance that ever fettered and cursed a suffering world. For long centuries, even from Constantine to Pope Gregory VII, the conflict between church and state waxed stronger and stronger, and the encroachments and usurpations became more deadly and devastating. When Christianity first found its way into the city of the Caesars it lived at first in cellars and alleys, but when Constantine crowned the union of the church and state, the church was stamped with the impress of the Roman idea and fanned with the spirit of the Caesars. Soon we see a Pope emerging, who himself became a Caesar, and soon a group of councilors may be seen gathered around this Pope, and the supreme power of the church is assumed by the Pope and his councilors.

The long blighting record of the medieval ages is simply the working out of that idea. The Pope ere long assumed to be the monarch of the world, making the astounding claim that all kings and potentates were subject unto him. By and by when Pope Gregory VII appears, better known as Hildebrand, his assumptions are still more astounding. In him the spirit of the Roman church became incarnate and triumphant. He lorded it over parliaments and council chambers, having statesmen to do his bidding, and creating and deposing kings at his will. For example, when the Emperor Henry offended Hildebrand, the latter pronounced against Henry a sentence not only of excommunication but of deposition as Emperor, releasing all Christians from allegiance to him. He made the Emperor do penance by standing in the snow with his bare feet at Canossa, and he wrote his famous letter to William the Conqueror to the effect that the state was subordinate to the church, that the power of the state as compared to the church was as the moon compared to the sun.

This explains the famous saying of Bismarck when Chancellor of Germany, to the German Parliament: "We will never go to Canossa again." Whoever favors the authority of the church over the state favors the way to Canossa.

When, in the fulness of time, Columbus discovered America, the Pope calmly announced that he would divide the New World into two parts, giving one part to the King of Spain and the other to the King of Portugal. And not only did this great consolidated ecclesiasticism assume to lord it over men's earthly treasures, but they lorded it over men's minds, prescribing what men should think and read and write. Nor did such assumption stop with the things of this world, but it laid its hand on the next world, and claims to have in its possession the keys of the Kingdom of Heaven and the kingdom of purgatory so that it could shut men out of heaven or lift them out of purgatory, thus surpassing in the sweep of its power and in the pride of its autocracy the boldest and most presumptuous ruler that ever sat on a civil throne.

The Reformation Incomplete

The coming of the sixteenth century was the dawning of a new hope for the world. With that century came the Protestant Reformation. Yonder goes Luther with his theses, which he nails over the old church door in Wittenberg, and the echoes of the mighty deed shake the Papacy, shake Europe, shake the whole world. Luther was joined by Melancthon and Calvin and Zwingli and other mighty leaders. Just at this point emerges one of the most outstanding anomalies of all history. Although Luther and his compeers protested vigorously against the errors of Rome, yet when these mighty men came out of Rome, and mighty men they were, they brought with them some of the grievous errors of Rome. The Protestant Reformation of the sixteenth century was sadly incomplete—it was a case of arrested development. Although Luther and his compeers grandly sounded out the battle cry of justification by faith alone, yet they retained the doctrine of infant baptism and a state church. They shrank from the logical conclusions of their own theses.

In Zurich there stands a statue in honor of Zwingli, in which he is represented with a Bible in one hand and a sword in the other. That statute was the symbol of the union between church and state. The same statute might have been reared to Luther and his fellow reformers. Luther and Melancthon fastened a state church upon Germany, and Zwingli fastened it upon Switzerland. Knox and his associates fastened it upon Scotland, Henry VIII bound it upon England, where it remains even till this very hour.

These mighty reformers turned out to be persecutors like the Papacy before them. Luther unloosed the dogs of persecution against the struggling and faithful Anabaptists. Calvin burned Servetus, and to such awful deed Melancthon gave his approval. Louis XIV revoked the Edict of Nantes, shut the doors of all the Protestant churches, and outlawed the Huguenots. Germany put to death that mighty Baptist leader, Balthaser Hubmaier, while Holland killed her noblest statesman, John of Barneveldt, and condemned to life imprisonment her ablest historian, Hugo Grotius, for conscience' sake. In England, John Bunyan was kept in jail for twelve long, weary years because of his religion, and when we cross the mighty ocean separating the Old World and the New, we find the early pages of American history crimsoned with the stories of religious persecutions. The early colonies of America were the forum of the working out of the most epochal battles that earth ever knew for the triumph of religious and civil liberty.

America and Religious and Civil Liberty

Just a brief glance at the struggle in those early colonies must now suffice us. Yonder in Massachusetts, Henry Dunster, the first president of Harvard, was removed from the presidency because he objected to infant baptism. Roger Williams was banished, John Clarke was put in prison, and they publicly whipped Obadiah Holmes on Boston Common. In Connecticut the lands of our Baptist fathers were confiscated and their goods sold to build a meeting house and support a preacher of another denomination. In old Virginia, "mother of states and statesmen," the battle for religious and civil liberty was waged all over her nobly historic territory, and the final triumph recorded there was such as to write imperishable glory upon the name of Virginia until the last syllable of recorded time. Fines and imprisonments and persecutions were everywhere in evidence in Virginia for conscience' sake. If you would see a record incomparably interesting, go read the early statues in Virginia concerning the Established Church and religion, and trace the epic story of the history-making struggles of that early day. If the historic records are to be accredited, those clergymen of the Established Church in Virginia made terrible inroads in collecting fines in Baptist tobacco in that early day. It is quite evident, however, that they did not get all the tobacco.

On and on was the struggle waged by our Baptist fathers for religious liberty in Virginia, in the Carolinas, in Georgia, in Rhode Island and Massachusetts and Connecticut, and elsewhere, with one unyielding contention for unrestricted religious liberty for all men, and with never one wavering note. They dared to be odd, to stand alone, to refuse to conform, though it cost them suffering and even life itself. They dared to defy traditions and customs, and deliberately chose the day of non-conformity, even though in many a case it meant a cross. They pleaded and suffered, they offered their protests and remonstrances and memorials, and, thank God, mighty statesmen were won to their contention, Washington and Jefferson and Madison and Patrick Henry, and many others, until at last it was written into our country's Constitution that church and state must in this land be forever separate and free, that neither must ever trespass upon the distinctive functions of the other. It was pre-eminently a Baptist achievement.

A Lonely Struggle

Glad are our Baptist people to pay their grateful tribute to their fellow Christians of other religious communions for all their sympathy and help in this sublime achievement. Candor compels me to repeat that much of the sympathy of other religious leaders in that early struggle was on the side of legalized ecclesiastical privilege. Much of the time were Baptists pitiably lonely in their age-long struggle. We would now and always make our most grateful acknowledgment to any and all who came to the side of our Baptist fathers, whether early or late, in this destiny determining struggle. But I take it that every informed man on the subject, whatever his religious faith, will be willing to pay tribute to our Baptist people as being the chief instrumentality in God's hands in winning the battle in America for religious liberty.

The Present Call

And now, my fellow Christians, and fellow citizens, what is the present call to us in connection with the priceless principle of religious liberty? That principle, with all the history and heritage accompanying it, imposes upon us obligations to the last degree meaningful and responsible. Let us today and forever be highly resolved that the principle of religious liberty shall, please God, be preserved inviolate through all our days and the days of those who come after us....

Liberty Not Abused

It behooves us now and ever to see to it that liberty is not abused. Well may we listen to the call of Paul, that mightiest Christian of the long centuries, as he says: "Brethren, ye have been called unto liberty: only use not your liberty for an occasion to the flesh, but by love serve one another." This ringing declaration should be heard and heeded by every class and condition of people throughout all our wide stretching nation.

It is the word to be heeded by religious teachers, and by editors, and by legislators, and by everybody else. Nowhere is liberty to be used "for an occasion to the flesh." We will take free speech and a free press, with all their excrescences and perils, because of the high meaning of freedom, but we are to set ourselves with all diligence not to use these great privileges in the shaming of liberty. A free press—how often does it pervert its high privilege!

Things Worth Dying For

When this nation went into the world war a little while ago, after her long and patient and fruitless effort to find another way of conserving righteousness, the note was sounded in every nook and corner of our country that some things in this world are worth dying for, and if they are worth dying for they are worth living for. What are some of the things worth dying for? The sanctity of womanhood is worth dying for. The safety of childhood is worthy dying for, and when Germany put to death that first helpless Belgian child she was marked for defeat and doom. The integrity of one's country is worth dying for. And, please God, the freedom and honor of the United States of America are worth dying for. If the great things of life are worth dying for, they are surely worth living for.

A League of Nations

Standing here today on the steps of our Nation's capitol, heard by the chamber of the Senate of the United States, I dare to say as a citizen and as a Christian teacher, that the moral forces of the United States of America, without regard to political parties, will never rest until there is a worthy League of Nations. I dare to express also the unhesitating belief that the unquestioned majorities of both great political parties in this country regard the delay in the working out of a League of Nations as a national and worldwide tragedy.

The moral and religious forces of this country could not be supine and inactive as long as the saloon, the chief rendezvous of small politicians, that chronic criminal and standing anachronism of our modern civilization, was legally sponsored by the state. I can certify all the politicians of all the political parties that the legalized saloon has gone from American life, and gone to stay. Likewise, I can certify the men of all political parties, without any reference to partisan politics, that the same moral and religious forces of this country, because of the inexorable moral issues involved, cannot be silent and will not be silent until there is put forth a League of Nations that will strive with all its might to put an end to the diabolism and measureless horrors of war. I thank God that the stricken man yonder in the White House has pleaded long and is pleading yet that our nation will take her full part with the others for the bringing in of that blessed day when wars shall cease to the ends of the earth.

The Right Kind of Christians

This noble doctrine and heritage of religious liberty calls to us imperiously to be the right kind of Christians. Let us never forget that a democracy, whether civil or religious, has not only its perils, but has also its unescapable obligations. A democracy calls for intelligence. The sure foundation of states must be laid, not in ignorance, but in knowledge. It is of the last importance that those who rule shall be properly trained. In a democracy, a government of the people, for the people, and by the people, the people are the rulers, and the people, all the people, are to be informed and trained.

My fellow Christians, we must hark back to our Christian schools, and see to it that these schools are put on worthy and enduring foundations. A democracy needs more than intelligence, it needs Christ. He is the light of the world, nor is there any other sufficient light for the world. He is the solution of the world's complex questions, the one adequate Helper for its dire needs, the one only sufficient Savior for our sinning race. Our schools are afresh to take note of this supreme fact, and they are to be fundamentally and aggressively Christian. Wrong education brought on the recent world war. Such education will always lead to disaster.

The Christian School

The time has come when, as never before, our beloved denomination should worthily go out to its world task as a teaching denomination. That means that there should be a crusade throughout all our borders for the vitalizing and strengthening of our Christian schools. The only complete education, in the nature of the case, is Christian education, because man is a tripartite being. By the very genius of our government, education by the state cannot be complete. Wisdom has fled from us if we fail to magnify, and magnify now, our Christian schools. These schools go to the foundation of all the life of the people. They are dispensable to the highest efficiency of the churches. Their inspirational influences are of untold value to the schools conducted by the state, to which schools also we must ever give our best support.

The one transcending inspiring influence in civilization is the Christian religion. By all means, let the teachers and trustees and student bodies of all our Christian schools remember this supremely important fact, that civilization without Christianity is doomed. Let there be no pagan ideals in our Christian schools, and no hesitation or apology for the insistence that the one hope for the individual, the one hope for society, for civilization, is the Christian religion. If ever the drum beat of duty sounded clearly, it is calling to us now to strengthen and magnify our Christian schools.

The Task of Evangelism

Preceding and accompanying the task of building our Christian schools, we must keep faithfully and practically in mind our primary task of evangelism, the work of winning souls from sin unto salvation, from Satan unto God. This work takes precedence of all other work in the Christian program. Salvation for sinners is through Jesus Christ alone, nor is there any other name or way under heaven whereby they may be saved. Our churches, our schools, our religious papers, our hospitals, every organization and agency of the churches should be kept aflame with the passion of New Testament evangelism.

While thus caring for the homeland, we are at the same time to see to it that our program is co-extensive with Christ's program for the whole world. The whole world is our field, nor may we, with impunity, dare to be indifferent to any section, however remote.

A Glorious Day

Glorious it is, my fellow Christians, to be living in such a day as this, if only we shall live as we ought to live. Irresistible is the conviction that the immediate future is packed with amazing possibilities. We can understand the cry of Rupert Brooke as he sailed from Gallipoli, "Now God be thanked who hath matched us with this hour!" The day of the reign of the common people is everywhere coming like the rising tides of the ocean. The people are everywhere breaking with feudalism. Autocracy is passing, whether it be civil or ecclesiastical. Democracy is the goal toward which all feet are traveling, whether in state or in church.

The Price to Be Paid

Are we willing to pay the price that must be paid to secure for humanity the blessings they need to have? We say that we have seen God in the face of Jesus Christ, that we have been born again, that we are the true friends of Christ, and would make proof of our friendship for Him by doing His will. Well, then, what manner of people ought we to be in all holy living and godliness? Surely we should be a holy people, remembering the apostolic characterization, "Ye are a chosen generation, a royal priesthood, an holy nation, a peculiar people: That we should shew forth the praises of Him who hath called you out of darkness into His marvelous light, who in time past were not a people but are now the people of God."

Let us look again to the strange passion and power of the early Christians. They paid the price for spiritual power. Mark well this record: "And they overcame him by the blood of the Lamb, and by the word of their testimony; and they loved not their lives unto the death." O my fellow Christians, if we are to be in the true succession of the mighty days and deeds of the early Christian era, or of those mighty days and deeds of our Baptist fathers in later days, then selfish ease must be utterly renounced for Christ and His cause, and our every gift and grace and power utterly dominated by the dynamic of His cross. Standing here today in the shadow of our country's capitol, compassed about as we are with so great a cloud of witnesses, let us today renew our pledge to God, and to one another, that we will give our best to church and to state, to God and to humanity, by His grace and power, until we fall on the last sleep.

Chapter Eleven

Questions for Personal Reflection and Group Study

An Enquiry . . . by William Carey

1. What plea does Dr. Carey make in this *Enquiry* to his fellow Christian brethren?

2. Discuss the meaning of Matthew 28:19 and Mark 16:15 in Carey's day and in our present day. How does Dr. Carey interpret these Scriptures?

3. How did Dr. Carey feel about the conversion of the world's heathen?

4. Reflect on some of the history in which Dr. Carey makes his points.

5. What are some of the practical ways Dr. Carey states for the conversion of the heathen?

6. What were the consequences of his speech in the years to come?

The Virginia Chronicle (1790) by John Leland

1. Who were the first settlers in the state of Virginia?
2. Describe the life and worship of the Quakers.
3. What does the author write about slaves in Virginia?
4. What is the author's opinion of the
   Presbyterians?
   Methodists?
   Tunkers?
   Mennonists?
5. What does the name "Tunkers" mean?
6. Who was Menno Simon?
7. When did the Baptists "take their rise in Virginia"?
8. Who were the "Regular Baptists" and "Separate Baptists"?
9. How were Baptists persecuted in Virginia?
10. What did the "act of toleration," passed in the first of William and Mary's reign, do for the Baptists?
11. According to Frederick, in his "Memoirs of the House of Brandenburg," what was the "cause of the Reformation" in England? In Germany? In France?
12. Why can "no national church . . . in its organization, be the Gospel Church"?
13. What is meant by "the Church of England has a human head"?
14. What does the author say about the "three great principles": fate, free-will, and restitution?
15. What was the controversy in Virginia concerning marriage?
16. How does the author Leland describe Virginia in the times of revival?
17. What was the mode of dress among the Baptists? How did the Revolution change Virginia's dress codes?
18. What is meant by "dry christening" and what does the author write about it?

19. How did the "Virginia Baptists" compare with the Germans?

20. Describe the "rights and bonds of conscience."

21. What are Elder Leland's "thoughts on systems"?

22. What was happening politically in the United States and the world at the time of this writing (1790)?

Selections from *Manual of Theology* by John L. Dagg

Doctrine Concerning Divine Grace: "Duty of Gratitude for Divine Grace"

1. Discuss the author's opening sentence: "As love is the affection which should arise in our hearts, from a view of God's character, so gratitude is the affection which should be produced, by a view of the benefits that He confers." What does he mean by this statement?

2. What does the author write about "our gratitude for the blessings of salvation"?

3. How can our "gratitude to God . . . be proportional to the blessing received"?

Doctrine Concerning the Will and Works of God: "Duty of Delighting in the Will and Works of God"

1. Ponder this statement: "Our happiness is not merely the absence of grief and pain, but it is positive delight." Do you agree? Why or why not?

2. What is meant by "religious truth," and why should it "stimulate to diligence and perseverance"?

3. What lies at the foundation of true religion, according to the writer?

4. How is "the trial of our delight in God . . . experienced when affliction comes"?

"Three Changes in Theological Institutions" by James Petigru Boyce

1. At the writing of this chapter, what was the "demand" for theological education? How has that demand changed over the years?

2. What does the author mean by "the existing evils" and what are these evils?

3. What has been the "primary object of all our educational efforts" according to the writer?

4. What does the author write about the subject of "knowledge"?

5. What are some of the changes and ideas the author discusses within the text of his chapter? List and discuss.

"Circular Letter on Confessions of Faith" by S. M. Noel

1. What does the author believe about creeds? What does he mean by a "creed"?

2. Why are "our confessions" "human productions"? What does the author mean by this?

3. Discuss the meaning of the following statement: "If there be any divine warrant for a church (in this day) there is a divine warrant for a creed as a test of union, a bond of fellowship, a fence against error, and a shield against that spirit of restless innovation which esteems every novelty an improvement."

"High Doctrine and Broad Doctrine" by Charles H. Spurgeon

1. Discuss the meaning of John 6:37 as Dr. Spurgeon expounds on it.

2. To what does the author refer when he writes: "No, I never reconcile friends"?

3. Describe his experience in the western Highlands. What spiritual example does he bring from this experience?

4. What is the "eternal purpose"?

5. How does the writer present "the everlasting gospel"?

6. What is meant by the statement "a river is free to every dog that runs along the bank..."? To what is the author referring?

"The Duties of Pastors to Their Churches" by Elder John W. Brown

1. Discuss Acts 20:28. How does Elder Brown use this Scripture?

2. According to the author, what are the duties of churches to their pastors?

3. Why is there an obligation of the pastor to preach the gospel to his flock? Why is this listed as the "first and most important duty of the pastor"?

4. What does the author write about "expository preaching"? Do you agree?

5. How should the gospel be preached?

6. Why should a preacher be "argumentative" and "eloquent"? Why should he "labor for his intellectual improvement"?

7. Why and how should the preacher "give himself wholly to the gospel and the services of the church"? What situations would render it impossible for him to do so?

8. What kind of example should a pastor be for his church?

9. What are the pastor's responsibilities regarding visiting his members?

10. How should a pastor "exercise his judgment and influence to guard the church against the admission of unworthy members"? What makes an "unworthy member"?

"Dangers of Denominational Prosperity" by the Reverend Jacob R. Scott

1. Discuss the meaning of 1 Corinthians 10:12. What is meant by this Scripture?

2. What does the author warn about Christian purity? Why does he see prosperity "threatening to mar it"?

3. Discuss why rapid growth is an "increased liability to disunion."

4. Why does a large denomination "threaten our humility"? Do you agree or disagree? Why?

5. Ponder the following statement: "Another danger to which our prosperity renders us peculiarly liable, is a diminution of energy in propagating the truth."

6. What does the author mean by this statement: "I refer to the danger of activity not being so general throughout the churches as when they were smaller, of every church and every individual not coming up so much, as a body, to the help of the Lord." Would you agree that as the "members and resources of a church increase," members will no longer share the responsibility of church work?

7. What is the danger, as the author points out, of "our denomination becoming secularized by its prosperity"?

8. What does the writer mean when he writes on the "influence of denominational prosperity on the toleration of others"?

9. How does a "proud" denomination "incur heaven's displeasure"?

Reminiscences of the Old-Time Baptists by S. G. Hillyer

1. What is meant by "regeneration"?

2. Describe the old-time Baptist meeting-house.

3. What was the difficult schedule of the Baptist preacher in those days?

4. What happened in the "conferences"?

5. What is meant by "church discipline"? Why is it not practiced as strictly today as it was in the day in which Hillyer writes?

6. Why did early Georgia Baptists reject theaters, operas, circuses, etc.? What was their intention?

7. How did early Baptists receive new members?

8. What is the "offense of the cross"?

9. Describe their "baptisms." What were their customs?

10. How was a preacher called to the ministry in earlier days?

11. What were listed as some of the "tests" of a divine call?

12. What constituted a call to the ministry in those days?

13. Describe the case of Dr. W. Kilpatrick.

14. What took place at the ordination of deacons? Of ministers?

15. Describe the social life of early Georgia Baptists. Why was it difficult? Where were the churches located?

16. What were some opportunities of social gatherings?

17. What is meant by "social worship." How did it take place?

18. What happened at "prayer meeting." Where was it held and why?

19. Describe the early Baptists' "public worship."

20. How did early Baptists use music and song?

21. List and discuss some of the doctrinal views of early Georgia Baptists. What did they believe?

"Baptists and Religious Liberty" by George W. Truett

1. Where and when was this sermon given by Dr. Truett?

2. What does Dr. Truett describe as the "doctrine of religious liberty"?

3. "Baptists have one consistent record concerning liberty throughout all their long and eventful history," writes the author. What is it?

4. What are the "fundamental Baptists principles"?

5. Discuss the following:
   - The absolute Lordship of Christ
   - The Bible as our rule of faith and practice

6. To Baptists, why is "infant baptism unthinkable"?

7. Why does the author emphasize that "these two ordinances [baptism and Lord's Supper] are not sacramental, but symbolic"? Why do Baptists believe that the ordinances are symbols?

8. Why is Christ's church a "pure democracy"? "A free church in a free state"?

9. What is meant by the statement: "We will never go to Canossa again"?

10. Why was "the Protestant Reformation of the sixteenth century . . . sadly incomplete" according to Dr. Truett?

11. What are the "things worth dying for" and why?

12. Discuss the following statement: "Civilization without Christianity is doomed." What is the "one hope"?